# WOMEN'S STUDIES QUARTERLY

VOLUME 51   NUMBERS 1 & 2   SPRING/SUMMER 2023

An educational project of the Feminist Press at the City University of New York, the College of Staten Island, City University of New York, and Kingsborough Community College, City University of New York, with support from the Center for the Study of Women and Society and the Center for the Humanities at the Graduate Center, City University of New York

**EDITOR**
Red Washburn, Kingsborough Community College and The Graduate Center, CUNY

**EDITORIAL DIRECTORS**
Dána-Ain Davis and Kendra Sullivan

**GUEST EDITORS**
Christina B. Hanhardt, University of Maryland, College Park
Dayo F. Gore, Georgetown University

**POETRY EDITORS**
Cheryl Clarke
JP Howard
Julie R. Enszer

**CREATIVE PROSE EDITORS**
Keisha-Gay Anderson
Lauren Cherelle
Vi Khi Nao

**VISUAL ARTS EDITOR**
Maya von Ziegesar

**EDITORIAL ASSISTANTS**
Googie Karrass
Maya von Ziegesar

**EDITORIAL INTERN**
Angela Boscarino

**SOCIAL MEDIA & EVENTS MANAGER**
Juwon Jun

**EDITORS EMERITAE**
Brianne Waychoff 2020–2022 ▪ Natalie Havlin 2017–2020
Jillian M. Báez 2017–2020 ▪ Matt Brim 2014–2017 ▪ Cynthia Chris 2014–2017
Amy Herzog 2011–2014 ▪ Joe Rollins 2011–2014 ▪ Victoria Pitts-Taylor 2008–2011
Talia Schaffer 2008–2011 ▪ Cindi Katz 2004–2008 ▪ Nancy K. Miller 2004–2008
Diane Hope 2000–2004 ▪ Janet Zandy 1995–2000 ▪ Nancy Porter 1982–1992
Florence Howe 1972–1982; 1993–1994

## The Feminist Press at the City University of New York

**EXECUTIVE DIRECTOR & PUBLISHER**
Margot Atwell

**EDITORIAL DIRECTOR**
Lauren Rosemary Hook

**ASSISTANT EDITOR**
Nick Whitney

**ART DIRECTOR**
Drew Stevens

**SENIOR SALES & MARKETING MANAGER**
Jisu Kim

**EXECUTIVE OPERATIONS & DEVELOPMENT COORDINATOR**
Rachel Page

*WSQ: Women's Studies Quarterly*, a peer-reviewed, theme-based journal, is published by the Feminist Press at the City University of New York.

**COVER ART**
*Stop Empire* by Kyle Goen

**WEBSITE**
feministpress.org/wsq
womensstudiesquarterly.com

**EDITORIAL CORRESPONDENCE**
*WSQ: Women's Studies Quarterly*, The Feminist Press at the City University of New York, The Graduate Center, 365 Fifth Avenue, Suite 5406, New York, NY 10016; wsqeditorial@gmail.com and wsqeditors@gmail.com.

**PRINT SUBSCRIPTIONS**
Subscribers in the United States: Individuals—$60 for 1 year; $150 for 3 years. Institutions—$85 for 1 year; $225 for 3 years. Subscribers outside the United States: Add $40 per year for delivery. To subscribe or change an address, contact *WSQ* Customer Service, The Feminist Press at the City University of New York, The Graduate Center, 365 Fifth Avenue, Suite 5406, New York, NY 10016; 212-817-7915; info@feministpress.org.

**FORTHCOMING ISSUES**
*WSQ Nonbinary*, JV Fuqua, Queens College, Red Washburn, Kingsborough Community
   College and Graduate Center
*WSQ Pandemonium*, Tracey Jean Boisseau, Purdue University, Adrianna L. Ernstberger,
   Marian University

**RIGHTS & PERMISSIONS**
Fred Courtright, The Permissions Company, 570-839-7477; permdude@eclipse.net.

**SUBMISSION INFORMATION**
For the most up-to-date guidelines, calls for papers, and information concerning forthcoming issues, write to wsqeditors@gmail.com or visit feministpress.org/wsq or womensstudiesquarterly.com.

**ADVERTISING**
For information on display-ad sizes, rates, exchanges, and schedules, please write to *WSQ* Marketing, The Feminist Press at the City University of New York, The Graduate Center, 365 Fifth Avenue, Suite 5406, New York, NY 10016; 212-817-7918; sales@feministpress.org.

**ELECTRONIC ACCESS AND SUBSCRIPTIONS**
Access to electronic databases containing backlist issues of *WSQ* may be purchased through JSTOR at www.jstor.org. Access to electronic databases containing current issues of *WSQ* may be purchased through Project MUSE at muse.jhu.edu, muse@muse.jhu.edu; and ProQuest at www.il.proquest.com, info@il.proquest.com. Individual electronic subscriptions for *WSQ* may also be purchased through Project MUSE.

ISSN: 0732-1562   ISBN: 978-1-55861-231-0   $25.00

Gunja SenGupta, Brooklyn College
Barbara Shaw, Allegheny College
Lili Shi, Kingsborough Community College
Robyn Spencer, Lehman College
Saadia Toor, College of Staten Island
Laura Westengard, New York City College of Technology, CUNY
Kimberly Williams, Mount Royal University
Kimberly Williams Brown, Vassar College
Karen Winkler, Psychotherapist

# Contents

# Editor's Note

Red Washburn

This issue, *State/Power*, addresses the many bureaucratic and problematic faces of the state—the carceral state, the straight state, the anti-choice state, the anti-immigrant state, the white supremacist state, the fascist state, and the cis state, among others. It explores many critical issues connected to state formations, historical legacies, and structures of power. Some such issues include the following: mutual aid, housing insecurity, reproductive rights, land sovereignty, familial disappearances, juvenile rights, and social movements. The focus on racialized resistance to state power is incisive, allowing for a rich centering of BIPOC identity, history, and struggle at this moment of interminable and egregious anti-Black, anti-trans, white nationalist, and misogynist hatred. Basic human access to jobs, housing, health care, and a livable life are essential at any temporal juncture, though as the global pandemic continues, state power must be excoriated and reenvisioned. Alternatives for a better world are possible with a restructuring and dismantling of social institutions, multinational corporations, and global capitalism. In particular, the academic and activist work on trans of color critiques of carceral states and abolitionist futures as well as the historical remembering of the Third World Women's Alliance and the lessons and possibilities it holds at this current moment are captivating. This issue points to the problems and promises of challenging state power.

*State/Power* is indebted to numerous scholars, writers, artists, editors, and/or editorial staff and boards. During a very difficult time, namely the tragic passing of *WSQ* general editor Brianne Waychoff, I want to extend a huge thank-you to the *WSQ* team and editorial board for all their commitment and labor. In particular, I want to thank Dána-Ain Davis at the Center

*WSQ: Women's Studies Quarterly* 51: 1 & 2 (Spring/Summer 2023)

for the Study of Women and Society and Kendra Sullivan at the Center for Humanities for coming on board as interim editorial directors to oversee managerial operations and funding as *WSQ* transitions to new general editors later in 2023. Their work has been invaluable to helping the journal grow and thrive. I also want to extend a hearty thank-you to the editorial assistants, Googie Karrass, Maya von Ziegesar, and Angela Boscarino, all of whom worked tirelessly on communicating with the scholars, writers, and artists to make this issue happen. I want to thank the guest editors, Christina Hanhardt and Dayo Gore, for curating and editing this issue. I also want to thank the poetry editors, Cheryl Clarke, Julie R. Enszer, and JP Howard, as well as the prose editors, Keisha-Gaye Anderson, Lauren Cherelle, and Vi Khi Nao. In addition, I want to extend a generous thank-you to Eileen Liang and Natalie Ruby for their administrative assistance with internships in feminist publishing for graduate students in women's and gender studies at the City University of New York. Our partnership has significantly enriched the quality of the journal for our feminist communities across CUNY and beyond. I also wish to thank Sampson Starkweather and Juwon Jun at the Center for Humanities for collaborating with *WSQ*, especially aiding with publicity. Most importantly, I am extremely grateful for the Feminist Press leadership for all their help with scheduling, production, and distribution, especially executive director Margot Atwell, editorial director Lauren Rosemary Hook, and assistant editor Nick Whitney. I cannot thank you enough for your help and support. I appreciate the entire *WSQ* community for everything, and I look forward to future issues, including *Nonbinary* next in the queue!

**Red Washburn**
Professor of English and Women's, Gender, and
  Sexuality Studies
Director of Women's, Gender, and Sexuality Studies
Kingsborough Community College and the
  Graduate Center
City University of New York

# Introduction

Dayo F. Gore and Christina B. Hanhardt

In 2020 the Movement for Black Lives, drawing on what it describes as an "ecosystem of over 170 organizations," relaunched its 2016 Vision for Black Lives platform to build "political will and power" (Movement for Black Lives 2020). Two aspects of the platform stand out to us: first, that an intersectional analysis is at the center of all demands; and second, that "the state" is theorized as a source of punishment that activists reject and as a set of resources that activists might make claims upon. Given our respective research on twentieth-century U.S. social movements (Christina on lesbian, gay, bisexual, transgender and queer activism, and Dayo on Black women's radicalism and the U.S. Left) and investments in contemporary left movements, these issues have long preoccupied our work on and engagement with political organizing.

In the last three years the stakes have only intensified. Social and economic conditions in the United States and around the globe demonstrate the necessity of addressing categories of difference while confronting state power, its resources, and institutional reach. From abolitionist demands to "defund the police and invest in communities" to calls for protecting rights such as access to abortion and health care, these years of pandemic, protests, and legal mandates have laid bare the power of the state to shape everyday life and survival. This is especially the case in the context of the recalibration of neoliberalism and white nationalism.

Counter to claims on the left and right that identity politics stand in contrast to class politics, or that movements named by single-identity frames are necessarily delimited, many activist responses to the COVID-19 pandemic and leadership during the Black Lives Matter uprisings of the

*WSQ: Women's Studies Quarterly* 51: 1 & 2 (Spring/Summer 2023)

summer of 2020 treated race, gender, sexuality, and class as tightly interwoven social categories that are essential to building justice movements and radical change. In addition, many of these movements have directly engaged the state, be that in supporting socialist- and progressive-identified political candidates or demanding economic resources for state health infrastructure, even as they have also participated in local mutual aid networks and called for the end of carceral systems, borders, and even the U.S. nation-state itself. We have been struck by how these organizing efforts speak to histories that we have studied of political movements that center identity and economic politics and also urge a revisiting of the ways states mobilize power and belonging through interconnected systems of benefits, discipline, and violence.

In considering this special issue we were inspired by important debates about the state that have long animated social movement organizing as well as left and feminist scholarship, such as the place of liberal reforms in radical strategy, the value or limits of centralization and seeding electoral power from below, the challenges of forging new visions on an international scale while sustaining local engagement, and how to recognize the state's co-optation of radical terms without ceding discursive and political ground. We also sought to highlight scholarship and activism emerging from feminists of color that have long made visible the capitalist state's use of social locations beyond class to structure resource distribution.

We seek in this issue on *State/Power* to provide productive insights and provoke further conversation. The articles that follow reroute expected histories and dominant discourses about state power and track how people, particularly Black and other racialized communities, have organized in response. They also take up some precise issues from recent years that have been at the forefront of discussions about the state, such as practices of mutual aid and collective care, the expansion of state punishment alongside the retraction of public resources, and the relationship between local, federal, and global power. Throughout, they explore what directly engaging the state might offer and restrict, and they do so with an attentiveness to identity and difference.

The first two articles approach these issues through an analysis of the place of bodily regulation in the operation of the carceral state. In "'The Potential That Was in All of Us': Carceral Disability and the Japanese American Redress Movement," Adria L. Imada looks at how organizers with the Redress Movement argued that the incarceration of Japanese Americans during World War II led to mass disablement. Mobilizing people with disabilities, the chronically ill, and the mad, the movement drew on feminist principles to center the expertise of those who refused normative decorum and legalistic remedy even as they also did not adopt the explicit terms of disability rights. These efforts relied on an intergenerational group of activists including a number in leadership who applied skills, strategies, and analyses of power to the Redress Movement that they had developed as part of "Serve the People" programs, Asian American activism, and Third World Women's movements of the 1960s and 1970s.

By contrast, Lauren Jae Gutterman outlines some of the stakes when liberal reformers center legal protection counter to the expressions and experiences of those most harmed by carceral systems. In "Queering *Morales v. Turman*: Gender, Sexuality, and Juveniles' Right to Treatment," Gutterman shows how in this landmark case liberal advocates made demands for incarcerated juveniles' right to rehabilitative treatment by arguing that incarceration pushed young people into homosexuality and/or nonconventional gender roles. In this way, liberal advocates enforced racialized gender and sexual norms alongside their challenges to certain forms of carceral power, even as Gutterman also highlights everyday acts of sex/gender defiance by mostly Black and Mexican American incarcerated youth that made their way into the public record. But these were far from the only contradictions of legal reform; Gutterman ends by noting how, in the years after *Morales v. Turman*, the expansion of so-called community-based rehabilitative treatment programs increased the number of youth within Texas's carceral system, most especially Black youth, who were thus also increasingly subject to sex/gender surveillance and forced normalization.

The tension between grassroots and more policy-focused resistance in the fight for rights and resources is at the center of Robert Thomas Choflet's "'We Wanted to Talk Plumbing': Organizing and Mutual Aid in Baltimore's High-Rise Public Housing," which examines Black women's organizing for equitable housing in Baltimore since the 1990s. Choflet shows that residents' acts of mutual aid, such as collectivized repair work, became a means to claim public resources and to develop a materialist critique of privatized housing as a form of state neglect. These arguments and strategies also served to challenge developers and other municipal players who pointed to privatization as a solution to so-called family dysfunction rather than an inadequate way to address structural racism, sexism, and poverty. In this way, Black women activists moved between different scales and strategies of state engagement and also crafted critiques of the political economy of the city by mobilizing kinship networks and other intimate relations between women of color.

Kinship networks are also central to Amina Zarrugh's look at how family-led and women-led social movements have emerged in response to the use of disappearance as a tool of political and social terror in many different national contexts. Zarrugh's "Uncertainty as Statecraft: Family Movements Contesting Disappearance" charts the ways state actors often rely on inaction and the uncertainty of disappearance as a source of disruption and power as families are left wondering what has happened to their kin and are forced to negotiate the ambiguous emotional, political, and legal consequences produced by these practices. Yet, out of this uncertainty, Zarrugh argues, activists have deployed these circumstances and the moral force of the family to build collective action and contest state power. The article speaks to how activists might launch successful challenges to discursive strategies of state actors by embracing certain liberal discourses and normative identities like parent, mother, and family.

Yet as Zarrugh and others in this special issue note, such strategies that mobilize normative structures of state power do not come without often unintended consequences. The tensions, pitfalls, and complications of liberal strategies of resistance are mapped out in Sara Clarke Kaplan's article "After *Roe*: Race, Reproduction, and Life at the Limit of Law." Kaplan seeks to reorient the liberal discourse emerging from abortion rights supporters who decry the overturn of *Roe v. Wade* as a crisis in reproductive politics reflective of a broader crisis in liberal governance. She excavates how such arguments purport to highlight the "unplanned consequences" of the state's overreach but also elide any analysis of racial power and difference that continue to structure reproductive policies and practices in the United States. Kaplan urges an alternative perspective that resists upholding liberal governance long managed through the policing of bodies deemed nonnormative and instead views abortion rights as deeply linked to broader struggles for racial, sexual, and gender freedom.

The second section of this special issue includes some of the most insightful new scholarship that engages issues regarding political organizing and activist encounters with state power. Drawing from their own book-length studies, the four scholars in this section give context and specificity to some of the common threads woven throughout this issue. They also provide new approaches to thinking through the routes and strategies of grassroots and international movements that have challenged state forces, policies, and resource distribution. We are pleased to include Christina Heatherton's "How to Make Revolution," which introduces us to the "convergence spaces" of internationalism in the era of the Mexican Revolution; Ren-yo Hwang's "Trans of Color Entrapments and Carceral Coalitions," which examines mainstream protrans identity politics in relation to mandates emerging from California's carceral state; Jennifer Dominique Jones's investigation of the postwar military policies that imbricated gay and Black identities in "Black Liberals, the Cold War Straight State, and the Politics of Ambivalence"; and Rosemary Ndubuizu's "Gendering the Politics of Black Displacement," which analyzes the racialized and gendered local and federal politics of affordable housing in Washington, DC.

Each author considers community-based activism and organizational efforts to address the struggles of minoritized and marginalized people facing the crushing burdens of war, capitalism, and the carceral state. They are also attentive to internal and external tensions that emerge around making strategic demands on the state and the often coercive power and violence of state-led accommodations and reforms. These points reveal common through lines between these short pieces and the issue's lead articles, such as the ways community-based and activist-oriented programs have often empowered the carceral state; the force and far reach of the normative state (from its co-optation of radical discourse to coercive laws and practices); and how grassroots activists and broad mobilizations can open up key points of leverage by reclaiming or reframing state-sanctioned identities or mobilizing under the banner of successful legacies of resistance.

One such legacy of resistance is featured in our Classics Revisited section, which is on the first issue of *Triple Jeopardy* published by the Third World Women's Alliance (TWWA) in 1971. We include images of the cover of the newspaper, an editorial statement detailing the group's vision, and the "Tuesday Schedule" of political education sessions held in New York City. Responding to these sources, the three essays in this section chart the role of political education in building a mass movement, the need for a multifaceted and internationalist strategy to resist state violence, and the central place of women of color in the history of radical political visions. Vani Kannan focuses on the "Tuesday Schedule," highlighting the importance of writing—be it in magazines, newspapers, newsletters, journals, or books—as a part of building organizations, and thus a key concern, too, for those who write, teach writing, or study writing as political work today.

Lenora R. Knowles also examines how the TWWA adopted *Triple Jeopardy* as a political education tool and its continued relevance today. Knowles focuses on their use of the rhetorical device of the question, their analysis of state power, and efforts to link Third World communities. She thinks through these lessons in relation to her own participation in political education and leadership development as an organizer in Baltimore. And finally, Tiana U. Wilson provides a close reading of the *process* of creating *Triple Jeopardy*. Drawing on her oral history with TWWA cofounder and lead editor of *Triple Jeopardy*, Frances Beal, Wilson traces Beal's political and journalistic path and how it shaped some of the collective's editorial, labor, and distribution strategies. She also emphasizes the role the newspaper played in situating women of color as leaders in socialist organizing at that time.

Revisiting the TWWA history of political writing as political practice provides a perfect transition to the final section of our special issue: book reviews. We feature reviews of four new books that analyze state power by centering gender, sexuality, and racialization; engaging the history of social movements; and analyzing the state, without treating any of these topics in isolation. Instead, these books look at how the state functions as a precise set of punitive forces, but also as an abstract form that might be reimagined. This includes Erica R. Edwards's *The Other Side of Terror: Black Women and the Culture of U.S. Empire*, reviewed by Roderick A. Ferguson; *Love's Next Meeting: The Forgotten History of Homosexuality and the Left in American Culture* by Aaron Lecklider, reviewed by Zifeng Liu; *Red Scare: The State's Indigenous Terrorist* by Joanne Barker, reviewed by Juliana Hu Pegues; and *Abolition. Feminism. Now.* by Angela Y. Davis, Gina Dent, Erica R. Meiners, and Beth E. Richie, reviewed by Barbara Ransby. The issue closes out with two short pieces selected by the journal's poetry and general editors. We hope that the interventions and provocations offered up in this collection of writings on state power provide some insights into how activists and social movements imagine new paths to justice and liberation.

### Acknowledgments
We would like to thank the editors, editorial board, and leadership of *WSQ* for their support for this issue. We are particularly grateful for the editorial acumen of Googie Karrass and Nick Whitney, as well as the numerous peer reviewers who helped to strengthen this issue.

**Dayo F. Gore** is associate professor in the Department of African American Studies at Georgetown University and has previously taught in the Department of Ethnic Studies and Critical Gender Studies Program at the University of California, San Diego. She is the author of *Radicalism at the Crossroads: African American Women Activists in the Cold War* and coeditor of *Want to Start a Revolution: Radical Women in the Black Freedom Struggle*. She can be reached at dg1013@georgetown.edu.

**Christina B. Hanhardt** is associate professor in the Department of American Studies and an affiliate of the Department of Women, Gender, and Sexuality Studies at the University of Maryland, College Park. She is the author of *Safe Space: Gay Neighborhood History and the Politics of Violence*, which was awarded the Lamdba Literary Award for Best Book in LGBT Studies. She can be reached at hanhardt@umd.edu.

## Works Cited

Movement for Black Lives. 2020. "The Preamble: The Vision for Black Lives." Movement for Black Lives. https://m4bl.org/policy-platforms/the-preamble/.

PART I. **ARTICLES**

# "The Potential That Was in All of Us": Carceral Disability and the Japanese American Redress Movement

Adria L. Imada

**Abstract:** The mass incarceration of more than 120,000 Japanese Americans during World War II has usually been assessed in terms of devastating economic and property losses, racist profiling, and the abrogation of constitutional rights. However, survivors also claimed incarceration as an experience of individual and collective disablement. In a break from decorum, survivors testified about a range of mental and physical disabilities at the U.S. Commission on Wartime Relocation and Internment of Civilians Hearings (CWRIC) held across the United States in 1981. This article discusses how a grassroots redress movement for government restitution brought the experiences of disabled, chronically ill, and mad people into the Commission hearings. Informed by 1960s–1970s Asian American and Third World Women's movements, intergenerational redress organizing transmitted and amplified the subjugated knowledge of disabled survivors. These efforts to involve ordinary people in redress produced an unanticipated yet profound record of what I call *carceral disability*: the aggregate disabling effects of mass incarceration and state violence. I further deliberate on the unresolvable ambiguities and ongoing anticarceral legacies of the Redress Movement. **Keywords:** Japanese American wartime incarceration; redress and reparations; grassroots organizing; disability; anticarceral activism

Several Japanese American women testified before a U.S. congressional commission held in a Los Angeles state government building on August 4, 1981. Of different ages and occupations, all had been removed forcibly from the West Coast following Japan's attack on Pearl Harbor. They and their families had been incarcerated in U.S. concentration camps, also known

*WSQ: Women's Studies Quarterly* 51: 1 & 2 (Spring/Summer 2023)

euphemistically as "relocation centers" or "internment camps," which operated for nearly four years between 1942 and 1945.[1] Each witness presented
short oral testimonies to the fact-finding panel about the disabling effects
of wartime mass incarceration.

Mary Sakaguchi Oda, a doctor, spoke of her college-age sister's nervous
breakdown, which required five months' psychiatric hospitalization, as well
as the deaths of another sister, her father, and her brother. Mabel T. Ota,
a retired school principal who had been deprived of obstetric care while
incarcerated, testified about the permanent brain damage sustained by her
daughter during birth. Her developmentally disabled daughter had grand
mal seizures and was still being cared for at home nearly forty years later.
Mary Fumiko Kurihara, a former garment worker, described her "mental
anguish" and deteriorating health as she tried to work and provide for her
child during and after incarceration. Akiyo DeLoyd said she recently began
undergoing therapy to cope with forty years of feeling like a second-class
citizen (Herzig Papers 1981b, box 193, folder 3, 86–89; 93–112; "Commission on Wartime Relocation and Internment Testimony," *Rafu Shimpo*,
August 5, 1981).

Halted occasionally by tears, their testimonies were observed by a larger
audience of men and women sitting behind them in a nondescript government auditorium. In videotaped footage of the hearing, Japanese American
women in attendance can be seen crying softly and wiping their eyes (Visual
Communications 1981a).[2] Oda, Ota, Kurihara, and DeLoyd were but a
few of approximately five hundred Japanese American survivors of different generations, class backgrounds, and immigration statuses who testified
at the U.S. Commission on Wartime Relocation and Internment of Civilians (CWRIC) hearings. Ten hearings were convened during the summer
and fall of 1981 in nine U.S. locations. The bipartisan federal CWRIC was
a temporary body established by an act of Congress in 1980 to study the
World War II incarceration of 120,000 Japanese Americans and "recom-
mend appropriate remedies" (*Personal Justice Denied* 1997, 1).[3]

The overwhelming majority of attestants at the hearings were not professional "experts" or community leaders but survivors contributing their
stories for the first time on the official record. Although they described
devastating economic and property loss, interrupted educational opportunities, racist targeting, and the abrogation of constitutional rights during
and after incarceration, Japanese American survivors also narrated ongoing
disabilities, trauma, institutionalization, severe depression, and exposure to

suicide, to a degree unheard of and undocumented to date. Such disabilities became visible within demands for government reparations.[4]

What brought survivors to disclose such disabilities in public? The hearings were the culmination of nearly a decade of grassroots agitation for government redress. This redress movement for U.S. government apology and restitution recruited the participation of ordinary Japanese Americans who considered themselves neither experts nor activists.[5] In this article, I discuss how intergenerational organizing during the hearings phase of redress transmitted and amplified the subjugated knowledge and experiences of disabled survivors. Grassroots organizers' goals could be summarized as follows: "Bring the hearings to the people, and the people to the hearings." At times explicitly informed by feminist principles, this collective work allowed Japanese American incarceration to emerge as an experience of mass disablement.

Despite the prominence of disabled, chronically ill, and mad people in the CWRIC hearings, disability has not garnered much attention in the breadth of scholarship on the Japanese American Redress Move-ment (Daniels, Taylor, and Kitano 1991; Hatamiya 1993; Takezawa 1995; Maki, Kitano, and Berthold 1999; Shimabukuro 2001; Murray 2008). This omission may be because redress activists did not deploy the language of disability rights per se, nor did they frame redress as a disability movement. Nevertheless, activists' extensive outreach to, and recruitment of, diverse people for the hearings disclosed disability as a significant force shaping Japanese American life at the time. These public testimonies disrupted prevailing ableist representations of Japanese Americans who had mended from incarceration.

Thus, grassroots redress activism produced an unanticipated yet profound outcome: a record of what we might call *carceral disability*, or the aggregate disabling effects of mass incarceration. The hearings provided stark evidence of what Liat Ben-Moshe has called "disablement as a form of state violence" (2020, 156).[6] In a break from decorum, survivors conveyed the cumulative and ongoing toll of state violence on themselves and their loved ones. Sally Kirita Tsuneishi, who had been uprooted from Kohala, Hawai'i, to the Jerome, Arkansas, camp, lamented, "Our family's greatest loss was in the potential that was in all of us" (Herzig Papers 1981b, box 193, folder 3, 118). However, "all of us" took on new meanings beyond collective loss, as redress organizers sought to harness the potential of a more complex cross-section of community members. I further deliberate

on the unresolvable ambiguities and the anticarceral legacies of redress that
continue to unfold.

### Mobilizing Diverse Voices

Participation in the CWRIC hearings posed significant barriers. Some individuals and organizations who had been pressing for redress and reparations
were incensed by the very creation of the Commission in 1980, viewing
it as a backsliding step or stalling tactic (Hohri 1988, 87; Maki, Kitano,
and Berthold 1999, 88).[7] The CWRIC would delay restitution as Issei
(first-generation) elders were dying. Furthermore, most Japanese Americans were either wary, or knew little, of redress rationales, nor were they
inclined to trust a commission run by the government that had imprisoned them. The requirement that potential witnesses submit a form with a
personal profile made survivors balk. What might the federal government
do with this personal information (NCRR 2018, 201)?

Grassroots redress organizers, thus, faced formidable obstacles from the
start. First, Japanese Americans were reluctant to talk about incarceration,
even within their own families. Instead, "social amnesia," internal silence, and
assimilation became characteristic responses in the postwar era (Kashima
1980, 13; Nagata 1993, 99; NCRR 2018, 144). Second, claiming stigmatized
experiences of bodily impairment, madness, and ongoing mental disabilities
in public was unprecedented, particularly for older Japanese Americans.[8]
However, a coalition of grassroots activists approached the CWRIC and its
upcoming hearings as a useful means to unite Japanese Americans, educate
the broader public about wartime incarceration, and agitate for redress.
Founded in 1980, the National Coalition for Redress/Reparations (NCRR)
was a network of progressive Nisei (second-generation Japanese Americans,
that is, born of immigrant parents) and Sansei (third-generation Japanese
Americans). NCRR had its largest base in Los Angeles, California, with
regional affiliates in San Diego, Sacramento, San Francisco, San Jose, and
New York (*NCRR Banner*, May 1981, June–July 1981).[9]

The community organizing of the leftist, Los Angeles chapter of NCRR
has been the best known and most documented to date, via oral histories
and members' autoethnographic writings that account for their motivations
and approaches to redress. Indeed, LA NCRR was influential and visible in
redress organizing; it mobilized the largest constituency of survivors for the
first CWRIC fact-finding hearings held outside of Washington, DC. While

this article discusses Los Angeles as a pivotal and influential center of redress activism, it also provides assessments of grassroots redress activities in other regions. Lesser-known and smaller groups outside of Los Angeles—whether NCRR affiliates or other coalitions—also recruited attestants for hearings. Not all redress groups identified as leftist or feminist, but many had female leaders or a core membership of women volunteers of different ages, as in New York City and Seattle.[10]

Activists in NCRR aimed to mobilize a diverse community for the hearings (Murray 2008, 314, 318; "Community Group Airs Views on Nikkei Redress," *Rafu Shimpo*, February 22, 1980). Lillian Nakano of Los Angeles NCRR described their objective: "This should be testifiers coming from the community. The real people, people who suffered, people who have something to say, and they should be able to say it" (Nakano 2009). The more conservative Japanese American Citizens League (JACL), a mainstream national civil rights organization, pursued top-down legislative lobbying for redress in Washington, DC. Although some regional JACL chapters assembled a broad array of witnesses, others strategized to seat upstanding Japanese American community leaders and veterans who would impress the CWRIC with wartime patriotism and military sacrifice (Murray 2008, 305–6).[11]

By contrast, to recruit "many voices of the Nikkei community," such as nonexperts, women, working-class people, the elderly, and noncitizens, NCRR went to places where Japanese Americans lived, shopped, worked, and worshipped.[12] Sansei and Nisei organizers tabled with leaflets and petitions at the Village Plaza in Little Tokyo, Los Angeles. At the 1980 mochitsuki (mochi pounding), an important year-end community event in Little Tokyo, volunteers brought a literature table and talked to people about redress goals (*NCRR Banner*, February 1981). Nisei and Sansei volunteers were busy giving presentations and workshops at Christian, Buddhist, and Shinto churches and distributing newsletters throughout the summer of 1981 ("Educators Endorse NCRR Goals," *Rafu Shimpo*, May 18, 1981; "'Camp Experience' Topic of Redress Workshop," *Rafu Shimpo*, July 17, 1981).

In various locations, local redress volunteers publicized upcoming hearings, provided updates on their communications with CWRIC, and mobilized witnesses. In New York City, Concerned Japanese Americans (CJA), a NCRR affiliate, conducted outreach in a very different environment from Los Angeles. As New York had a dispersed Japanese American community with no geographic center, CJA tapped into networks of progressive

activists, artists, cultural workers, Japanese American churches, and veterans.[13] They held community meetings, potluck dinners, fundraising drives,
and a media campaign in 1981 (Fujino 2005, 263–64; Hohri Collection).
One CJA cultural program featured Asian American playwrights Philip Kan
Gotanda and David Henry Hwang, among others. With persistent peti-
tioning, CJA was able to secure New York City as an additional hearing site
from the CWRIC and ultimately seated witnesses of various generations
and carceral experiences from the Northeast.

### The Emergence of Grassroots Redress

What gave rise to this grassroots activism? In the 1960s and 1970s, Sansei
(third-generation Japanese Americans) converged in an inchoate "structure of feeling"—a lived experience of social contestation (Williams 1977,
130–32). Many Sansei had not been incarcerated themselves, but were
the children and grandchildren of survivors. This younger generation had
learned little about wartime incarceration from their families, but they
sought to understand and address the mental illness, alienation, alcoholism, drug abuse, and poverty they witnessed within their families or wider
communities. In Southern California, Alan Nishio's father, for example,
had been forced to give up his grocery business when he was incarcerated,
and as a result he took up gardening, a job he hated. He died of alcoholism
in 1968 (Nishio 1994; NCRR 2018, 61). Among Miya Iwataki's revela-
tions was seeing many unmarried elderly Issei men, "some abandoned by
their own families, living in rat-trap rooms in Little Tokyo" (NCRR 2018,
103). Sansei drew upon this collective feeling of distress as a resource for
an umbrella of political, cultural, and social work projects, and later for the
Redress Movement.

   Involvement in broader Asian American, Black Power, and Third World
anti-imperial movements also energized Sansei activists. Protesting the Vietnam War, they developed critiques of systemic racism, capitalism, and the
exploitation of people of color. Some enrolled in Asian studies and ethnic
studies courses at institutions like UCLA, UC Berkeley, and San Francisco
State. They began to investigate wartime concentration camps and organize early community pilgrimages to the Manzanar and Tule Lake camps
(*Gidra*, January 1970).[14]

   As California activists witnessed ill health, housing insecurity, and
poverty in their communities, they traced these contemporary conditions

to economic racism and wartime incarceration. In Los Angeles, Sansei activists created "Serve the People" community projects that supported neglected Japanese Americans (NCRR 2018, 35, 76, 103; *Gidra*, December 1973). These programs provided social services, counseling, and self-help drug intervention to a broad swath of vulnerable and abandoned people, including recently released felons, sick and disabled people, blind people, impoverished elderly Issei, and adolescent girls (Hamano Quon 2001, 214; *Gidra*, December 1973).

When elderly male Issei and working-class Japanese American residents were evicted and displaced by the redevelopment of Little Tokyo, the Little Tokyo People's Rights Organization (LTPRO) protested. Organizers viewed the proposed 1970s "relocation" of these undesirable residents as an extension of the unjust 1942 removal and incarceration of unwanted Japanese Americans ("Community Group Airs Views on Nikkei Redress," *Rafu Shimpo*, February 22, 1980; NCRR 2018, 54).

Inspired by Third World feminism, Japanese American women in Los Angeles, most of whom were Sansei, founded the feminist group Asian Sisters. In response to the crisis of adolescent young women's drug addiction and overdoses in the early 1970s, they provided space for Asian American women to counsel younger peers (Hamano Quon 2001, 212). Asian Sisters also created meetings for immigrant parents to support each other and communicate more effectively with their children. The Sisters organized weekly carpools for parents who did not own cars and drove them to sessions (Fu 2008, 91). Merilynne Hamano and the Asian Sisters' astute diagnosis was that the current drug abuse epidemic and suicides among Sansei youth were outcomes of assimilation and a silent response to wartime incarceration and racial and capitalist exploitation (Hamano 1972, 8; Fu 2008, 87). In their quest for solutions, the Asian Sisters and their allies were unafraid of exposing trauma and ugliness. Some of these Los Angeles Sansei—including Hamano, Kathy Nishimoto Masaoka, Miya Iwataki, and Alan Nishio—brought these energies and strategies to the Redress Movement and the newly formed NCRR in California.

### Gender Equity and Intergenerational Negotiation

Grassroots redress relied on the active participation of women and on intergenerational labor. NCRR in particular was committed to men and women of different generations sharing equitably in decision-making and administrative labor. It was loosely structured and did not operate by strict age-based hierarchy or patriarchal governance. Lillian Nakano, a Nisei who worked alongside her husband, Bert Nakano, in LA NCRR, said many women took on leadership roles in their group. She emphasized, "Not just token things where the men do all the talking and the women do the staffing!" (*NCRR Reader* 2006).[15] Nakano and other women were quick to alert male peers to sexist or disparaging behavior. Addressing "chauvinism," they cleared the way for Japanese American women to participate more freely in community spaces (Nakano 2009). Alan Nishio of LA NCRR concurred that grassroots redress was a feminist environment: "If you were strongly chauvinistic in your attitude as a man, you would either have to change dramatically and quickly or you would not feel comfortable within NCRR!" (*NCRR Reader* 2006).

Such feminist practices in grassroots work had been forged by Japanese American women during prior 1960s–1970s Asian American and Third World women's movements. As historian Valerie Matsumoto has analyzed, Sansei women shaped these movements with astute critiques of their gendered racialization (2016, 184). Merilynne Hamano Quon, a founder of Asian Sisters and a NCRR Southern California outreach organizer between 1980 and 1985, argued of women in the Asian American movement: "We were not just 'warm and cuddly' basically 'brainless' women waiting for the 'line' to be handed down by men. We wrote theory; debated strategy; chaired meetings; spoke at rallies; and organized workers, youth, elderly, and the poor on an equal footing with the men" (Hamano Quon 2001, 211).

Two female cochairs led the New York City–based East Coast Japanese Americans for Redress (ECJAR), a redress coalition that had developed from the work of CJA members. These women were Sasha Hohri, a younger Sansei, and Michi Kobi, a Nisei. In Seattle, two women, Cherry Kinoshita and Karen Seriguchi, did most of the groundwork in Community Committee on Redress/Reparations (CCRR), a redress group unaffiliated with NCRR. In their respective regions, these women did extensive outreach to prepare and seat witnesses (Shimabukuro 2001, 71; NY JAOH 2021). As Nisei and Sansei women took on leadership roles in redress organizing, Lillian Nakano of LA NCRR recalled how the CWRIC took notice. Joan Bernstein, the chairperson of the nine-person CWRIC and its only woman commissioner, remarked on how NCRR had so many women involved compared to JACL (Nakano 2009).

Feminist grassroots organizing for redress meant that some Japanese American men, Nisei and Sansei alike, took on labor historically considered female work. Men staffed literature tables and spoke at churches and house meetings (Matsuoka 2010; *NCRR Reader* 2006; NCRR 2018, 209). In New York's ECJAR, husband-and-wife activists William (Bill) and Yuri Kochiyama worked on media outreach for the upcoming CWRIC hearing in New York. Both drew on their wide political and cultural networks to fundraise, write press releases, inform community members, and publicize the November 23, 1981, hearing (Fujino 2005, 263–64).

### Preparing for the Hearings

Redress organizers recruited a heterogenous set of witnesses and prepared them to contribute their stories in a public setting. One of their steepest tasks was convincing surviving Issei to testify. As first-generation immigrants, Issei had experienced direct harm during and after incarceration. They were now elderly, often isolated, and primarily spoke Japanese. Nisei and Sansei organizers met them at their homes, senior citizen centers, and churches and did their best to communicate redress goals in Japanese, even if their language skills were not stellar (Matsuoka 2010). In New York, ECJAR held community outreach meetings in 1981 that included Issei; they printed flyers in English and Japanese and provided Japanese translators (Hohri Collection). In Seattle, organizer Karen Seriguchi set up meetings with Issei at local churches and brought translators. The Seattle group also published a Japanese-language version of its redress survey in the local Japanese newspaper (Shimabukuro 2001, 68).

Embodied, face-to-face interactions helped to persuade reluctant Issei to participate. In San Jose, California, Richard Katsuda, a Sansei from the Nihonmachi Outreach Committee (NOC) approached Umeno Fujino, a feisty Issei elder, about whether she might testify at the hearings. She declined, replying in Japanese that the government would not listen to an old lady like her. Finally, Katsuda told her, "But Fujino-san, *kodomo no tame ni*, you need to do it for the sake of your children and grandchildren." Fujino paused a moment, then concluded, "*Mmmm, so da ne* [Hmmm, that's right]," and agreed to testify. Four more Issei followed Fujino's lead and signed up as witnesses for the San Francisco hearings held in August 1981 (NCRR 2018, 208–9). From personal encounters like these, organizers were able to fill CWRIC hearing agendas.

While convincing community members to testify was a critical step, activists also tackled an onerous amount of clerical labor under tight deadlines, since potential witnesses were vetted and selected by CWRIC staff in Washington, DC. Getting seated on a hearing panel was a bureaucratic process beset with daunting barriers to most laypeople. Anyone wishing to present testimony needed to send a sheet with a personal profile and "summary of key areas of testimony" as well as a full copy of written testimony in advance to CWRIC ("Redress Reports," *Pacific Citizen*, July 10, 1981). Organizers explained these rules at community workshops. In advance of the Los Angeles hearings, for instance, NCRR members transcribed oral testimony, provided translations for Japanese speakers, and typed, photocopied, and mailed documents (NCRR 2018, 202).

Furthermore, redress organizers prepared witnesses to deliver oral testimonies since many had never spoken in public before. They held mock hearings in Seattle, Chicago, New York, and Los Angeles where people practiced giving their testimony in small groups or in front of audiences (NY JAOH 2021). In Seattle, the CCRR-organized mock hearing in May 1981 brought two hundred audience members and speakers to Nisei Veterans Committee Hall. Hearing people share their stories led to more witnesses at the official hearing in Seattle (Shimabukuro 2001, 71). LA NCRR, as well as local JACL chapters in California, held sessions for people to practice delivering condensed three to five minutes of testimony. At some sessions, judges role-played as the commissioners ("Seek Redress Hearing Testimony," *Rafu Shimpo*, March 24, 1981; Maki, Kitano, and Berthold 1999, 99). It was not uncommon for witnesses to break down crying during their testimonies, however. The redress committee of JACL Chicago may have anticipated how emotional this preparation would be for survivors. It brought a psychiatric nurse, a Sansei woman, to assist witnesses at its mock hearing (Tomihiro 1997).

Though this labor was often invisible or behind the scenes, it made people's access to the hearings possible. New York activists pushed the CWRIC to add New York City as an additional hearing site in order to allow Japanese Americans in that region, particularly elderly Issei survivors, to attend. After CJA leaders assembled petitions and testified at the Washington, DC, July hearings, the Commission added a New York City hearing date to its agenda (Hohri Collection, Sasha Hohri letter to Joan Bernstein, June 12, 1981; Sasha Hohri testimony July 16, 1981).

Realizing it would be difficult for working people to participate in daytime hearings, LA NCRR demanded that the Commission hold evening sessions in accessible community locations. They ultimately secured an evening hearing at Little Tokyo Towers on Tuesday, August 4, 1981. Little Tokyo Towers housed senior citizen apartment units, largely occupied by elderly Issei who had no other family. NCRR also stipulated that Japanese-language interpreters provide simultaneous translation for Issei who did not speak English, and it later coordinated these services with CWRIC staff for the Los Angeles hearings (*NCRR Banner*, February 1981; NCRR 2018, 203).

Redress groups also took care to provide transportation to the San Francisco and Los Angeles hearings, especially for elderly people who did not drive and lived far from hearing sites. At the Los Angeles hearings, NCRR members arranged headphones for Japanese speakers to hear simultaneous translation, overflow rooms and speakers to accommodate more attendees, bento (box lunches) so people could commune during lunch, and daily press releases for community updates (NCRR 2018, 202, 209). Miya Iwataki, a NCRR cofounder, was so occupied with these preparations that she herself was not able to testify, to her later regret (*NCRR Reader* 2006).

### Disrupting Assimilation and Ableism

Although grassroots redress organizing was not oriented specifically toward disability or gender justice per se, intensive outreach to ordinary community members meant that hundreds of women, elderly people, and people with disabilities who would not have been seated as witnesses ultimately contributed testimony to ten CWRIC hearings in nine locations.[16] Among those testifying about mental illness was a Nisei man named George Morimoto in Los Angeles. He offered composed testimony about his mental breakdowns and severe depression since his family's incarceration at the Heart Mountain, Wyoming, concentration camp. Morimoto witnessed how his father's "years of detention and institutionalization destroyed his independence and initiative." Morimoto's own anxiety and "emotional stress" caused him to lose his hair and suffer episodes of depression. While seeking periodic counseling and therapy, Morimoto decided to bring his testimony to the CWRIC to find a remedy for his "repressed anger" (Visual Communications 1981b).

Witnesses like Morimoto contributed their stories at great personal risk, forming a substantial and expressive record of carceral disability unheard publicly until this time. In doing so, this record neutralized ableist assumptions and assertions of divergent political actors, whether they were opponents or supporters of redress. One of the most extreme anti-redress positions was exemplified by Republican U.S. senator Samuel Ichiye (S.I.) Hayakawa of California. Born in Canada, Hayakawa was a naturalized U.S. citizen of Japanese ancestry. As the first speaker at the Los Angeles hearings, he argued that Japanese Americans had no need for restitution, since they had recovered since incarceration and perhaps even benefited from it. Hayakawa claimed that wartime incarceration was a "three-year vacation" in which Japanese Americans led "trouble free and relatively happy lives." He further argued that the monetary restitution demanded by redress activists would be a travesty and insult, since Japanese Americans had flourished into an "almost a privileged class" with "notorious scholastic aptitude" (Herzig Papers 1981b, box 193, folder 3, 17, 19, 23).

Hayakawa's portrayal of an unscathed, prosperous Japanese American community enjoying educational and professional achievement was far from an outlier.[17] The *Wall Street Journal* slammed redress proposals in 1978 as "guilt mongering" by "self-appointed ethnic spokesmen." It asserted that compensation was unnecessary since Japanese American "passion for upward mobility [. . .] led them to position of prestige and power ("Guilt Mongering," August 11, 1978). These commentaries presented Japanese Americans as nondisabled achievers—immigrants who had assimilated and seized the classic, ableist American paradigm of self-reliance, "hard work and determination" (Nielsen 2012, xii).

Yet another stinging ableist critique arrived from the opposite end of the political spectrum. Frank Chin, the rabble-rousing contrarian Chinese American playwright who had instigated important redress direct action events in Seattle, jeered the Los Angeles CWRIC hearings as a "circus of freaks."[18] In a lengthy opinion piece published on the front page of the *Rafu Shimpo* newspaper, Chin decried the "sobstory testimony" of "victim after victim" who offered but shallow insights into their incarceration experience. Asking for scholars and experts instead, Chin dismissed the stories of ordinary people: "as expert as the testimony of the mentally retarded on retardation" ("Unfocused L.A. Hearings: 'A Circus of Freaks,'" August 21, 1981). In this view, witnesses sorely lacked the knowledge and intelligence to interpret their own histories.

To be sure, some redress activists eschewed the airing of personal distress in government testimony, viewing this as a tactical misstep and exploitative spectacle. William Hohri, leader of the Chicago-based National Council for Japanese American Redress (NCJAR), testified on the first day of the Washington, DC, hearings that his members were "offended" by the idea of reliving their ordeals in an "upsetting and distasteful" public exhibition (Hohri Collection, Hohri CWRIC testimony, July 16, 1981; Herzig-Yoshinaga and Lee 2011, 18). Similarly, Shosuke Sasaki, a retired statistician and activist in Seattle who worked closely with Hohri on redress, objected to the disability narratives emerging from CWRIC testimonies.[19] Three days before the hearings were scheduled to begin in Seattle, Sasaki's op-ed criticized the "demeaning" testimonies at Los Angeles and San Francisco to date. He argued, "[T]he heavy concentration on recitals of stories of humiliation, suffering and property loss is diverting attention away from the serious constitutional issues involved." Instead, Sasaki suggested, testimonies, if they were to be used at all, should be contributed by "prominent scholars" and "experts" ("Commission Is an Evasion of the Demand for Redress," *Seattle Post-Intelligencer*, September 6, 1981).

Despite his apparent antipathy to the hearings, Sasaki did not dispute the suffering of survivors. Indeed, as author of an early direct redress plan in 1975, Sasaki had relied on the categories of "mental and emotional suffering" and "psychological injuries" as reparations rationales (Shimabukuro 2011, 122). Ironically, Sasaki and the Seattle redress group's language referencing mental disabilities became incorporated into the core vocabulary of redress activism and the structure of the Commission agenda itself (e.g., its panels on "psychological impact").

### Redress Outcomes and Ambiguities

Against this backdrop of ableist praise and criticism, survivors nonetheless provided compelling evidence of aggregate disablement. Beginning in July in Washington, DC, and concluding in November 1981 in New York City, witnesses described a range of mental and physical disabilities: not being able to hold down jobs and experiencing their own mental illnesses as well as the mental hospital commitments, early deaths, and suicides of family members and friends.[20]

NCRR organizers considered the hearings a success, strengthening solidarity. After the CWRIC hearings, NCRR itself grew from about one thousand to eight thousand members (Murray 2008, 314). Miya Iwataki effused about Los Angeles, "In the hearing room, the empathy and support was palpable. Every story and every day created a group catharsis" (NCRR 2018, 202). The hearings also appeared to broker greater intergenerational understanding between the Nisei who had been incarcerated and their Sansei children. Some Sansei, seeing their parents and elders speaking out against the government for the first time, forgave the older generation for not protesting earlier. In turn, elders appreciated younger Sansei who worked so hard on redress actions (NCRR 2018, 209).

The Commission hearings marked a turning point in the Redress Movement, convincing more Japanese Americans of the need for restitution. The CWRIC drew on the oral and written witness testimonies for its comprehensive report, *Personal Justice Denied*, issued in 1982–83. It assessed that incarcerated people had suffered "enormous damages, both material and intangible," including injuries to the body and spirit (*Personal Justice Denied* 1997, 459–60). The CWRIC issued unanimous recommendations, including that Congress pass a joint resolution for a public apology and establish a redress fund for twenty-thousand-dollar payments to individual survivors, as well as an educational fund (*Personal Justice Denied* 1997). These recommendations were implemented five years later in the 1988 Civil Liberties Act (CLA) passed by Congress and signed by President Ronald Reagan.[21]

These legislative successes were celebrated by redress activists and many Japanese American survivors as victories for individuals and U.S. civil rights (Hohri 1988; Maki, Kitano, and Berthold 1999; Tateishi 2020). However, scholars have also examined the fragile and contradictory outcomes of the Japanese American Redress Movement as a set of social and legal remedies. In seeking accountability from the state that perpetrated these wrongs, redress outcomes were, by definition, narrow. The CLA bestowed apologies and reparations to a specific class of beneficiaries, but with limited effects on institutional and state racism (Yamamoto 1992, 240; 1999, 12). Furthermore, the United States, by acknowledging and correcting its abrogation of rights via the Japanese American redress process, may claim a restoration of liberal democracy while hiding other acts of state violence and racism (Paik 2016, 30).

The inadequacy of state-enacted remedies is suggested by survivor testimonies themselves. As dictated by the testimonial format and the state's demand for truth claims, witnesses provided empirical evidence with names, dates, and sequences of events. However, many narratives also engendered ambiguity and ellipses, hinting at unpredictable psychological fragmentation and nonlinear experiences of disability and madness that survivors would continue to experience over time. In San Francisco, for instance, a man named Shin Mune described how his life had begun to change over the past five years as he became more aware of his own childhood memories in camp and his mother's suffering. Mune experienced an "inward" turn, becoming "almost a recluse," with a need to wander. His testimony ended with a polite "thank you very much" (Herzig Papers 1981c, box 194, folder 4, 35–36). However, where his wandering would lead and for how long could not be known. Such ambiguities exceeded the hearing format and the temporality of the Redress Movement itself.

For some witnesses, speaking brought relief, release, and hope. Ichiro Matsuda, the pseudonym of a Nisei man in Seattle, debated whether to testify or not. After he did, he said, "I became a new person. [ . . . ] All the stigma, all this anguish, just went out of my body" (Takezawa 1995, 164). Yet for many, survivorship, as a public action, demands remembering, which can bring pain instead of catharsis. Those who are the most vulnerable or traumatized may suffer during and after testifying. Mei Nakano, organizer of a Japanese American women's history exhibit, reflected, "Rather than confer catharsis and release [ . . .] the act of giving testimony appeared to rekindle bitter memories" as it spurred survivors' determination (Nakano 1990, 203). Journalist Robert Shimabukuro recalled one survivor in Seattle telling him he had ruined her day by making her remember the incarceration (Shimabukuro 2001, xv–xvi).

For secondary survivors and Sansei like Margene Fudenna, the San Francisco hearings of four to five hundred people amounted to the largest discussion of Japanese American incarceration she had experienced to date. Fudenna was motivated to query her own family about the camps, only to have her own mother refuse to talk (Six Sansei 1992, 92–93). The hearings marked the symbolic beginning of a much longer and more uncertain quest for answers. Furthermore, survivors who were the most injured by mass incarceration were the least likely to benefit from individual reparations or community-oriented projects that were funded by the CLA. Even as hundreds of survivors like Shin Mune chose to speak of mental and bodily vulnerabilities, other stories were lost. Many survivors did not join the Redress Movement, while some remained too economically and socially marginalized to be located.[22] After the 1988 passage of the CLA, the U.S. Office of Redress Administration began to issue twenty-thousand-dollar payments to documented survivors. Tsuyako "Sox" Kitashima of Seattle, a Nisei who became an activist after testifying at CWRIC hearings, volunteered to assist Japanese Americans with the necessary restitution paperwork. Though persistent in her efforts, Kitashima had uneven success in the 1990s with survivors who were disabled, mentally ill, homeless, or living without family members in congregant institutions (Kitashima and Morimoto 2003, 113–15, 121).

### Conclusion: Lessons of Carceral Disability

Still another afterlife of redress that remains underexplored is whether its record of carceral disability produced its own legacies.[23] How might this record shape reparative changes, as in the sense of repairing damage and relationships beyond monetary compensation (Yamamoto 1999, 15)? Has carceral disability stimulated post-redress social and political transformations? Redress could neither fully encompass healing nor resolve persistent wounds. However, grassroots activists continue to address evolving challenges. In the four decades since the CWRIC hearings, the anticarceral lessons of redress inform and galvanize responses to recurring state racism.

Organizers with NCRR did not see the apology as the end of their struggle. NCRR changed its name to Nikkei for Civil Rights and Redress after the 1988 CLA passage and turned its attention to anticarceral and reparations coalitions. NCRR, in its early formation, asserted that redress included "supporting others who are suffering from unjust actions taken by the United States government" ("Educators Endorse NCRR Goals," *Rafu Shimpo*, May 14, 1981). Though NCRR was a relatively small group, its principles and practices were informed by allied struggles with African Americans, working class immigrants, and Indigenous people (NCRR 2018, 353). Its members rallied in support of Navajo sovereignty in 1986 after the government issued an eviction order for Navajo people living in Big Mountain, Arizona. NCRR explicitly likened this action to the unjust removal of Japanese Americans (NCRR 2018, 322–23). It also pivoted to anticarceral causes, such as opposition to the 9/11 racial profiling of Muslim Americans.

More recently, members coordinated letter-writing campaigns in support of H.R. 40, a reparations bill for African Americans introduced to Congress in 2021. H.R. 40 proposes a federal commission similar to the CWRIC that would study the U.S. government's role in supporting the institution of slavery and develop reparation proposals (Commission 2021). Kathy Masaoka, a longtime NCRR organizer, declared in her February 2021 testimony to the House Judiciary Committee that African American demands for civil and equal rights in housing and education had "opened the door" for Japanese American redress. She argued that, as the CWRIC hearings did for Japanese American incarceration, "H.R. 40 is an opportunity to learn about the institution and legacy of slavery. [. . .] What we must do is listen and learn from these stories" (H.R. 40 2021).

Some Japanese American survivors have focused on the anticarceral causes of immigrant justice, the issue of migrant family reunification, and the project of ending police violence. Chizu Omori, a Nisei living in Seattle, became involved in redress in her late forties (Takezawa 1995, 48). Incarcerated at the age of twelve with her family at the Poston, Arizona, camp, Omori testified at the Seattle CWRIC hearings in 1981. There she described her mental distress as a "shroud-like covering" keeping her silent (Omori 1981). Spurred by their traumatic childhoods during incarceration, she and other Japanese American survivors founded Tsuru for Solidarity in 2019. This intergenerational group, primarily composed of Japanese American incarceration descendants of varied generations and ages, opposes the federal government's opening or repurposing of detention sites and prison camps for migrants and asylum seekers. Tsuru for Solidarity members, while not using the explicit language of disability rights, support the abolition of prisons to halt what could be called the disabling effects of state detention practices.

In June 2019, Omori and five other survivors traveled with younger Asian Americans to Fort Sill, Oklahoma, to protest the planned detention of unaccompanied migrant children from Mexico and Central America (Ben Fenwick, "'Stop Repeating History': Plan to Keep Migrant Children at Former Internment Camp Draws Outrage," *New York Times*, June 22, 2019). Now a U.S. Army installation, Fort Sill was used as a prison for Chiricahua Apache people, including the leader Geronimo, in the 1890s. It also housed a boarding school for American Indian children and a detention facility for seven hundred Japanese immigrants during World War II.

Chizu Omori and the Japanese American contingent gathered with Apache and Kiowa tribal members and immigrant activists at the gates of Fort Sill. The then-ninety-year-old Omori, referring to her three-and-a-half-year incarceration, said, "I'm here to bear witness to the travesty of the American justice system. [. . .] The family separation policy is ruining the lives of these children. We the people have to stand up and protest this" (Kondo 2019).[24]

In the wake of the successful 1988 CLA passage, observers cautioned that redress must push beyond its immediate beneficiaries, lest reparations preserve the "illusion of change" with little lasting structural or political transformation (Yamamoto 1992, 240). To be sure, state power shifts and changes form, imperiling different communities, whether inside, outside, or between the formal boundaries of the U.S. nation-state. Yet the "all of us" ethos of grassroots redress continues to animate responses to state violence. As she stood on the lands of the Apache people, Chizu Omori's demand for an anticarceral future was a reverberating echo of 1980s redress. This work of redress may become its most persistent legacy.

### Acknowledgments
This article is dedicated to my uncle and aunty, Atsumi Eto and Yemi Eto, who survived incarceration at Tule Lake, California; Jerome, Arkansas; and Heart Mountain, Wyoming. Support for this research was provided in part by a grant from Carnegie Corporation of New York. The staff of UCLA Library Special Collections, especially Molly Haigh, facilitated access to the Jack and Aiko Herzig Papers at a critical stage. I also warmly thank Glen Mimura, Sunyoung Lee, and Duncan Williams for sharing their insights, and Arnold Pan and Marjorie Lee of the UCLA Asian American Studies Center for lending time and expertise. *WSQ State/Power* special issue editors Christina Hanhardt and Dayo Gore, as well as two readers, provided generative feedback that greatly improved the ideas within.

**Adria L. Imada** is professor of history at University of California, Irvine, and a 2021 Andrew Carnegie Fellow. She is author of *Aloha America: Hula Circuits through the U.S. Empire* and *An Archive of Skin, An Archive of Kin: Disability and Life-Making during Medical Incarceration*. She can be reached at aimada@uci.edu.

### Notes
1. After Executive Order 9066 was issued by President Franklin D. Roosevelt in February 1942, "alien" noncitizen Japanese and Japanese Americans with citizenship living on the West Coast of the United States were sent to ten concentration camps run by the War Relocation Authority (WRA). Some Issei (first-generation, in other words, Japanese immigrants) and Japanese Americans living in Hawai'i also were sent to WRA camps on the U.S. continent or a separate internment camp in Hawai'i run by the U.S. Army. In addition, the U.S. Department of Justice (DOJ) imprisoned Japanese, Italian,

and German nationals with supposedly "suspect" loyalties in maximum-security "internment camps." I rely on "mass incarceration" to describe the forcible removal and imprisonment of people of Japanese descent during World War II. "U.S. concentration camp" refers to the ten WRA-run sites, while "internment camp" refers to the DOJ- or U.S. Army–run camps. Although out of favor with contemporary scholars and activists, the terms "internment camp" and "camp" were in wide use among Japanese Americans during and after redress activism. They also persist in the vernacular of some Japanese American survivors, regardless of official government designations and scholarly conventions. I retain the selective use of "internment" as used in original source materials.

2. The Los Angeles hearings were videotaped by Visual Communications (VC), an Asian American activist media organization. The video recording consists of over twenty-five hours of testimony given by 153 witnesses (Ichioka 1998). On the fortieth anniversary of the CWRIC hearings in August 2021, VC and NCRR (Nikkei for Civil Rights and Redress) posted its digitized hearings on the former's website. The Chicago hearings at Northeastern Illinois University were filmed on September 22–23, 1981, and some of the New York City hearing was videotaped on November 23, 1981.

3. After years of grassroots redress organizing, the temporary commission of nine appointees emerged as a series of compromises. The primary focus of the CWRIC was on Executive Order 9066 and Japanese Americans, but its mandate was broadened to include Alaska Natives who had been forcibly removed from the Aleutian and Pribilof Islands ("Aleut civilians" and "permanent resident aliens of the Aleutian and Pribilof Islands"). The addition of Aleuts to the CWRIC senate bill resulted in support from Alaska's senate delegation and inoculated the bill from criticism that it would benefit only Japanese Americans (Maki, Kitano, and Berthold 1999, 91). Of the oral testimonies provided by the 790 witnesses, approximately five hundred were from survivors. Edited summaries of CWRIC hearing transcripts and a list of attestants are in Herzig-Yoshinaga and Lee 2011, but the full oral and written transcripts have not been published.

4. Redress and reparations demands included a government apology, direct monetary compensation to survivors, and a community fund to compensate the entire community; the latter ultimately was not funded. The direct payments were intended to prevent the U.S. government from committing similar violations in the future.

5. The Japanese American Redress Movement consisted of multiple phases, including early 1970s discussions of monetary reparations, the establishment

of the CWRIC in 1980, the passage of the 1988 Civil Liberties Act (CLA) that funded twenty thousand dollars in restitution to each survivor, and the subsequent distribution of these reparations to survivors through 1998.

6. Japanese American mass incarceration was but one outcome of interlocking processes of state violence that some progressive redress activists addressed, and continue to address, in coalitional calls to action. Though outside the scope of this article, it is crucial to understand that colonial regimes produced disablement through genocidal practices of settler colonization, reservations, boarding and residential schooling, institutionalization, medical incarceration, starvation, and land privatization (Lomawaima 1994; McCallum 2017; Burch 2021; Imada 2021; Justice and O'Brien 2021; Whitt 2021). In the U.S. expansion of mass incarceration, people who are poor, disabled, and racialized have been disproportionately policed and imprisoned. At the same time, incarceration accelerates conditions of disability and ill health in these communities (Ben-Moshe, Chapman, and Carey 2014).

7. Some JACL chapters responded angrily to the national JACL recommendation for a commission. Another redress/reparations group emerging from Seattle dissented by forming the National Council on Japanese American Redress (NCJAR). Led by William Hohri in Chicago, NCJAR pursued $27 billion class-action litigation against the federal government instead of a legislative remedy (Hohri 1988, 191–224).

8. As social scientists and psychologists have noted, there is evidence suggesting Japanese Americans were reticent about disclosing mental illness. They also were more inclined to care for mentally ill family members at home, rather than place them in psychiatric hospitals (Fujii, Fukushima, and Yamamoto 1993, 336). Disability studies scholar Margaret Price, citing Cynthia Lewiecki-Wilson, argues for the use of the term "mental disability," as it encompasses "madness" as well as cognitive and intellectual disability (2013, 305). The previously pejorative terms "mad" and "madness" have been reinvigorated by psychiatric system survivors and the field of mad studies. In my use here, madness is more than a medical condition, and it includes the recognition that (1) inequitable social and economic conditions have led to diagnoses of mental illness (Staub 2011; Metzl 2011), and (2) psychiatric differences have been used to justify disenfranchisement (Aho, Ben-Moshe, and Hilton 2017, 293).

9. NCRR also had affiliations with Asian American student unions at University of California, Berkeley, and San Francisco State University.

10. The core membership of NCRR was composed of mostly Left-identified Sansei, but it also included Nisei and others who held more conservative political views (Murray 2008, 317).

11. The San Fernando chapter of the JACL in Southern California, for instance, urged Nisei veterans and families whose sons had died in war to show up in force at the Los Angeles hearings (*Rafu Shimpo*, August 1, 1981). Japanese Americans in the 1970s–80s remained ambivalent about the JACL due to its wartime policies and leadership. JACL had adopted a polarizing, hyper-American stance of urging compliance with the government's removal and evacuation order of Nikkei. Encouraging Nisei men to prove their loyalty through voluntary military service, it advocated the segregation of those who defied the draft (Lyon 2020; Masaoka and Hosokawa 1987; Murray 2008, 308). William Hohri of NCJAR excoriated the national JACL for packing the CWRIC hearings with its leaders and feting Commissioners with parties (Hohri 1988, 95).

12. Nikkei means emigrants of Japanese descent; here it refers to people of Japanese descent living in the United States, regardless of formal citizenship status.

13. In May 1981, Concerned Japanese Americans formally joined NCRR. CJA had attended the NCRR national conference in late 1980 and decided to join the redress coalition (Hohri Collection, Sasha Hohri Letter to CJA, January 1, 1981). CJA would later work on organizing for the New York hearing within a larger coalition called East Coast Japanese Americans for Redress (ECJAR).

14. The first organized pilgrimage to the former Manzanar concentration camp was December 1969.

15. Lillian Nakano, née Lillian Sugita, and Burt Nakano were Nisei born in Hawai'i.

16. Ten hearings were held over nineteen days in Washington, DC, Los Angeles, San Francisco, Seattle, Anchorage, Unalaska (Aleutian Islands, AK), St. Paul (Pribilof Islands, AK), Chicago, and New York. At the Alaska hearings, Aleut and Nikkei witnesses spoke of their continuing trauma (Herzig Papers 1981a). The United States had acted on different rationales for these groups' respective removal and imprisonment: Japanese and Japanese Americans were imprisoned for their perceived danger to national security, while Aleuts were relocated to protect them from invasion (Madden 1992, 56).

17. Japanese Americans in the Los Angeles CWRIC audience responded with loud boos and hisses, interrupting Hayakawa several times (Visual Communications, 1981a). Hayakawa had not been incarcerated during the war. He had become an "archenemy" of Japanese Americans, and his unpopular, extreme position against redress may have roused community members to move toward supporting the movement (Tateishi 2020, 192, 251).

18. Frank Chin made a significant contribution to redress by instigating the first Day of Remembrance (DOR) in Seattle over Thanksgiving weekend in 1978. The event reenacted the removal of Seattle Japanese Americans to the Puyallup Assembly Grounds and drew a few thousand community members, revitalizing support for redress. As DOR programs were adopted by other cities in the 1980s, they too reignited community support for redress and expanded media coverage of wartime incarceration (Shimabukuro 2001, 41–48; Nakagawa 2020).

19. Hohri's and Sasaki's critiques of the testimonials can be interpreted within the context of a broader disagreement over redress strategies and the creation of the blue-ribbon Commission. An Issei who had emigrated to Washington state as a child, Sasaki had been imprisoned with his family at the Minidoka, Idaho, concentration camp. Sasaki was a statistician and active member of the Seattle Evacuation Redress Committee (SERC), which developed an early template for individual reparations known as the Seattle Plan. A reparations bill developed by SERC, the World War II Civil Liberties Violation Redress Act (H.R. 5977), was introduced to Congress in 1979, but it failed. Instead, in the same year, the JACL National Committee for Redress (NCR) supported a congressional study commission bill, which passed with the support of Japanese American senators Daniel Inouye and Spark Matsunaga and representatives Norman Mineta and Robert Matsui. Opposing this strategy of a commission, Sasaki refused to testify at the 1981 CWRIC hearings (Shimabukuro 2001, 25–30, 73; Niiya 2016).

20. The opening Washington, DC, hearings held on July 16, 1981, were dominated by representatives of organizations, but a few individuals provided testimonies about carceral disabilities, illness, and death. Individual testimonies of disablement took center stage, however, at subsequent hearings in Los Angeles on August 4–6, 1981, through the final hearings in New York City on November 23, 1981 (Herzig Papers 1981a; Herzig-Yoshinaga and Lee 2011).

21. The monetary distribution for the CLA totaled over $1.5 billion. An affiliated Aleut Restitution Act in 1988 provided twelve thousand dollars for each Aleut survivor; Aleuts had been forcibly relocated by the United States from the Aleutian and Pribilof Islands to detention camps in southeastern Alaska.

22. Few of those most grievously injured by incarceration were likely to have become witnesses, although some of their family members referred to their injuries and absences in testimonies. Many had died; others had renunciated their U.S. citizenship under duress during incarceration.

23. Film and literature by Japanese American survivors and their relations is one significant legacy. Though momentary, the redress hearings introduced

the widespread presence of disablement, psychological distress, mental illness, and absent memories. These incomplete and "uncanny" memories of survivors can be explored more fully in what scholar Glen Mimura calls "post-Redress media." As Mimura analyzes, feminist Japanese American filmmakers Rea Tajiri, Janice Tanaka, and Lise Yasui rely on experimental formats, rather than documentary narrative, to probe the lingering effects of incarceration on public and private relations (2009, 81–82).

24. Less than a week after this protest, the U.S. Department of Health and Human Services announced that it no longer needed to house migrant children at Fort Sill (Ken Miller, "Plan Halted to House Migrant Kids at Oklahoma's Fort Sill," *Associated Press*, July 27, 2019).

## Works Cited

Aho, Tanja, Liat Ben-Moshe, and Leon J. Hilton. 2017. "Mad Futures: Affect/Theory/Violence." *American Quarterly* 69, no. 2 (June): 291–302.

Ben-Moshe, Liat. 2020. *Decarcerating Disability: Deinstitutionalization and Prison Abolition*. Minneapolis: University of Minnesota Press.

Ben-Moshe, Liat, Chris Chapman, and Allison C. Carey, eds. 2014. *Disability Incarcerated: Imprisonment and Disability in the United States and Canada*. New York: Palgrave Macmillan.

Burch, Susan. 2021. *Committed: Remembering Native Kinship in and beyond Institutions*. Chapel Hill: University of North Carolina Press.

Commission to Study and Develop Reparation Proposals for African Americans Act, H.R. 40, 117th Cong. (2021). https://www.congress.gov/bill/117th-congress/house-bill/40.

Daniels, Roger, Sandra C. Taylor, and Harry H. L. Kitano. 1991. *Japanese Americans: From Relocation to Redress*. Revised edition. Seattle: University of Washington Press.

Fu, May. 2008. "'Serve the People and You Help Yourself': Japanese-American Anti-Drug Organizing in Los Angeles, 1969 to 1972." *Social Justice* 35, no. 2: 80–99.

Fujii, June S., Susan N. Fukushima, and Joe Yamamoto. 1993. "Psychiatric Care of Japanese Americans." In *Culture, Ethnicity, and Mental Illness*, edited by Albert C. Gaw, 305–46. Washington, DC: American Psychiatric Press.

Fujino, Diane Carol. 2005. *Heartbeat of Struggle: The Revolutionary Life of Yuri Kochiyama*. Minneapolis: University of Minnesota Press.

*Gidra* Collection. Densho Digital Repository. https://ddr.densho.org/ddr-densho-297/.

Hamano, Merilynne. 1972. "Thoughts of Remembrance for Clara." *Gidra* 4, no. 5 (May): 8.

Hamano Quon, Merilynne. 2001. "Individually We Contributed, Together We Made a Difference." In *Asian Americans: The Movement and the Moment,* edited by Steve Louie and Glenn Omatsu, 206–19. Los Angeles, CA: UCLA Asian American Studies Center Press.

Hatamiya, Leslie T. 1993. *Righting a Wrong: Japanese Americans and the Passage of the Civil Liberties Act of 1988.* Stanford, CA: Stanford University Press.

Herzig, Jack, and Aiko Herzig. 1981a. Papers. Commission on Wartime Relocation and Internment of Civilian Public Hearings Transcripts, expanded and edited. Collection 451. UCLA Library Special Collections.

———. 1981b. Papers. August 4, 1981. Box 193, folder 3. Commission on Wartime Relocation and Internment of Civilian Public Hearings Transcripts, expanded and edited. Collection 451. Los Angeles, CA, UCLA Library Special Collections.

———. 1981c. Papers. August 13, 1981. Box 194, folder 4. Commission on Wartime Relocation and Internment of Civilian Public Hearings Transcripts, expanded and edited. Collection 451. San Francisco, CA, UCLA Library Special Collections.

Herzig-Yoshinaga, Aiko, and Marjorie Lee, eds. 2011. *Speaking Out for Personal Justice: Site Summaries of Testimonies and Witness Registry, from the U.S. Commission on Wartime Relocation and Internment of Civilians (CWRIC) Hearings, 1981.* Los Angeles, CA: UCLA Asian American Studies Center; Civil Liberties Public Education Fund.

Hohri, Sasha. Collection. Densho Digital Repository. https://ddr.densho.org/ddr-densho-352/.

Hohri, William Minoru. 1988. *Repairing America: An Account of the Movement for Japanese-American Redress.* Pullman: Washington State University Press.

*H.R. 40: Exploring the Path to Reparative Justice in America, House Judiciary Committee, 117th Cong.* (2021). YouTube, 3:09:26. February 17, 2021. https://youtu.be/KoWfrexyi84.

Ichioka, Yuji. "Introduction." 1998. In *Speak Out for Justice: Viewer's Companion,* 5. Los Angeles, CA: Nikkei for Civil Rights & Redress; Visual Communications. https://ncrr-la.org/speakout/speakout_ViewersComp.pdf.

Imada, Adria L. 2021. "Family History as Disability History: Native Hawaiians Surviving Medical Incarceration." *Disability Studies Quarterly* 41, no. 4. https://doi.org/10.18061/dsq.v41i4.8475.

Justice, Daniel Heath, and Jean M. O'Brien, eds. 2021. *Allotment Stories: Indigenous Land Relations under Settler Siege.* Minneapolis: University of Minnesota Press.

Kashima, Tetsuden. 1980. "Japanese American Internees Return, 1945 to 1955: Readjustment and Social Amnesia." *Phylon* 41, no. 2: 107–15.

Kitashima, Tsuyako (Sox), and Joy K. Morimoto. 2003. *Birth of an Activist: The Sox Kitashima Story*. San Mateo, CA: Asian American Curriculum Project.

Kondo, Alan. 2019. "2019-06-22 Fort Sill Protest." Filmed June 22, 2019, in Fort Sill, OK. Vimeo, 18:56. https://vimeo.com/345825703.

Lomawaima, K. Tsianina. 1994. *They Called It Prairie Light: The Story of the Chilocco Indian School*. Lincoln: University of Nebraska Press.

Lyon, Cherstin. 2020. "Japanese American Citizens League." *Densho Encyclopedia*. Last modified October 8, 2020. https://encyclopedia.densho. org/Japanese%20American%20Citizens%20League.

Madden, Ryan. 1992. "The Forgotten People: The Relocation and Internment of Aleuts during World War II." *American Indian Culture and Research Journal* 16, no. 4: 55–76.

Maki, Mitchell T., Harry H. L. Kitano, and S. Megan Berthold. 1999. *Achieving the Impossible Dream: How Japanese Americans Obtained Redress*. Urbana: University of Illinois Press.

Masaoka, Mike M., and Bill Hosokawa. 1987. *They Call Me Moses Masaoka: An American Saga*. New York: Morrow.

Matsumoto, Valerie J. 2016. "Sansei Women and the Gendering of Yellow Power in Southern California, 1960s–1970s." In *Trans-Pacific Japanese American Studies: Conversations on Race and Racializations*, edited by Yuko Takezawa and Gary Y. Okihiro, 183–209. Honolulu: University of Hawaiʻi Press.

Matsuoka, Jim. 2010. "Jim Matsuoka Interview by Martha Nakagawa." May 24, 2010. Densho Digital Repository. https://ddr.densho.org/media/ddr-densho-1000/ddr-densho-1000-281-transcript-36babc846d.htm.

McCallum, Mary Jane Logan. 2017. "Starvation, Experimentation, Segregation, and Trauma: Words for Reading Indigenous Health History." *The Canadian Historical Review* 98, no. 1: 96–13.

Metzl, Jonathan. 2011. *The Protest Psychosis: How Schizophrenia Became a Black Disease*. Boston: Beacon Press.

Mimura, Glen M. 2009. *Ghostlife of Third Cinema: Asian American Film and Video*. Minneapolis: University of Minnesota Press.

Murray, Alice Yang. 2008. *Historical Memories of the Japanese American Internment and the Struggle for Redress*. Stanford, CA: Stanford University Press.

Nagata, Donna K. 1993. *Legacy of Injustice: Exploring the Cross-Generational Impact of the Japanese American Internment*. New York: Plenum Press.

Nakagawa, Martha. 2020. "Days of Remembrance." *Densho Encyclopedia*. Last modified June 19, 2020. https://encyclopedia.densho.org/Days%20of%20 Remembrance.

Nakano, Lillian. 2009. "Lillian Nakano Interview." July 8, 2009. Densho Digital Repository. https://ddr.densho.org/media/ddr-densho-1000/ddr-densho-1000-254-transcript-0d151f25db.htm.

Nakano, Mei T. 1990. *Japanese American Women: Three Generations, 1890–1990.* Berkeley, CA: Mina Press Publishing.

NCRR (Nikkei for Civil Rights and Redress). 2018. *NCRR: The Grassroots Struggle for Japanese American Redress and Reparations.* Los Angeles: UCLA Asian American Studies Center Press.

*NCRR Banner* Archives. NCRR. https://ncrr-la.org/NCRR_archives/ncrr_banners.htm.

*NCRR Reader: A Reader on the History of the NCRR.* 2006. NCRR. Last modified April 17, 2006. https://ncrr-la.org/reader/.

Nielsen, Kim E. 2012. *A Disability History of the United States.* Boston: Beacon Press.

Niiya, Brian. 2016. "Shosuke Sasaki." *Densho Encyclopedia.* Last modified February 17, 2016. https://encyclopedia.densho.org/Shosuke%20Sasaki.

Nishio, Alan. 1994. "Oral History with Alan Nishio by Traci Kiriyama." May 5, 1994. OH 2371. Japanese American Oral History Project. Center for Oral and Public History, California State University, Fullerton.

NY JAOH (New York Japanese American Oral History Project). 2021. "The 1981 NYC JA Commission Hearings Story." Vimeo, 25:50. https://vimeo.com/645145420.

Omori, Chizuko. 1981. "Chizuko Omori Written Testimony, Seattle, Washington." September 9, 1981. Densho Digital Repository. Commission on Wartime Relocation and Internment of Civilians Collection. https://ddr.densho.org/ddr-densho-67-170/.

Paik, A. Naomi. 2016. *Rightlessness: Testimony and Redress in U.S. Prison Camps since World War II.* Chapel Hill: University of North Carolina Press.

*Personal Justice Denied: Report of the Commission on Wartime Relocation and Internment of Civilians.* 1997. Washington, DC: Civil Liberties Public Education Fund; Seattle: University of Washington Press.

Price, Margaret. 2013. "Defining Mental Disability." In *The Disability Studies Reader,* edited by Lennard J. Davis, 303–12. 4th ed. New York: Routledge.

Shimabukuro, Robert Sadamu. 2001. *Born in Seattle: The Campaign for Japanese American Redress.* Seattle: University of Washington Press.

Six Sansei. "The Sansei Experience." 1992. *U.S.-Japan Women's Journal. English Supplement,* no. 2: 77–95.

Staub, Michael E. 2011. *Madness Is Civilization: When the Diagnosis Was Social, 1948–1980.* Chicago, IL: University of Chicago Press.

Takezawa, Yasuko I. 1995. *Breaking the Silence: Redress and Japanese American Ethnicity.* Ithaca, NY: Cornell University Press.

Tateishi, John. 2020. *Redress: The Inside Story of the Successful Campaign for Japanese American Reparations.* Berkeley, CA: Heyday.

Tomihiro, Chiye. 1997. "Chiye Tomihiro Interview." September 11, 1997. Densho Digital Repository. https://ddr.densho.org/interviews/ddr-densho-1000-93-1/.

Visual Communications. 1981a. "Speak Out for Justice. August 4, 1981." Filmed Tuesday, August 4, 1981, Los Angeles, CA. https://vcmedia.org/latest-news/speakout-aug4.

———. 1981b. "Speak Out for Justice. August 5, 1981." Filmed Wednesday, August 5, 1981, Los Angeles, CA. https://vcmedia.org/latest-news/speakout-aug5.

Whitt, Sarah. 2021. "'Care and Maintenance': Indigeneity, Disability and Settler Colonialism at the Canton Asylum for Insane Indians, 1902–1934." *Disability Studies Quarterly* 41, no. 4. https://doi.org/10.18061/dsq.v41i4.8463.

Williams, Raymond. 1977. *Marxism and Literature.* Oxford, UK: Oxford University Press.

Yamamoto, Eric K. 1992. "Friend, or Foe or Something Else: Social Meanings of Redress and Reparations." *Denver Journal of International Law and Policy* 20, no. 2 (Winter): 223–42.

———. 1999. "What's Next?: Japanese American Redress and African American Reparations." *Amerasia Journal* 25, no. 2: 1–17.

# Queering *Morales v. Turman*: Gender, Sexuality, and Juveniles' Right to Treatment

Lauren Jae Gutterman

**Abstract:** This article complicates understandings of *Morales v. Turman*, a class action lawsuit filed in 1971 on behalf of juveniles in six Texas Youth Council (TYC) institutions, as a victory for incarcerated youth. Drawing on *Morales*'s substantial legal archives, this article highlights the ways the lawyers, social workers, psychologists, and psychiatrists who came together on behalf of incarcerated youth in this case understood the state's capacity to foster and enforce gender and sexual conformity as a social good. While they hoped to protect incarcerated children from state violence and to affirm their constitutional rights, these experts helped to embed a pathological conception of homosexuality and gender nonconformity into the broader legal battle for juvenile offenders' "right to treatment." In ushering in a treatment-focused juvenile justice regime, the expert witnesses who testified on behalf of the plaintiffs also helped to foster the TYC's turn away from traditional carceral institutions toward community-based residential facilities. **Keywords:** LGBTQ; carceral studies; juvenile justice; Black studies; *Morales v. Turman*; community-based treatment

Scholars and journalists have long recognized the importance of *Morales v. Turman*, a class action lawsuit filed in 1971 on behalf of juveniles in six Texas Youth Council (TYC) institutions across the state (McNeely, Frucht, and Filvaroff 1973; Wooden 1976; Martin and Ekland-Olson 1987; Redding-ton 1990; Kemerer 1991; Bush 2010).[1] This landmark federal civil rights case against James Turman, TYC's executive director, as well as TYC's members, school supervisors, and employees, revealed widespread due process violations as well as horrifying physical and psychological abuse against incarcerated minors, who were predominantly Black and Mexican American.[2] *Morales v. Turman* was part of a broader legal revolution to

*WSQ: Women's Studies Quarterly* 51: 1 & 2 (Spring/Summer 2023)

protect young people's constitutional rights, and it was one of a number of cases in the lower federal courts in the early 1970s that established a foundation for juvenile offenders' right to rehabilitative treatment (Blasko 1985; Roth 1985; Alexander 1995). The case resulted in the closing of the two TYC institutions with the gravest abuses, the creation of a committee to oversee institutional reforms, and a statewide shift in TYC commitments to community-based treatment programs (Bush 2010; O'Brien 2021). It also helped to create national benchmark standards for the care of juveniles in state reformatories (National Center for Youth Law, n.d.).

This article complicates understandings of *Morales* as a victory for incarcerated youth by focusing on the racialized ways the case enforced gender and sexual norms. In what follows, I provide a queer reading of the case in two senses. First, I show how mental health experts and attorneys for the plaintiffs and amici argued that TYC practices fostered boys' and girls' homosexuality and gender nonconformity. Such practices, they claimed, were "anti-rehabilitative" or contra to delinquents' reform and as such constituted evidence of cruel and unusual punishment prohibited under the Eighth Amendment. In his defining study of the juvenile justice system in Texas, historian William Bush examines these aspects of the case and notes that *Morales* "participated in the era's debate over gay rights and identity" without fully addressing the connection it made between straightness and "rehabilitation" (Bush 2010, 194). Although *Morales* affirmed juveniles' "right to treatment," the argument for this right rested, in part, on an understanding of sexual and gender variance as pathological. Second, I demonstrate how TYC staff members and racially liberal juvenile justice advocates similarly conflated Blackness with sexual and gender deviance (Ferguson 2003). Despite their different goals and motivations, both groups of people understood Black boys and girls as in particular need of "straightening" through punishment or reform, respectively. While it might be expected that TYC staff treated Black youth as inherently nonnormative, expert witnesses for the plaintiffs perceived Black youth's gender and sexual expression as culturally produced and changeable but no less in need of remedy and intervention.

The expert witnesses who testified on behalf of the plaintiffs reflected activists' and intellectuals' long-standing efforts to counter stereotypes of Black and Mexican American youth as irredeemably deviant. As scholars have shown, since its beginning in the late nineteenth century the juvenile justice system has fostered racist stereotypes of children of color in order to justify their disproportionate incarceration and even forced sterilization while denying them resources used to "rehabilitate" their white counterparts (Chávez-García 2012; Lira 2022; Agyepong 2018). Meanwhile, by the mid-twentieth century, psychologists, psychiatrists, and social workers who were critical of racial discrimination, especially against African Americans, sought to counter these ideas by arguing that Black children's gender and sexual nonconformity was a product of racial discrimination. These racial advocates advanced an understanding of gender and sexual normativity as integral to mental health, and the experts testifying on behalf of TYC youth echoed their arguments (Doyle 2016; Ramos 2019). Furthermore, in the wake of Assistant Secretary of Labor Daniel Patrick Moynihan's notorious 1965 report, *The Negro Family: The Case for National Action*, which depicted Black familial "dysfunction"—specifically, emasculated Black men and dominant Black matriarchs—as the cause of Black poverty, urban crime, and national unrest, preparing incarcerated Black boys and girls to take on their proper gender roles in the heterosexual family was of urgent importance to juvenile justice advocates in *Morales* (Moynihan 1965; Mumford 2012).

Drawing on *Morales*'s substantial legal archives, including court transcripts and TYC records, as well as expert witnesses' notes, reports, and depositions, this article highlights the ways the lawyers, social workers, psychologists, and psychiatrists who came together on behalf of incarcerated youth in this case understood the state's capacity to foster and enforce gender and sexual conformity as a social good. Even as they criticized the violence and abuse the state meted out, they argued that it could and should work to ensure incarcerated juveniles' straightness. In other words, they welcomed the state's capacity for "intimate governance," its ability to shape our most personal desires, relationships, and self-expressions (Canaday, Cott, and Self 2021). I begin by showing how lawyers and expert witnesses for the plaintiffs and amici accused TYC staff and institutions of harming incarcerated youth by inculcating homosexuality and gender nonconformity among them. In particular, these juvenile justice advocates objected to TYC practices of sex segregation: labeling and separating suspected homosexual boys, while over-policing and inadvertently encouraging affection between girls. Juvenile justice advocates also criticized the ways TYC institutions stymied girls'—especially Black girls'—femininity. Next, I use the records generated by *Morales* to uncover how young people in TYC institutions understood their own behavior and identities, as well as the ways they sought out affection, pleasure, and support from one another despite staff's attempts to demonize and obstruct their same-sex bonds. TYC youth's refusal or inability to conform to the gender and sexual rules staff set out for them demonstrates both their rejection of conventional standards of heteronormativity and their determination to persevere within a brutal institution.

While they hoped to protect incarcerated white working-class and Black and Mexican American children from state violence and to affirm their constitutional rights, the experts who testified on behalf of the plaintiffs helped to embed a pathological conception of homosexuality and gender nonconformity into the broader legal battle for juvenile offenders' "right to treatment" as well as into the standards of care that *Morales* established. Rather than labeling, isolating, and punishing minors who troubled gender and sexual norms, juvenile justice experts encouraged TYC staff and institutions to straighten youth less directly by utilizing the power of suggestion and reverse psychology. They called for gentler but, in some ways, more insidious state practices that would transform young people's sexual desires and gender identifications from the inside out. In ushering in a treatment-focused juvenile justice regime, the expert witnesses who testified on behalf of the plaintiffs also helped to foster the TYC's turn away from traditional carceral institutions toward community-based residential facilities. *Morales* suggests, then, that liberal reformers' understanding of carceral institutions as fostering queerness undergirded the rise of community treatment infrastructure in the 1970s.

### Heteronormativity and Juvenile Rehabilitation

Two young juvenile justice lawyers, Steven Bercu and William Hoffman, initially filed suit in *Morales v. Turman* after TYC officials tried to prevent them from interviewing juveniles they suspected had been incarcerated without hearings or legal counsel in violation of their right to due process (*In re Gault* 1967). After interviewing hundreds of the 2,500 TYC inmates during the case's investigatory phase in 1972, Bercu and Hoffman amended their original pleading to include a wider range of violations and to argue that juveniles in TYC institutions had a right to rehabilitative treatment. The Mental Health Law Project (MHLP) and the U.S. Department of Justice supported this line of argument after joining the case as amici. A group of lawyers and mental health practitioners founded the Mental Health Law Project in 1972 to protect the rights of the "mentally handicapped" and improve their quality of life (Mental Health Law Project 1977). In *Morales*, the MHLP represented five national organizations as amici: the American Orthopsychiatric Association, the American Psychological Association, the American Association on Mental Deficiency (now the American Association on Intellectual and Developmental Disabilities), the National Council on Crime and Delinquency, and the Child Welfare League. These organizations provided access to expert witnesses who investigated the general environment in TYC institutions and the question of whether or not they facilitated "desirable" changes among juveniles in the state's reformatories (Pre-trial Brief, n.d., 2).

In their pre-trial brief, the MHLP argued that the TYC had a constitutional duty to provide rehabilitative treatment to youths in its care. While the goal of rehabilitation may have appeared progressive, within the carceral system the language of medical "treatment" and "cure" had long been linked with the criminalization and forcible "healing" of homosexuals through electroshock therapy, for example (Kunzel 2017). In keeping with this history, the lawyers and experts representing the MHLP understood heterosexuality as synonymous with well-being. The MHLP's pre-trial brief noted that the witnesses would point to practices at TYC institutions that they believed to be "counter-habilitative" (Pre-trial Brief, n.d., 3). These included the "callous labelling and segregating of certain youngsters at Mountain View" as homosexual, which the brief argued was an example both of "cruel and unusual punishment" and of treatment "inconsistent with rehabilitation" because it ascribed a stigmatizing sexual label on youth "still in search of [their] sex identity" (Pre-trial Brief, n.d., 24–25). The idea that incarceration contributed to homosexuality was hardly new. As historian Regina Kunzel has shown, by the mid-twentieth century "there was a growing fear that prison, rather than simply collecting perverts, played an active part in producing them" (2008, 88). In the post–World War II period, rising rates of juvenile delinquency, combined with a growing faith in psychoanalytic theories about adolescence, heightened American concerns about the effects of incarceration on young people's sexuality, in particular.

This anxiety provided a crucial backdrop for *Morales*. During the trial, which began in Tyler, Texas, on July 2, 1973, attorneys for the plaintiffs and amici pointed to several ways TYC institutions pushed adolescents into homosexual behaviors or identities and, as such, undermined their right to treatment. To begin with, expert witnesses in *Morales* expressed concern that sex segregation itself was fostering incarcerated juveniles' homosexuality.

For example, in his testimony before the court, psychiatrist and professor Robert Baxter argued that sex-segregated reform schools directed boys toward homosexuality by exposing them to "people who are involved in homosexual experiences" and by leaving them no heterosexual "outlet" for their sexual desires. Voicing an idea that would come up repeatedly during the trial, Baxter argued that one of the core developmental tasks adolescents need to accomplish is "to learn to adjust to a heterosexual world." Lacking opportunities to adapt to a heterosexual environment, Baxter warned, could have "very long-range consequences" for incarcerated youth. "You mean damaging consequences?" Peter Sandmann, attorney for the plaintiffs, asked Baxter, to which he responded, "Yes, I do" (Record of Proceedings 1973a, 164–65). Baxter and Sandmann's interchange on the very first day of the trial defined homosexuality as a harmful mental problem and a sign of failed psychological adjustment.

In addition to the sex-segregation of TYC institutions, attorneys and witnesses for the plaintiffs and amici argued that the placement of suspected homosexual boys at Mountain View State School in certain dorms was encouraging their sexual deviance. Boys at Mountain View, a maximum-security unit for boys deemed the "most challenging" juvenile offenders, were sexually and racially segregated in two "punk dorms": Dorm 1, which housed Black boys, and Dorm 9, which housed Anglo and Mexican American boys. The term "punk," derived from a broader vernacular among incarcerated men and itinerant male laborers stretching back to the early twentieth century (Boag 2003; Kunzel 2008), implied youth, physical weakness, a "passive" role in homosexual sex, and often economic dependence on an older male "wolf" or "jocker." Commentators typically saw "punks"—within and outside of prison—as the sexual victims of stronger and more dominating men (Donaldson 2001). At Mountain View, the term was used somewhat differently to refer to all potential male participants in same-sex sex, regardless of their gender presentation or sexual role. Black "punk" boys' additional racial separation reflected long-standing stereotypes of Black men as sexual aggressors. It also reflected more recent understandings of rape in male prisons as an expression of power and racial resentment perpetrated by Black men against their white counterparts in an attempt to "repair" their masculinity (Kunzel 2008).

According to multiple expert witnesses in *Morales*, punk dorms pushed boys toward permanent homosexuality. In his testimony, Leonard Lawrence, a San Antonio–based child psychiatrist and professor, condemned the practice of segregating suspected queer boys in specific dorms, arguing that it "does more to increase the likelihood that this will be his ultimate adult mode of sexual expression than any other factor." Doing so, Lawrence testified, "strip[s] a child of an appropriate identity" and is a "very anti-therapeutic type of approach" (Lawrence 1973, 3134–35). Lawrence's testimony was in line with contemporary medical understandings of adolescent homosexuality. Psychological and psychiatric writing about adolescent sexuality in the 1960s stressed young people's sexual malleability and portrayed homosexuality as both harmful and avoidable (Bieber et al. 1962). As increasingly militant gay and lesbian activists denounced the medicalization of homosexuality, adolescent and pediatric psychiatrists continued to believe that homosexuality was less stable and more treatable among children (Shearer 1966; Symmonds 1969; Davenport 1972). After the American Psychiatric Association removed homosexuality from the *Diagnostic and Statistical Manual of Mental Disorders II* (*DSM-II*) in late 1973, many psychiatrists— even those who supported demedicalization for adults—continued to believe that they should prevent homosexuality and gender nonconformity among children whenever possible (Sedgwick 1991).

Echoing these medicalized understandings of juvenile gender and sexual variance, Lawrence, along with several other expert witnesses in *Morales*, expressed concern that staff members at Mountain View were improperly diagnosing boys as homosexual and overstepping professional boundaries in doing so. Even as Lawrence's psychiatric colleagues were questioning the medicalization of homosexuality among adults, Lawrence persisted in describing homosexuality among juveniles as a mental condition that required an involved "psychiatric diagnosis," including an examination of the patient's childhood experiences and family background. He also disapproved that "untrained" individuals at Mountain View were making such determinations (Lawrence 1973, 3066). Howard Ohmart, a consultant with the American Justice Institute and a well-known expert on juvenile corrections, agreed. "It is particularly disturbing," he testified, "when the determination is made by the correctional officer, who quite clearly is the least educated, and in my judgement least qualified to hand those kinds of labels on people" (Record of Proceedings 1973c, 1251). Such statements about TYC staff, who were drawn primarily from rural areas surrounding TYC institutions, suggested a sense of class and educational superiority on the part of the expert witnesses for the plaintiffs.

At the same time, experts like Lawrence and Ohmart had a clear self-interest in arguing that only educated professionals, like themselves, were qualified to label a juvenile as homosexual. In doing so, these experts both affirmed a medicalized understanding of adolescent homosexuality and shored up psychiatrists' authority. The field of psychiatry was in crisis in the 1970s as a variety of leftist activists critiqued psychiatric understandings of mental illness and portrayed psychiatrists as enforcing systems of oppression (Staub 2011). Historian Abram Lewis has argued that the campaign to remove homosexuality from the *DSM-II* was one way that psychiatrists sought to protect their profession and reestablish psychiatry as "an impartial expert discourse and a proponent of social diversity" (Lewis 2016, 4). Although the psychiatric and juvenile justice experts who testified in *Morales* did not see homosexuality as a legitimate option for adolescents, they similarly sought to protect and defend the psychiatric profession by arguing that untrained correctional officers were improperly labeling incarcerated youth as homosexual and undermining their rehabilitation.

Expert witnesses for the plaintiffs and amici argued that TYC practices were driving girls to homosexuality, as well, albeit by different means. Several expert witnesses argued that due to an excessive and unwarranted fear of homosexuality, TYC staff were too harshly policing girls' demonstrations of affection, including hugging, holding hands, or sharing clothing. Doing so was preventing girls from building friendships with each other in "healthy" and necessary ways, while making homosexuality into an appealing form of rebellion and perhaps a lasting identity. Clinical psychologist Patricia Blakeney, who lived at Gainesville for several days while examining the institution, insisted that what incarcerated girls referred to as "love business" or "L.B. stuff" was not authentic lesbianism but "just a game" that the staff's anxiety encouraged (Record of Proceedings 1973b, 994). Echoing earlier sociological studies of incarcerated women's cultures, Blakeney argued that homosexuality in the girls' reform schools was merely a manifestation of their desire for familial connections (Giallombardo 1966; Kunzel 2008).

According to Blakeney, while Gainesville staff were pushing girls into pseudohomosexuality in some ways, they were encouraging girls' more lasting gender and sexual deviance in others. Blakeney was quite concerned that the institution was prohibiting girls from expressing their femininity and developing what she called an "appropriate sexual identity" (Record of Proceedings 1973b, 981–82). She complained that the dorm she lived in at Gainesville had only one mirror, which was made of metal and inadequate, thus preventing girls from paying sufficient attention to their looks and experimenting with hairstyles and makeup in age-appropriate ways. Blakeney disapproved of the "starchy diets" and lack of exercise the girls received, which was making them "pudgy" and implicitly unattractive (Record of Proceedings 1973b, 953). She worried that the girls' lack of interactions with boys and men was disrupting their femininity. What one would hope to see in a typical adolescent girl, Blakeney explained, "is that she would come to see that being a woman is really something to be proud of, that she would like to be pretty," and that she would "relate to men as a woman, rather than relating to a man as, you know, one of the guys" (982). This developmental task was impossible in a sex-segregated environment without "men around to reward feminine behavior" (982). For Blakeney, heterosexuality was the ultimate marker of successful femininity.

Blakeney, among other experts for the plaintiffs and amici, was particularly concerned about the effect of incarceration on Black girls' femininity. Their worries reflected a broader discourse, stretching back to enslavement, that marked Black girls and women as always already outside of normative standards of femininity if not womanhood itself (Morgan 2004; Haley 2016; Snorton 2017). Throughout the trial, attorneys for the plaintiffs made a point of affirming the right of Black girls and boys to express their racial identity through their hairstyles and modes of dress, but this right extended only to conventionally gendered fashions. In his examination of Blakeney, Louis Thrasher, attorney for the Justice Department, brought up the fact that Gainesville's rules and regulations penalized hairstyles favored by Black girls, specifically multiple braids or ponytails that required more than two ties or rubber bands (Record of Proceedings 1973b, 1065). In her testimony, Gisela Konopka, social worker, professor, and author of the classic study *The Adolescent Girl in Conflict* (1966), claimed that Black girls at Gainesville "had unusually short-cut hair," which not only differed from the longer Afros she believed were more common among Black youth but also "made them immediately somehow look like the butch in their homosexual relationship which added to the problem" (Record of Proceedings 1973e, 2157). In his cross-examination, Assistant Attorney General of Texas Larry York tried to suggest that Black girls at Gainesville had a range of hair lengths by presenting Konopka with a photograph of a girl at the institution with a longer Afro, but Konopka was unconvinced by this argument, and no one pursued the possibility that some Black girls might simply prefer shorter hair.

TYC staff shared an understanding of Black girls as insufficiently feminine. Rather than perceiving Black girls' femininity as undermined by a cultural "tangle of pathology" induced by enslavement, however, TYC's staff more likely subscribed to racist stereotypes that cast Black girls and women as biologically less feminine, vulnerable, and moral than white women (Moynihan 1965, 29). Since the late nineteenth century, these stereotypes had worked to justify the disproportionate incarceration of Black women across the nation, as well as their exploitation and denigration within prison (Gross 2006; Hicks 2010; LeFlouria 2015; Haley 2016). At the same time, ideas about Black girls as irredeemable justified Southern state leaders' opposition to funding segregated juvenile reformatories for them (Cahn 2007). In Texas, despite Black female reformers' efforts to create an institution specifically for Black girls beginning in the Progressive Era, it was not until 1927 that the Texas State Legislature authorized the creation of such a facility, and not until 1945 that the state appropriated any funding for the school. The Brady State School for Negro Girls opened on the site of a former prisoner of war camp in 1947. Only in 1966 did the state racially integrate its girls' reformatories (Bush 2010). Reflecting long-standing practices at Southern carceral institutions, staff at Gainesville routinely labeled white girls as more capable of reform than Black girls. As Blakeney explained to the court at trial in *Morales*, the "ideal" inmate at Gainesville was typically "a nice, quiet, docile, passive girl preferably with blond hair and blue eyes" (Record of Proceedings 1973b, 968).

Even as experts like Blakeney criticized pervasive racism within TYC institutions, however, they agreed with TYC staff that Black girls were in need of feminization. This consensus was made evident by what the attorneys chose to discuss in court, as well as what they did not. For example, in her expert report on the girls' institutions, social worker Margaret Sheely noted that one of the Black girls she spoke to at Crockett complained that the staff forced her and other Black inmates to shave their legs. The girl told Sheely that she had never shaved before being committed to Crockett, but staff assumed that by not shaving the girls were "playing like a man, or acting like a stud" (Sheely 1972, 3). Staff often sent girls who refused to shave to the Security Treatment Cottage, where they were separated from the other juveniles and deprived of regular activities and privileges. Although being sent to the Security Treatment Cottage was a more severe punishment than girls received for wearing multiple braids, attorneys for the plaintiffs and amici chose not to bring up the issue in court. What is more, the experts and attorneys most likely agreed with Crockett staff that Black girls *should* shave their legs. In fact, Blakeney noted in court that policies at Gainesville had previously—and problematically, she implied—afforded insufficient time for girls to "wash their hair, shave their legs, [and] that kind of grooming" (Record of Proceedings 1973b, 1048).

In short, neither these expert witnesses nor the lawyers for the plaintiffs argued that Black girls—or any girls, for that matter—had a right to engage in styles of self-presentation that white, middle-class people like themselves perceived as masculine. Doing so would have contradicted their case that TYC institutions were inculcating juveniles' homosexuality and gender nonconformity and, thus, violating their right to treatment. It also would have challenged their notion that in order to achieve full incorporation into the nation's economic and social order, Black children needed to be brought into line with white, middle-class gender and sexual norms. To fail to do so, as the TYC had, was a profound injustice in the eyes of these juvenile justice advocates, one that marked Texas's Black youth for a future on the margins of society.

### Incarcerated Youth and the Question of Self-Perception

Attorneys and expert witnesses for the plaintiffs and amici clearly conveyed their understandings of adolescent gender and sexuality, but incarcerated juveniles' conceptions of their own identities and behaviors are much harder to document. This is due, in part, to the way lawyers shaped juvenile witnesses' testimonies at trial. In arguing that TYC institutions were pushing juveniles toward homosexuality, the plaintiffs' attorneys repeatedly amplified the voices of youth who feared or felt alienated by homosexuality in TYC institutions.[3] They also simultaneously evaded other juveniles' potentially nonnormative sexual and gender self-identifications. In several instances, the attorneys chose not to question incarcerated youth about their sexual identities or relationships when their straightness seemed uncertain. For example, one seventeen-year-old girl from Corpus Christi, then in her eleventh month of incarceration at Gainesville, testified that she did not trust the house parents at the institution because one had taken a ring from her that belonged to another girl. Perhaps because of the romantic symbolism involved in exchanging rings, Bercu did not ask this young witness if she was "in" homosexuality as he did other girls, nor did he ask her about her relationship with the inmate whose ring she had been wearing (Testimony 1973b). William Logan, attorney for the Justice Department, likewise avoided issues of sexual identity in questioning a boy, C.W., who had purposefully sought out placement in Dorm 9 at Mountain View, the "punk" dorm for white and Mexican American boys (Testimony 1973c, 61).

During the trial, the attorneys also attempted to undermine the staff's labeling of certain youth as gay, as the testimony of one sixteen-year-old Black girl, G.G., from Bryan, Texas, demonstrates.[4] G.G., who had been incarcerated at Gainesville for eleven months, testified that staff accused her of being "in" homosexuality or the "love business" (Record of Proceedings 1973d, 1839). They told G.G. they disapproved of the ways "girls just [ran] up to" her when she walked, as if the very way she moved inspired other girls' homosexuality (1841). Staff reported her for holding hands with another girl and for sitting at the same table with another Black girl in violation of house rules. On the stand, G.G. recalled how her house mother, case worker, and homemaking teacher had all called her by a slew of degrading and racist names in front of her peers; they insulted her mother and accused her of engaging in prostitution. Staff even accused G.G. of trying to rape another inmate, an allegation they used to isolate her in the Security Treatment Cottage. By the time she testified, staff had sent G.G. to the Security Treatment Cottage three times, the last for two weeks. During that period, G.G. remained alone, barred from participating in schooling, therapy, or recreational activities, until the staff finally admitted that their accusations against her had been baseless.

Lawyers for the plaintiffs and amici objected to the racist treatment G.G. experienced at Gainesville, the harsh punishment she endured, and the rules that prevented her from expressing affection and developing relationships with other girls, especially other Black girls. They also worked hard to imply that G.G. was, in fact, straight and that any suggestion of sexuality or romance between her and other girls was a product of the staff's imagination. In his direct examination, Bercu highlighted that the staff punished G.G. and other girls for engaging in homosexual behavior for merely touching, holding hands with, or combing another girl's hair, and he pointed out that there had been no coeducational activities at Gainesville during G.G.'s time there. Then, in her cross-examination, Patricia Wald, attorney for the MHLP, made clear that G.G. had a boyfriend "on the outside," but that staff had unjustly prevented G.G. from writing to him, telling her she could only correspond with members of her family (Record of Proceedings 1973d, 1862). In short, the attorneys refused to consider—or to provide G.G. any opportunity to affirm—that she was involved in sexual or romantic relationships with other girls. In doing so, they suggested that if G.G. had engaged in the "love business" she would have been less deserving of sympathy, her accusations of racist treatment might have been less believable, and her punishment by Gainesville staff more understandable.

The court attempted to erase juveniles' potential queerness in other ways as well. One seventeen-year-old Black boy, J.H. from Amarillo, testified about the abuse he endured and witnessed while housed in Mountain View's Dorm 1, the dorm for Black suspected homosexuals. Despite being housed in a "punk" dorm, J.H. rejected this designation and described himself as a "dude," meaning "you ain't no homosexual" (Testimony 1973d, 42). He testified that white staff members had beaten, kicked, and slapped him on multiple occasions. He also testified about the staff's abuse of his Black peers, including a queer inmate in Dorm 1 who was singled out by staff for particularly brutal treatment. It is impossible to know how this second juvenile, whom I'll refer to as X, identified their own gender or sexuality, but J.H. referred to them alternately as "he" and "she" because, as he told the defense, "she's a homosexual" (22).[5] J.H.'s use of "she" seems to have been intended in a derogatory way, but whether it also reflected X's own gender identity and linguistic preferences is unclear. As historian Jules Gill-Peterson has shown, since the early twentieth century, gatekeeping clinicians had largely excluded Black children and other children of color from the emerging field of trans medicine by imagining white children as more "plastic" and capable of transition. By contrast, medical professionals were more likely to label trans kids of color as mentally ill or homosexual (Gill-Peterson 2018).

Whatever their own identity, X's gender and sexual nonconformity troubled both the TYC's policies and the proceedings in the courtroom that day. Judge William Wayne Justice ordered the witness to refer to X as "he," but, whether out of habit or willful resistance, the witness persisted in alternating between masculine and feminine pronouns, thereby confounding the court's attempt to "straighten" X's story. By testifying about the severe abuse X experienced at the hands of Mountain View staff, J.H. affirmed their dignity. He also revealed that the staff's abuse of X was targeted and intentional. Before the court, J.H. relayed how, in March of 1973, he and X were pulling grass as a punishment when the guards attacked X. In order to make this forced labor as uncomfortable as possible, staff prohibited juveniles from bending their knees, forcing them to lean over at the waist for hours at a time. When X began to bend their knees, one employee, Mr. Shnick, kicked them in the head. Shnick then declared, "I've been wanting to get you anyway," because X had been "trying to make a fool of him" (Testimony 1973d, 21). X then refused to work at all, so Shnick beat X again until they tried to run to the gym to escape and another student caught them. J.H. later learned that after X was caught the school supervisor poured tear gas on them, a punishment not without precedent at the school. When J.H. saw X the next day in the infirmary, "the skin was peeling off her face" (24).

Youth like X may have been unable to assert their own gender and sexual identities at trial, but within TYC institutions they expressed nonnormative gender identities and same-sex desires in ways that staff members and even expert witnesses were forced to acknowledge. In a transcript of their conversations while living at the Gainesville State School for Girls, Blakeney and psychiatrist Gerda Hansen Smith described how the school's review committee tried to reform girls who were "trying to act like a boy," by forcing them to wear dresses (Smith and Blakeney, n.d. a, 6). One housemother at Gainesville expressed to Blakeney that she was quite pleased that a Black girl—who had previously been forced to wear dresses to school every day—was looking more feminine, but Blakeney did not agree. "She's an attractive girl but she dresses in a masculine kind of way," Blakeney noted, and she told Smith that the girl had a way of making even very feminine clothing appear more boyish, for instance, by putting a T-shirt under a shirtwaist dress to give it a different neckline (2). Rather than seeing this girl's style as reflecting a strong and independent personal identity, Blakeney understood it as a sign of the Gainesville staff's ineptitude.

Based on existing archival records, we cannot know exactly how this girl conceived of her gender or what words she used to describe herself, but it is worth noting that her strategy of layering a T-shirt under a dress echoes the actions of contemporary masculine-identified people in women's prisons who have found creative ways of resisting what they term "forced feminization" by remaking standard-issue clothing (Girshick 2015, 99). As one such individual incarcerated in California told sociologist Lori Girshick in the 2000s, "I'm not OK with those ugly wide-neck shirts. They try to make you look all feminine, I'm not wearing that. We just cut the sleeves, get it sewed up, get something to taper it [the neck] a little bit, make it so we can deal with it" (99). Whatever her gender identification, the Gainesville girl described above was similarly determined to remake the feminine clothing she had to wear in ways that she preferred.

Much as some girls thwarted staff attempts to feminize them, others undermined expert witnesses' analyses of their expressions of intimacy as purely asexual. In response to an order by the Department of Justice before the trial, each of the six TYC institutions was required to document the ways they punished homosexuality over the 1972 calendar year. Although Gainesville's report claimed that "overt homosexual acts" were not a problem, the school listed thirty-two incidents of "inappropriate affection" between girls, which included seventeen acts of kissing (at least one in which both girls were undressed), three acts of "rubbing legs," and one act of "having hand in blouse" (Gainesville State School for Girls, n.d.). The report of the Statewide Reception Center for Girls, which included staff members' handwritten notes, suggests similarly that TYC staff were preventing girls from doing more than holding hands: "It has been said by girls that [name redacted] and [name redacted] have been kissing in the bathroom," one logbook entry noted (Statewide Reception Center for Girls 1972a). "[Name redacted] and [name redacted] have lost their free time tonight for their behavior in the showers," another entry read (Statewide Reception Center for Girls 1972b). Furthermore, upon witnessing a lesbian or "L.B." wedding at Gainesville, which concluded with the couple kissing and licking blood off each other's fingers—even Blakeney conceded privately that she "got [the] feeling" that it was "a little more serious than just a game" (Smith and Blakeney, n.d. b, 16).

Reports compiled by the boys' schools for the Justice Department reflect a complex environment in which sex functioned as a tool of bartering and exchange, a means of control and abuse, and an expression of intimacy and affection. One typical incident report from the Terrace school at Gatesville documented a student who gave "hand jigs" to other students in exchange for cigarettes (Special Incident Report 1972b). Acts of sexual violence and assault appeared in TYC school records as well. In March of 1972, three boys in the Sycamore school at Gatesville raped another boy. They tied his hands together, walked him to the periphery of the school property, and threatened to hit him with a rock if he did not comply (Special Incident Report 1972a). Institutional reports, of course, cannot be taken as an entirely reliable source of information about juveniles' sexual encounters. Rape within Texas's juvenile institutions might have been underreported for a range of reasons, including victims' reluctance to come forward and staff members' willingness to ignore or actively condone such violence. Indeed, as historian Robert Chase has shown, during this same time period, adult prisons in Texas systematized sexual violence, rewarding prisoners who assisted guards and policed their peers with unfettered sexual access to other inmates' bodies (Chase 2020).

At the same time, brutal acts of violence may not have been the norm in juvenile reformatories: of approximately 140 acts or attempted acts of homosexual behavior punished with solitary confinement at all of the boys' institutions between 1964 and 1972, force was mentioned only three times (Sexual Treatment Center 1964–72). Tellingly, boys' acts of same-sex intimacy and their expressions of same-sex desire appear to have been punished just as harshly in TYC institutions as their acts of sexual violence, suggesting that TYC staff were concerned with policing not only sex but also affection. Unsurprisingly, TYC staff appear to have punished Black boys who expressed same-sex desire and affection most severely. According to the record of solitary confinements for sexual misconduct at all three boys' institutions between 1964 and 1972, only Black boys were punished for kissing other boys. In 1965 one Black boy was put into isolation for twenty-two days after merely talking about doing so. That same year, another Black boy was put into isolation for the same period of time for "crawling into another boy's bed" (Sexual Treatment Center 1964–72). Quantitative reports support these anecdotal examples about the racialization of punishment at TYC institutions: between 1962 and 1972, more Black boys (136 in total) were put into solitary confinement than either Anglo (84) or Mexican American boys (47) at all of the boys' schools (Sexual Treatment Center 1962–72). These statistics provide evidence of TYC staff members' racist understanding of Black boys as more sexually threatening than their peers and thus deserving of more severe punishment.

While expert witnesses insisted that homosexuality in TYC institutions was a product of sex-segregation and a form of mental illness, such analyses flew in the face of some juveniles' interpretations of their own behavior. A group of Black Gainesville girls who complained about not being able to wear pants told Smith explicitly that they were "lesbians 'in the free,'" a phrase TYC youth used to refer to life beyond the walls of the institution (Smith and Blakeney, n.d. a, 1). One boy at the Hilltop school complained to staff about another inmate who sexually approached him and who, it seems, identified as gay. As the first boy recalled, "He started to tell me about him and his men in the free and told me what he was. Then he told me that he wanted me to be his main thing" (Special Incident Report 1972c). Incident reports also document boys' defiant attitudes and lack of shame about their same-sex acts. "Admits to the allegation and does not attempt to rationalize his behavior," reads one report (Discipline Committee 1973). Austin MacCormick, a well-known criminologist and prison reformer who served as a witness for the defense, complained in his deposition about this seemingly new attitude among incarcerated men. What the TYC should really be trying to do, MacCormick insisted, "is to straighten out a few of them, except that nowadays nobody wants to be straightened out. They want to be accepted as homosexuals" (MacCormick 1973, 107).

Certainly, many juveniles in TYC institutions engaged in same-sex sexual acts without understanding themselves as homosexual. TYC staff categorized many young people as "punks" or "studs" who would not have claimed those labels for themselves. Furthermore, we cannot assume that even those youth who did use words like "gay" or "lesbian" to describe themselves in adolescence would continue to do beyond the walls of the reformatory, much less into adulthood. Still, without essentializing their behavior or overstating their agency within a brutal carceral system, it is possible to see the examples of gender nonconformity and nonviolent same-sex sexual expression above as conscious acts of self-preservation and sustenance. These acts both troubled the normalizing and dehumanizing logics of the juvenile reformatory and affirmed gender and sexual variance. In repeatedly challenging or simply ignoring the gendered and sexual rules TYC staff set out for them, Black youth, in particular, rejected conventional standards of gender and sexual respectability and flouted the stigma that staff and experts alike attributed to their behavior (Cohen 2004). The juvenile justice advocates misunderstood young people's gender and sexual nonconformity as evidence of their harm, when it was, in many cases, evidence of their strength, their resolution to survive and to resist the derogatory ways in which they were depicted.


### Conclusion

Judge Justice ultimately found persuasive the plaintiffs' argument that TYC institutions fostered incarcerated juveniles' homosexuality and thus violated their constitutional right to treatment. In his 1974 memorandum opinion, Justice made clear that he considered protecting juveniles' heterosexual development to be key to their rehabilitation and successful reintroduction into society. While Justice's opinion recognized and emphasized incarcerated juveniles' right to express their individual identities, including their racial, ethnic, and religious identities, he included no such right to express nonnormative gender or sexual identifications. Justice objected to the lack of opportunities for contact with "members of the opposite sex" in TYC institutions, which were, he stated, "an absolutely necessary condition for normal healthy adolescent growth." As a result, he concluded that juveniles in TYC institutions did "not learn to function in a heterosexual environment" (*Morales v. Turman* 1974, 43). With his recommendations for TYC institutions, Justice sought to reverse this practice and foster incarcerated juveniles' sexual normalcy through the coeducation of TYC institutions and a shift to community-based programs such as "group homes, halfway houses, day care programs, outpatient clinics, [and] home placements with close supervision" that would provide a "less restrictive, alternative form of rehabilitative treatment" (68–69).

Expert witnesses for the plaintiffs and amici were in consensus that the TYC should transition to community-based residential alternatives, and many experts had experience leading, or had advocated for, such programs before they testified. Leonard Lawrence served as the clinical director of a residential treatment center for "emotionally disturbed children" in San Antonio (Lawrence 1973, 3052). Patricia Blakeney directed a halfway house for runaway adolescents in Galveston. Gisela Konopka published an article in 1970 in the National Association of Social Workers' journal arguing that group homes and other residential units located within communities offered the best models for the treatment of juvenile delinquents (Konopka 1970). These experts also conveyed their belief that community-based programs and halfway houses would be better suited to facilitating normative gender and sexual development, as they would free juveniles from the detrimental effects of sex-segregated institutions, allowing them to date and socialize with the opposite sex and to wear clothing and hairstyles that were fashionable in their home communities, which experts considered particularly important for the development of heterofemininity. As Blakeney told the court, "just by sending a girl to a state school you almost certainly deny that she is going to have successful feminine experiences" (Record of Proceedings 1973b, 980).

Indeed, following James Turman's resignation, the TYC's next interim and eventually permanent director, Ron Jackson, oversaw a massive transition to community-based treatment programs before his retirement in 1993. In 1973, even before Justice issued his opinion in *Morales*, the TYC's board ordered Jackson to move to community-based programming. In 1974, TYC received a federal grant to initiate a residential contract program, and the following year the Texas legislature appropriated nine million dollars to be disbursed over the next two years for the creation of community-based residential programs for juvenile delinquents (Wilson 1978; General Appropriations Act 1975, 2503). This budget included the residential program as well as halfway houses and community assistance programs intended to increase the number of community alternatives to institutionalization. While only two such juvenile facilities existed when *Morales* was filed, ten years after *Morales*'s trial the state operated seven halfway houses and eighty-five privately contracted residential programs, which treated 1,981 youth (Texas Youth Commission 1983).[6]

The growth of treatment programs and residential facilities in the urban areas where most TYC youth lived, rather than the rural areas where TYC schools were located, did not signal a decline but rather an expansion of state power. As historian Cyrus O'Brien has pointed out, the rise of community-based programs in Texas ironically expanded the number of juveniles under TYC control by allowing for the confinement of "predelinquent" youth who had not violated criminal laws but were understood as at risk of doing so eventually (O'Brien 2021, 108). As could be expected, this transformation exacerbated racial injustice in the policing and incarceration of Texas youth. By 1992, the TYC was confining Black youth at eight times, and Hispanic youth at three times, the rate of their Anglo peers (Texas Youth Commission 1993, iv). The turn to community-based facilities then allowed the state to surveil the gender and sexuality of an even greater number of Texas juveniles and to heighten its focus on Black youth, who had long borne the brunt of the state's attempts at forced normalization.

The idea that community-based residential facilities provided a better likelihood of straightening juveniles was not often made explicit in TYC annual reports or other publications in the decades that followed *Morales v. Turman*'s trial. Nor was it apparent in the federal Juvenile Justice and Delinquency Prevention Act, passed by Congress on September 7, 1974, only a few days after Judge Justice issued his memorandum opinion in *Morales*. Among the central aims of this legislation was to incentivize states to "divert juveniles from the traditional juvenile justice system and to provide critically needed alternatives to institutionalization" through the creation of community-based programs and residences that could provide "psychological guidance among other medical and educational services" (Juvenile Justice and Delinquency Prevention Act 1974, 1111).

But the absence of clear language here about the ways carceral institutions seemed to foster gender and sexual deviance should not deceive us. The state's goal of compelling young people to comply with mainstream gender and sexual standards was critical as Texas and the nation shifted away from traditional institutions to seemingly straighter community alternatives.

**Lauren Jae Gutterman** is associate professor of American studies, history, and women's and gender studies at the University of Texas at Austin. She is the author of *Her Neighbor's Wife: A History of Lesbian Desire within Marriage.* She can be reached at lgutterman@utexas.edu.

## Notes

1. The six TYC institutions included the Brownwood State Home and School for Girls, Crockett State School for Girls, Gainesville State School for Girls, Giddings State Home and School for Boys, the Mountain View State School for Boys, and the Gatesville State School for Boys, which had seven internal schools. TYC also operated two Statewide Reception Centers, one for girls at Brownwood and one for boys at Gatesville.
2. According to Judge Justice's 1974 ruling, 34.1% of students in TYC institutions were Black, 23.9% were Mexican American, and 41.9% were Anglo (*Morales v. Turman* 1974, 108).
3. See, for example, Testimony 1973a.
4. Minor witnesses' initials are drawn, when available, from Bush 2010.
5. On the use of X to signify the connections between Blackness and transness, see Bey 2020.
6. The Texas Youth Council's name was changed to the Texas Youth Commission in 1983.

## Works Cited

Agyepong, Tera. 2018. *The Criminalization of Black Children: Race, Gender, and Delinquency in Chicago's Juvenile Justice System, 1899–1945.* Chapel Hill: University of North Carolina Press.

Alexander, Rudolph. 1995. "Incarcerated Juvenile Offenders' Right to Rehabilitation." *Criminal Justice Policy Review* 7, no. 2: 202–13.

Bey, Marquis. 2020. *The Problem of the Negro as a Problem for Gender.* Minneapolis: University of Minnesota Press.

Bieber, Irving, Harvey J. Dain, Paul R. Dince, et al. 1962. *Homosexuality: A Psychoanalytic Study.* New York: Basic Books.

Blasko, Marie L. 1985. "Saving the Child: Rejuvenating a Dying Right to Rehabilitation." *New England Journal on Crime and Civil Confinement* 11, no. 1: 123–59.

Boag, Peter. 2003. *Same-Sex Affairs Constructing and Controlling Homosexuality in the Pacific Northwest*. Berkeley: University of California Press.

Bush, William S. 2010. *Who Gets a Childhood? Race and Juvenile Justice in Twentieth-Century Texas*. Athens: University of Georgia Press.

Cahn, Susan K. 2007. *Sexual Reckonings: Southern Girls in a Troubling Age*. Cambridge, MA: Harvard University Press.

Canaday, Margot, Nancy F. Cott, and Robert O. Self, eds. 2021. *Intimate States: Gender, Sexuality, and Governance in Modern US History*. Chicago: University of Chicago Press.

Chase, Robert T. 2020. *We Are Not Slaves: State Violence, Coerced Labor, and Prisoners' Rights in Postwar America*. Chapel Hill: University of North Carolina Press.

Chávez-García, Miroslava. 2012. *States of Delinquency: Race and Science in the Making of California's Juvenile Justice System*. Berkeley: University of California Press.

Cohen, Cathy. 2004. "Deviance as Resistance: A New Research Agenda for the Study of Black Politics." *Du Bois Review* 1, no. 1 (March): 27–45.

Davenport, Charles W. 1972. "Homosexuality: Its Origins, Early Recognition and Prevention." *Clinical Pediatrics* 11, no. 1 (January): 7–10.

Discipline Committee, Valley School. October 1(8?), 1973, folder 4-A1-15, box 1999/085-16, Texas Youth Commission *Morales* Case Files, Texas State Library and Archives, Austin, Texas (hereafter MCF).

Donaldson, Stephen. 2001. "A Million Jockers, Queens and Punks." In *Prison Masculinities*, edited by Don Sabo, Terry A. Kupers, and Willie London, 118–26. Philadelphia, PA: Temple University Press.

Doyle, Dennis. 2016. *Psychiatry and Racial Liberalism in Harlem, 1936–1968*. New York: University of Rochester Press.

Ferguson, Roderick. 2003. *Aberrations in Black: Toward a Queer of Color Critique*. Minneapolis: University of Minnesota Press.

Gainesville State School for Girls. n.d. Response to Question 15 and 15a Addendum I. Folder #4-AI-15, box 1999/085-30, MCF.

General Appropriations Act. 1975. 64th Leg., R.S., ch. 743, art. II, 1975 Tex. Gen Laws 2417, 2443.

Giallombardo, Rose. 1966. *Society of Women: A Study of a Women's Prison*. New York: John Wiley & Sons.

Gill-Peterson, Jules. 2018. *Histories of the Transgender Child*. Minneapolis: University of Minnesota Press.

Girshick, Lori. 2015. "Out of Compliance: Masculine-Identified People in Women's Prisons." In *Captive Genders: Trans Embodiment and the Prison Industrial Complex*, edited by Eric A. Stanley, 96–104. Oakland, CA: AK Press.

Gross, Kali N. 2006. *Colored Amazons: Crime, Violence, and Black Women in the City of Brotherly Love, 1880–1910.* Durham, NC: Duke University Press.

Haley, Sarah. 2016. *No Mercy Here: Gender, Punishment, and the Making of Jim Crow Modernity.* Chapel Hill: University of North Carolina Press.

Hicks, Cheryl D. 2010. *Talk with You Like a Woman: African American Women, Justice, and Reform in New York, 1890–1930.* Chapel Hill: University of North Carolina Press.

*In re Gault.* 1967. 387 U.S. 1.

Juvenile Justice and Delinquency Prevention Act. 1974. vol. 42 USC series 5601 (1974). https://www.govinfo.gov/content/pkg/STATUTE-88/pdf/STATUTE-88-Pg1109.pdf.

Kemerer, Frank F. 1991. *William Wayne Justice: A Judicial Biography.* Austin: University of Texas Press.

Konopka, Gisela. 1966. *The Adolescent Girl in Conflict.* Englewood Cliffs, NJ: Prentice-Hall.

———. 1970. "Our Outcast Youth." *Social Work* 15, no. 4: 76–86.

Kunzel, Regina. 2008. *Criminal Intimacy: Prison and the Uneven History of Modern American Sexuality.* Chicago: University of Chicago Press.

———. 2017. "Sex Panic, Psychiatry, and the Expansion of the Carceral State." In *The War on Sex*, edited by David M. Halperin and Trevor Hoppe, 229–46. Durham, NC: Duke University Press, 2017.

Lawrence, Leonard. 1973. Transcript of Testimony. July 23, 1973, p. 3066, folder 9-37, box 1999/085-35, MCF.

LeFlouria, Talitha L. 2015. *Chained in Silence: Black Women and Convict Labor in the New South.* Chapel Hill: University of North Carolina Press.

Lewis, Abram J. 2016. "'We Are Certain of Our Own Insanity': Psychiatry and the Gay Liberation Movement, 1968–1980." *Journal of the History of Sexuality* 25, no. 1: 83–113.

Lira, Natalie. 2022. *Laboratory of Deficiency: Sterilization and Confinement in California, 1900–1950s.* Oakland: University of California Press.

MacCormick, Austin. Deposition. May 7, 1973, folder 5-36, box 1999/085-22, MCF.

Martin, Steve J., and Sheldon Ekland-Olson. 1987. *Texas Prisons: The Walls Came Tumbling Down.* Austin: Texas Monthly Press.

McNeely, Dave, Jamie Frucht, and Joan Filvaroff. 1973. "Kids in Court." *Texas Monthly*, June 30, 1973.

Mental Health Law Project. 1977. *Mental Health Law Project: Summary of Activities* 3, no. 1: 2.

*Morales v. Turman*, 383 F. Supp. 53 (E.D. Tex. 1974). Decided Aug. 30, 1974.

———. 562 F.2d 993 (5th Cir. 1977).

Morgan, Jennifer. 2004. *Laboring Women: Reproduction and Gender in New World Slavery*. Philadelphia: University of Pennsylvania Press.

Moynihan, Daniel Patrick. 1965. *The Negro Family: The Case for National Action*. Washington, DC: Office of Policy Planning and Research, United States Department of Labor.

Mumford, Kevin J. 2012. "Untangling Pathology: The Moynihan Report and Homosexual Damage, 1965–1975." *Journal of Policy History* 24, no. 1: 53–73.

National Center for Youth Law. n.d. "NYCL Lawsuit Reforms Texas Juvenile Institutions, Where Youth Were 'Tortured and Terrorized.' August 31, 1973." Accessed August 11, 2022. https://youthlaw.org/news/ncyl-lawsuit-reforms-texas-juvenile-institutions-where-youth-were-tortured-and-terrorized.

O'Brien, Cyrus J. 2021. "'A Prison in Your Community': Halfway Houses and the Melding of Treatment and Control." *Journal of American History* 108, no. 1: 93–117.

Pre-trial Brief of Amici on Behalf of American Orthopsychiatric Association et al. n.d. Folder B 2-48, box 1999/085-47, MCF.

Ramos, Nic John. 2019. "Pathologizing the Crisis: Psychiatry, Policing and Racial Liberalism in the Long Community Mental Health Movement." *Journal of the History of Medicine and Allied Sciences* 247, no. 1: 57–84.

Record of Proceedings. 1973a. July 2, 1973. Folder "Volume 1 File 2 of 2," box 1999/085-36, MCF.

———. 1973b. July 6, 1973. Folder "Volume 4 File 2 of 3," box 1999/085-37, MCF.

———. 1973c. July 9, 1973. Folder "Volume 5 File 1 of 2," box 1999/085-37, MCF.

———. 1973d. July 11, 1973. Folder "Volume 7 File 2 of 2," box 1999/085-37, MCF.

———. 1973e. July 18, 1973. Folder "Volume 9 File 1 of 2," box 1999/085-38, MCF.

Reddington, Mary Frances. 1990. "In the Best Interest of the Child: The Effects of *Morales v. Turman* on the Texas Youth Commission." PhD diss., Sam Houston State University.

Roth, Andrew. 1985. "An Examination of Whether Juveniles Are Entitled by the Constitution to Rehabilitative Treatment." *Michigan Law Review* 84, no. 2: 286–307.

Sedgwick, Eve Kosofsky. 1991. "How to Bring Your Kids Up Gay." *Social Text*, no. 29: 17–27.

Sexual Treatment Center for Sex Incidents. 1962–72. September 4, 1962 to December 18, 1972. Folder 3-12, box 1999/085-16, MCF.

———. 1964–72. September 15, 1964 to September 25, 1972. Folder 3-12, box 1999/085-16, MCF.

Shearer, Marshall. 1966. "Homosexuality and the Pediatrician: Early Recognition and Preventative Counselling." *Clinical Pediatrics* 5, no. 8: 514–18.

Sheely, Margaret. 1972. August 18, 1972. Folder 7-29, box 1999/085-27, MCF.

Smith, Gerda, and Patricia Blakeney. n.d. a. Transcription of Conversations during Inspections. Side 10. Folder, 7-36, box 1999/085-28, MCF.

———. n.d. b. Transcription of Conversations during Inspections. Side 5. Folder, 7-36, box 1999/085-28, MCF.

Snorton, C. Riley. 2017. *Black on Both Sides: A Racial History of Trans Identity.* Minneapolis: University of Minnesota Press.

Special Incident Report. 1972a. March 19, 1972. Folder 4-A1-15, box 1999/085-16, MCF.

———. 1972b. March 31, 1972. Folder 4-A1-15, box 1999/085-16, MCF.

———. 1972c. August 16, 1972. Folder 4-A1-15, box 1999/085-16, MCF.

Statewide Reception Center for Girls. 1972a. Addendum to Question 15. Undated log book entry. Folder #4-AI-15, box 1999/085-30, MCF.

———. 1972b. Addendum to Question 15. 1972. Log book entry May 6, 1972. Folder #4-AI-15, box 1999/085-30, MCF.

Staub, Michael E. 2011. *Madness Is Civilization: When the Diagnosis Was Social, 1948–1980.* Chicago: University of Chicago Press.

Symmonds, Martin. 1969. "Homosexuality in Adolescence." *Pennsylvania Psychiatric Quarterly* 9, no. 2: 15–24.

Testimony of [name redacted]. 1973a. July 5, 1973. Folder 9-35 "Testimony [minor]," box 1999/085 35, MCF.

———. 1973b. July 11, 1973. Folder 9-28 "Testimony [minor]," box 1999/085-35, MCF.

———. 1973c. July 19, 1973. Folder 9-31 "Testimony [minor]," box 1999/085-35, MCF.

———. 1973d. July 19–20, 1973. Folder 9-32 "Testimony [minor]," box 1999/085-35, MCF.

Texas Youth Commission. 1983. Annual Report. Austin, TX.

———. 1993. Overrepresentation of Minorities in the Juvenile Justice System. Austin, TX.

Wilson, R. 1978. "A State That Bucks the Trend." *Corrections Magazine* 4, no. 3 (September): 23–28.

Wooden, Kenneth. 1976. *Weeping in the Playtime of Others: America's Incarcerated Children.* New York: McGraw-Hill.

# "We Wanted to Talk Plumbing": Organizing and Mutual Aid in Baltimore's High-Rise Public Housing

Robert Thomas Choflet

**Abstract:** Federal and local campaigns to reform "distressed" high-rise public housing in the late twentieth century resulted in the elimination of thousands of public housing units from cities like Baltimore. Those reform campaigns often defined "distress" in cultural terms, imagining Black women residents as imperiled actors, public housing as an impediment to building normative family life, and housing demolition and privatization as a necessary and normalizing corrective. Oral histories with residents living in these disinvested spaces offer counternarratives and demonstrate how Black women residents theorized their own conditions, fashioned material political demands independent of policy makers and housing reformers, and worked to put these demands into practice. This piece reflects on the mutual aid organizing of two former residents of Baltimore's George B. Murphy Homes. Specifically, it analyzes the practical work they did to address the conditions that disinvestment produced, and the intellectual work they did to fashion a materialist vision for housing reform that pushed back against the drive toward demolition and privatization. **Keywords:** high-rise public housing; mutual aid; oral histories; National Commission on Severely Distressed Public Housing (NCSDPH); HOPE VI

The meeting was bigger and more spirited than she thought it was going to be. In fact, what Henrietta "Etta" Barnes imagined was something closer to "an instruction, a class" than a meeting—a skill share among a few friends who lived on the twelfth floor of 1058 Argyle Avenue, one of four high-rises in Baltimore's George B. Murphy Homes Family High-Rise Towers (Etta Barnes, pers. comm., November 7, 2012). The plan was to brainstorm and share some basic maintenance techniques. Through informal study, discussions with friends and relatives, and an ethos of "when you're

*WSQ: Women's Studies Quarterly* 51: 1 & 2 (Spring/Summer 2023)

poor, you teach yourself things," Barnes had developed a "handiness" that had raised her profile among her neighbors. She expected three people to be there. It turned out that something closer to a dozen came: "friends, people from other floors, someone from another building . . . some kids" (Barnes, pers. comm., January 1, 2013). Barnes intended to bring the group together in order to discuss rudimentary plumbing maintenance: "to teach [one another] how to change out the drain trap in the sink—Joanne's was clogged, no one from maintenance was coming to fix it" (Barnes, pers. comm., January 15, 2013). And while those who showed up to Joanne's meeting may have initially overestimated Barnes's skills—"they thought I knew how to do way more than I knew how to do. I rolled with it"—they agreed that it had become necessary for residents to learn how to make their own repairs (Barnes, pers. comm.).

Barnes no longer lives in public housing. The building she organized in no longer exists. It was demolished in 1999. Amid city officials, residents, and fanfare, the then president of the tenant's association, Mary Holmes, stood on a stage and pushed a prop dynamite plunger as a private demolitions company razed the buildings to the ground. In an instant, before a cheering crowd of hundreds of West Baltimore residents, the buildings that Barnes and Holmes had called home were gone, joining some two hundred thousand other public housing units that have been erased from the U.S. urban landscape in the years since Barnes organized her neighbors (Oakes and Pelton 1999; Pekkanen and Hughes 1999; Charles Cohen 2019).

That this loss of housing was met in Baltimore with excitement speaks to how effectively policy makers shaped the discourse in the years between Barnes's organizing work and Holmes's prop detonation. As Barnes's example demonstrates, conditions in the Murphy Homes had become so dire that residents felt it necessary to teach themselves building maintenance. Yet, as policy makers mounted their case for intervention and reform, they built it around a notion of building-wide "distress." Like the larger, national effort, local policy makers defined this "distress" in cultural terms.

The choice to narrate housing decline in terms of distress, and to define distress in cultural rather than material terms, relegated residents like Barnes to the margins of the discussion. This is not because policy makers ignored, categorically, resident voices. To the contrary, the reform campaigns expressed through both the congressional Commission on Severely Distressed Public Housing and Baltimore's Family High-Rise Modernization Task Force each made a point to include certain residents and present a picture of resident support. Rather, as I argue in this article, the loosely affiliated and informal movement Barnes was a part of, which focused on material interventions and improvements of housing conditions, challenged the prevailing material agenda, which worked to forgo improvements in favor of demolition and, ultimately, privatization of this once-public resource. I argue here that the forces of demolition and privatization cultivated a "cultural politics" through which they pursued these interests. By this, I mean that a politics whereby racialized, sexualized, and gendered signifiers; imagined norms; and the role that power assumes as arbiter of morality are all leveraged in pursuit of resource transfer. The tendency, for example, to elevate "family life" over specific housing conditions represents the type of cultural politics being considered here.

The choice by the media and the housing authority to narrate housing decline in a way that foregrounded some residents' performances of despair while ignoring other residents' organizing efforts—the ways that housing reformers mobilized and presented Black women as suffering subjects and public housing families as in peril—effaced the work of the building's organizers and their interventions in, and demands for, rehabilitation over demolition. Focusing on Baltimore's George Murphy Homes and working from a collection of oral histories that I have conducted with its former residents, this article looks at how planners fashioned a cultural politics that worked to displace the material demands made by residents. Further, this article looks at how Black women's intellectual labor and mutual aid produced a materialist critique of housing policy and offered alternative visions to the policies of demolition and privatization.

### Etta Barnes and Mutual Aid

Etta Barnes, currently in her late sixties, is the mother of three adult children and grandmother of two. She was a public housing resident for much of her adult life. She moved into the Murphy Homes when she was in her early twenties, and she lived there until they were demolished. While she now rents a two-story rowhouse in the southeast neighborhood of Patterson Park, the story of her public housing life and, in particular, her reluctant building organizing, provides insight and dimension to our understanding of public housing transformation, both locally in Baltimore as well as the larger urban United States.

Life in a place like the Murphy Homes in the late 1980s—that is to say, life within public housing in a moment of deep austerity—occasioned (invited, almost insisted on) this kind of community labor. As Rhonda Y. Williams has explored in detail in her study of mid-twentieth-century public housing communities, this mutual aid work was a register of residents' tenuous relationship to state resources as well as their capacity to reproduce their own social lives and conditions outside of and beyond state aid (Williams 2005). What Barnes and other Murphy Homes residents, as well as tenants in other high-rise complexes throughout the city proved through their collective practice was this: public housing communities existed not simply as objects of governance, nor as passive recipients of disinvestment, but as assemblies of people who constructed alternative forms of self-governance, in part through mutual aid.[1]

Barnes referred to her Murphy Homes work as "informal" organizing. In reflecting on that first meeting, she describes a coming-together of a working group of like-minded neighbors who wanted to do something about the deteriorating housing conditions they were living through. The "buildings were literally falling apart, killing people. These weren't trivial concerns," Baltimore resident Lorraine Greene remembered (pers. comm., April 18, 2015), referring to the tragic collapse of a balcony that killed twelve-year-old resident Raymond Toulson in 1989 (Ollove 1989). As Barnes noticed services diminishing, as broken elevators went unfixed, as leaky kitchen sinks and bathroom pipes became the norm, as trash began to accumulate in common areas, hallways, stairways, and so forth, she felt compelled to organize some kind of response. It was, by her admission, a "small" group, never more than fifteen people—one of what she estimates were many small groups of residents who were meeting and developing forms of mutual aid (Barnes, pers. comm., January 15, 2013).

"In those days, I learned what a drain trap was. Risers, a compression nut, watertight gaskets . . . ask me anything," she says jokingly about how she and other residents taught themselves plumbing basics—the kind of work she would do when maintenance ignored them (Barnes, pers. comm.). As local Black media reported at the time of the Murphy Homes demolition, "thirty percent of all maintenance work orders" in Baltimore high-rises concerned "plumbing problems" (White 1996). The group's work went beyond plumbing. They became skilled at other minor repairs and at identifying when the housing authority either dropped the ball or performed faulty maintenance. They fixed broken and moldy drywall. They repaired bowing and warped linoleum flooring. A member of their group who had done some side work for a carpeting company procured the use of a carpet stretcher and heavy-duty stapler that were used to address buckling carpeting. "We were the group who knew our way around the hardware store," Barnes recalls (pers. comm., May 20, 2013). These were skills that they felt were important to share with other residents. They became resident teachers. Residents who wanted to learn the art of repair regularly made their homes available for Barnes and others to provide classes, demonstrations, or workshops. After a particularly rainy spring, tenants experienced a mold outbreak. Residents gathered to share tips on how to abate the mold growing on the outdoor walls.

Barnes recalls organizing a training with people from another floor in her building. It focused on how to patch holes in ceilings and the walls— "there's a difference between patching drywall and patching plaster, you know" (pers. comm., May 21, 2013). Barnes recalled proudly the many times that she gave advice or counsel to a neighbor on how to address one or another maintenance concern.

Informal as the group may have been, they maintained a political vision and saw themselves as doing political work. They labored to hold maintenance staff accountable. As Barnes notes, because of how intimately familiar they had become with repair issues around their building and other buildings in the development, they often made attempts to bring such problems to the attention of the staff. Barnes states, "We'd run them down—'Did you get to such and such, yet?'—It got so they'd see us and turn the other way [*laughs*]" (pers. comm., January 15, 2013). It was this type of political work that led Barnes and others to develop a set of maintenance demands.

### Bonnie McKinley and "the Other Task Force"

Bonnie McKinley, too, lived in Murphy Homes. She moved into the building on the 900 block of Argyle in 1990, when she was thirty-eight years old. She raised two children there. Three of her sisters also lived in public housing, one in Murphy's "low-rises" and two in the neighboring Lexington Terrace, along with McKinley's six nieces and nephews. Over the years, McKinley had developed "a reputation in my building . . . for better or worse" (Bonnie McKinley, pers. comm., August 8, 2011). Like Barnes, she, too, gained experience in informal organizing activity. When her children were young, she pitched in with others in the building to make room in the courtyard for family activities:

It was that park at, I think, Hoffman and Argyle, that belonged to the project [HABC / Murphy Homes] . . . where my youngest and his friends couldn't play because there was just too much other activity if you know what I mean. . . . So some of us just started going out there. . . . You be visible. . . . We had this idea that if we wore these reflector vests—you know, the kind that a crossing guard has . . . this way of showing dealers that we weren't there for them . . . that maybe just being out there and around maybe would push some of them out and make more room for our kids. We had a lot of kids there that no one wanted getting involved with the drug dealing. (McKinley, pers. comm., August 8, 2011)

This work leveraged visibility and presence as a way of creating space. The ethic that McKinley and other residents developed was one that imagined a park as a commonly held resource available to the diversity of groups interacting with it. While there was clear unease in her discussion of drug dealing ("other activity"), she described working to fashion a community response that was not interested in moralizing or appeals to punitive power. Rather, there was the practical understanding that the "other activity" was potentially violent and particularly exploitative of younger, economically vulnerable people: "They're [people selling illicit drugs] in the park 'cause they look for project kids. . . . They get project kids wrapped up in that quick" (McKinley, pers. comm., August 1, 2011).

Their response was not an appeal to the police but an attempt to crowd out what they perceived to be a negative presence: "We decided to do soccer for the kids in that park. So on Saturday morning we'd bring out those nets and a ball and gather up the children we could and just let them play a game" (McKinley, pers. comm.). Like Barnes's, McKinley's work may not be immediately read as either issuing from or gesturing toward an overtly political imaginary. But in their practice, the women who donned reflective vests, set up soccer nets, and attempted to disrupt illicit markets in their backyard were making political claims on publicly held space, making an argument for a commons that existed in the service of communal rather than commercial (i.e., exploitative) aims.

As it happened, Barnes, McKinley, and the larger coalition of interested residents they worked with were not the only people meeting about the conditions of Murphy. In 1992, Congress committed two hundred million dollars in an effort to begin addressing public housing in need of "modernization" and "rehabilitation" (NCSDPH 1992). In an effort to efficiently utilize these funds, the National Commission on Severely Distressed Public

Housing (NCSDPH) was established. The commission was chaired by Congressman Bill Green of New York and Vincent Lane, director of the Chicago Housing Authority. The commission was populated by sixteen other people, a mix of other housing authority directors, former mayors, municipal employees, nonprofits, one tenant council president, a representative from the banking industry, and Richard D. Baron of McCormack Baron and Associates (now McCormack Baron Salazar), a nonprofit developer "and asset manager of economically-integrated urban neighborhoods" (McKormac Barron and Associates, n.d.).

The commission did not identify specific sites but rather produced a working definition that would then be used to assess local proposals for housing redevelopment through a series of working papers: "The NCSDPH developed the definition of severely distressed public housing with the intention that it be used so that PHAs (Public Housing Authority) can apply for severely distressed housing designation and for these housing developments to then qualify for remedies proposed by the NCSDPH and enacted by the Congress" (NCSDPH 1992). These working papers produced by the commission focused on "traditional measures," what the commission called "modernization," such as improving the physical conditions of a given public housing development. But they also focused on what it called "non-traditional measures."

Through public hearings the commission looked to identify examples of "severely distressed" housing. The hearings included "public testimony from residents, PHA staff and directors, and local government officials." They designed a "point system" for categorizing developments as severely distressed. The commission characterized severely distressed public housing through either a combination of several factors or an extreme degree of one. Alongside issues of "funding" and "age of housing stock," local housing authorities assessed things like access to employment, and factors such as "little exposure to people who might serve as constructive role models of economic success" were pointed to as reasons for "generations of families grow up thinking of public housing as permanent." "The factors chosen to be included in the definition combine[d] physical and social characteristics," and the commission enumerated four initial identifying characteristics, informed by those laid out in the congressional authorization language in the 1989 legislation: "500 or more units," "elevators," "vacancy rates of higher than 15 percent," and "tenants who are predominantly families with children"—put differently, high-rises, particularly those populated by children. Testimony from residents, PHA staff, and directors helped produce additional criteria: lack of applicant screening; housing stock age; lack of social services for residents in need, and most tellingly, "resident apathy" (NCSDPH 1992).

These criteria were then ranked and organized into groups: (1) conditions at the development itself, (2) conditions in the immediately surrounding neighborhood, and (3) factors relating to PHA's management capability. Based on these criteria, the commission found that 6 percent of U.S. public housing stock (totaling eighty-six thousand units) was "severely distressed." Their report recommended that Congress and HUD (U.S. Department of Housing and Urban Development) reform distressed housing by the year 2000, calling on them to support the "rehabilitation or replacement of existing units." However, this focus on the "physical and social characteristics" of public housing and its residents gave housing authorities "latitude in determining which public housing developments were severely distressed" (NCSDPH 1992, 1–2).

This effort was expressed and pursued locally in Baltimore through the Family High-Rise Modernization Task Force. While the organizing work of Barnes and McKinley did not intersect, they both found themselves interacting with this task force initiated by Baltimore's then mayor, Kurt Schmoke, and the executive director of the Housing Authority of Baltimore City at the time, Robert Hearn. It was chaired by Michael J. Kelley, dean of the University of Maryland law school (not to be confused with Michael P. Kelly, head of the DC Housing Authority from 2000 to 2010), and included politicians, education officials, lawyers, and leaders of housing advocacy groups, with fourteen members in all, including six public housing residents from across the city, McKinley being one.

Following Congress's lead, this task force also addressed itself to "non-traditional" measures of distress. The nine-month study it convened reviewed documents, heard oral testimony, and facilitated "lively" public exchanges in order to assess the "quality of life factors" within the city's high-rise public housing sites (Kelley 1991). While its stated purpose was to assess the relative "safety" of the city's high-rises for the nearly three thousand children who resided there, it also should be noted that its creation coincided with what the *Baltimore Sun* reported at the time was "$100 million in federal funds that the Housing Authority expects to receive over the next 10 years," incentivizing material intervention (Thompson 1990a).

"The task force gave them the ammo that they needed to look good on the news, even when they were putting people out of their housing," Lorraine Greene notes (pers. comm., April 18, 2015). An administrator at Morgan State University, Greene had been a West Baltimore resident as a teen and had "many, MANY" friends in the Murphy Homes and neighboring Lexington Terrace: "It was a home away from home," she notes, laughing (Greene, pers. comm.). Her observations align with the policy history. Baltimore Councilman William Cole IV, reflecting on this moment of transformation, noted the city's search for a residential "anchor" of downtown redevelopment (Capital News Service Staff 2008). The Housing Authority of Baltimore City revitalization plan appealed to developers that "it is feasible to redevelop obsolete and concentrated very low-income housing into more livable mixed income housing" (Capital News Service Staff 2008). By 1989 construction was already underway for the $104.5 million baseball stadium that would be sited just blocks from the Murphy Homes (Cassie 2022). Likewise, the area would soon benefit from a 1994 empowerment zone designation that would direct $100 million into economic development projects in the area (Baltimore Empowerment Zone Strategic Plan 1994).

As developers along with city planners began to rediscover the potential value in underdeveloped land downtown, and as that same cohort began to imagine a "new front door" to West Baltimore linking to the downtown area, private capital sought to harness and instrumentalize the state's claims to moral authority.[2] The underdeveloped public high-rises that lined the northwestern border of downtown and had for years been framed within public discourse as sites of criminality and sexual disrepute were increasingly imagined as impediments to private growth. The disreputable high-rises needed to go.[3]

While McKinley was ostensibly a central member of the task force, she never felt like an equal to the non–housing residents that she shared the work with. "They'd ask for your opinion and then ignore it," she notes. "Except when they needed us in front of the camera. They always encouraged us to go on and on about how bad the housing was when there were reporters around" (McKinley, pers. comm., August 8, 2011). She clarified as follows during one conversation:

> But look, the high-rises had real problems. But when I think about it now, what I think is that these lawyers, the mayor, these . . . I'll say it . . . these white people, they weren't really interested in us. Really. What I mean, is

they didn't care about how we struggled or what was happening to us—
even when they said they did. What they really wanted was to get us out. . . .
So they talked about how it was ruining our families. My entire family lived
there. It didn't ruin my family. (McKinley, pers. comm., August 8, 2011)

Her experience speaks to the complicated and sometimes contradictory relationships this process had with the Black women who lived in this
housing. The task force at once sought to incorporate the bodies and voices
of residents, yet these residents were presented a highly circumscribed set
of choices, ultimately all derived from outside of their own thoughts and
experiences as residents. As McKinley can attest, the task force made a
show of inviting and encouraging Black residents to join public meetings,
participate in surveys, and be included in the task force itself. Of the fourteen members who served on the task force, six, including McKinley, were
Black women and public housing residents.

Barnes's first exposure to the task force was at a meeting it convened at
the Murphy Homes many months into its research process. Entering the
meeting, she assumed the committee "was about finding solutions to the
problems" that disrupted public housing life (Barnes, pers. comm., May 20,
2013). As Barnes describes it, she and her neighbors attempted to participate in meetings but never felt as though there was any room for them or
for discussions that drew from their understanding of the buildings and
their problems or from their visions for solutions. They presented the task
force a list of recommendations, which they believed would be helpful and
reflective of their thinking, only to be rebuffed for not following protocol.

The recommendations as Barnes recalls them were straightforward:
(1) bolster the repair schedule, which had recently seemed to stall out, (2)
address the chronic slowing and breakdowns of the elevators, (3) address the
pest problem, which had spiraled out of control over the previous decade,
(4) address the crime, and (5) reopen a central paved courtyard, which was
home to basketball hoops and a site of socializing and which had recently
had its gates chained by HABC (Housing Authority of Baltimore City)
due to, as tenants tell it, an effort to appease Baltimore City Police. They
were moderate and grounded in explaining the need for material improvements—an effort to "improve those buildings." The city had other ideas.

Barnes and others were not completely ignored by the task force. They
were invited to meetings. As she describes it, they were effectively expected
to be an audience while the task force shared findings. Yet the material facts

"uncovered" by the task force presented in the reports back were not news to Barnes or to the other tenants present. The Murphy Homes were the most densely populated tract of public housing—and of residential space more broadly—in the city. Those who lived there "felt" the disinvestment, as one former Baltimore public housing resident described, particularly as the buildings aged and the political decisions accelerated disinvestment (Lawrence Tanner, pers. comm., February 11, 2013).

If they hadn't "felt" it, there was no shortage of local news segments, exposés, and newspaper articles that described in grim detail the conditions of Baltimore's public housing and their perceived effects on public housing communities, particularly the youth populations. A spate of articles that ran between 1989 and 1991 covering the mayor's task force offered many observations about the high-rises and their perceived nonnormative familial arrangements: "The buildings [. . .] house high numbers of pregnant teens and high school dropouts," one *Sun* article noted; another stated: "Most of the residents are single mothers with two children under age 12."[4]

Echoing the *Sun*, the task force published its final report, "New Lease on Life," in which it asserted that the high-rises as currently constituted were "unfit for family life." Its goal was to "make these communities more conducive for family living and revitalize the neighborhoods" (Thompson 1990a). In that spirit, the task force recommended that the HABC cut the number of high-rise housing units in Baltimore by 40 percent. "Demolish most of the Buildings," the task force recommended, "and replace them with new ones especially designed to strengthen family life." Practically speaking, doing so would have involved reducing the 2,750 units of high-rise public housing to 1,650 units and moving those who relied on the remaining 1,100 units, via a mix of housing vouchers and the scattered site-replacement units. In the Murphy Homes, this would mean reducing the 758-unit site to 455 units and displacing the remainder of the residents. It also recommended to expand education and job training efforts, as well as requiring tenants to contribute service to the community. It recommended that anyone with children should be relocated. Further, it "recommended that the Housing Authority implement a program in which relocated tenants could be taught basic life skills, such as how to manage a household, budget their money and care for their children" (Thompson 1990a).

While efforts to characterize the buildings as socially deforming and in need of demolition upset Barnes, what bothered her most (and continues to bother her) was not that the committee ignored the residents—it did not.

As noted, there were residents represented on the committee; likewise there were residents featured prominently at all press events: "they had a person who worked with residents to tell their stories to the media" (Barnes, pers. comm., January 15, 2013). What Barnes observed, however, was that there was no sincere effort made by the committee to connect to organizers in the buildings, to plug into and to draw from the mutual aid practices of those like Barnes and her cohort and to think through their vision for rehabilitation instead of demolition. "We weren't useful to them," she asserts. "The city was ready to tear those buildings down and they wanted the people who had given up . . . or the ones who would focus on the problems, the ones who weren't doing the work to make those apartments better, the ones without that vision for making it better." Here, Barnes's critique is sharp: "There were stories and there were politician visits and there was a lot of concern, but they didn't come to our meetings. . . . They didn't ask us what we were trying to get done to fix these problems. . . . They wanted the people who had given up, not the people who were working to get things better" (Barnes, pers. comm.).

The mutual aid work of Barnes, McKinley, and others should not be idealized. Nor should it be assumed that simply scaling up their work would have radically improved the high-rise towers. Rather, what discussions with residents reveal is that they maintained a materialist (rather than cultural) understanding of the very real problems with high-rise housing towers. In spite of housing authority gestures creating the illusion that they were expressing resident will, the reality was that they made political choices about how to narrate their intervention, the consequences of which obscured tenant organizing and gave the impression that demolition was inevitable. Barnes's slightly tongue-in-cheek observation rings very true: "They wanted to talk family dysfunction, we wanted to talk plumbing" (Barnes, pers. comm., May 21, 2013).

### "'Unfit' for Whose Family?"

McKinley described the task force as split in two. On the one hand, there were the residents. "We weren't unified," she noted of the group. "There were some folks who had more of a say than someone like me." Yet "we all lived in those towers." On the other hand, there were what she referred to as "the mayor's people." This group she described as primarily white, as members of the professional class, and as having had little exposure to public housing life and no experience living within it. According to McKinley, this group set the task force's *actual* agenda. While everyone was present at the meetings, they facilitated the meetings. They also wrote the reports and directed all of the interactions with the city, the housing authority, and HUD, and with the media. Further, they maintained a culture within the group that would keep the resident participants at arm's length: "We would be pleasant with each other, but we weren't friends or anything like that." "There wasn't much of a connection" between the residents and the other members of the task force (McKinley, pers. comm., January 5, 2012).

That divide, McKinley argues, went well beyond interpersonal insensitivities:

> When I think back on it, I think about who these people were and what they meant when they said "family"—again, this task force was about how the buildings weren't safe for families. [. . .] Their lives were so different from ours, so different. What did they think about when they thought about our families? [. . .] What did that white lawyer, who's from, I think, [the historically white and wealthy north Baltimore neighborhood of] Roland Park [. . .] What'd she know about Ms. Jean or this one right here [gesturing to a photo of Murphy Homes resident Elanor McDonald] or the other people they talked to or that she coached into running one of these meetings— what did she really know about their families? (McKinley, pers. comm., January 5, 2012)

"I'm not trying to say that rich white people understand their families different from poor people from the projects . . . from Black people," she said, then adding, "but . . . maybe I am [*laughs*]" (McKinley, pers. comm.).

When asked why the maintenance of competing ideas about family mattered, McKinley notes, "It meant they didn't need to solve our problems how they would solve their own" (McKinley, pers. comm., January 5, 2012). Roland Park has long been a signifier for what George Lipsitz would call the "white spatial imaginary" in Baltimore (Lipsitz 2011). Initially founded as a suburb of the city by upper-middle-class residents, the neighborhood was annexed by the city on January 1, 1919. It maintains a reputation as an over-resourced white enclave, marked by a concentration of large homes and winding tree-lined residential streets, exclusive private schools, and the kind of "exclusionary amenities" that have come to define a certain form of classed and raced residential segregation within the post–civil rights city.[5] Its enormous influence over both social and political life within the city, and its outsized claim to the city's resources, are often justified by its ability to make claims about itself as a site of "safety," "stability," and "family" life. Its over-resourced status has been justified precisely because of the role it plays in maintaining the "fit"-ness of family life within Baltimore. Likewise, its persistence as a site of concentrated resources for over a century could be attributed to its initial planning—its "defensive framework," among other factors (Sies 1997). By mobilizing the idea of Roland Park in discussing the demolition of the Murphy Homes, McKinley linked the over-accrual of resources necessary to produce Roland Park as a place "fit" for family life, with the extraction of resources from low-income Black residential space.

While spaces like the Murphy Homes high-rise development represent an attenuated extension of policy obligations to low-income families, their construction came with trade-offs. Because de-commodified housing represents a challenge to the prerogatives of racial capitalism, federal housing guidelines and funding stressed that public housing be for "nuclear, heterosexual families with children" (Norman 2012). Where European forms of social housing have often experimented with communal kitchens and other design approaches that invite alternatives to the nuclear family structure, mid-century proponents of U.S. public housing "held very conventional conceptions of family life and gender conceptions" (Marcuse 1995, 246). As a consequence, reinforcing "conventional family structure" has been an important pillar upon which public housing advocates initially built their support. Likewise, as those fashioning an image of "distress" demonstrated, building a perceived lack of stability has served as key to campaigns to undo public housing. That is, the public campaign against public housing, pursued through both Congress's National Commission and Baltimore's task force, turned on notions of familial instability.

The notion that "unfit for family life" should translate in policy terms to demolition, McKinley maintains, comes in part from this ideological insistence that working-class Black women and the kinship structures that policy makers encountered in public housing towers existed outside of normative definitions of family maintained by whites, particularly upper-middle-class white liberals, the kind who populate places like Roland Park. Where "family"—and in particular the preservation of family safety and stability, family "fit"-ness—is mobilized to justify the profound over-resourcing of an area like Roland Park, it furthers a political project that demolished housing and displaced Black women, pushing them from a public resource and into the private market.

The welfare state has historically set its claims of moral authority against a notion of Black female dysfunction, in particular the perceived dysfunction of Black mothers.[6] The findings of the Family High-Rise Modernization Task Force were in keeping with that tradition. The effects of disinvestment—from leaking faucets to crumbling balconies—which were at the center of Barnes's and McKinley's materialist politics, are evidence of state and capital neglect and as such, foreground the state's complicity in reproducing the suffering of public housing residents. These insights were displaced by a task force that, as Barnes notes, was more interested in the presentation of affect than of resident organizers' political observations or material and intellectual labor. To insist on the innate "harmfulness" of the space was to reposition those attempting to preserve their housing as negligent parents. Likewise, this notion of "harmfulness" provided ethical cover for the state to present its demolition campaign as acting in the interests of Black children, protecting them from their negligent parents. In spite of the state's own failures to look after the welfare of Black residents of public housing, it nevertheless mobilized possessive claims on the children living in high-rise housing, as a way of arguing for high-rise demolition.

This is not to say that the poor were malleable or easily manipulated. Rather, their lack of real power, combined with the overdetermined character of these struggles, allowed for the far more organized forces of upward redistribution to selectively appropriate their pain. Further, it allowed that appropriation to stand in for "resident voices." As Rosemary Ndubuizu's recent work demonstrates, disciplinary forces within housing policy have learned to make "use of Black women's voices" in their pursuit of austerity policies, painting a picture that their interventions "were the result of democratic inclusion of low-income (Black) residents' policy preferences" (Ndubuizu 2021, 153). Residents' frustrations in Baltimore and their public performances of suffering were instrumentalized by the task force. Their pain was massaged, and blanket expressions of alienation were transformed into a call for demolition.

Barnes's and McKinley's social practice—like that of many other high-rise residents—was occasioned by the presence of direct state aid, but was necessary precisely because that aid operated unevenly. The welfare state produced racialized asymmetries in resource distribution and, historically, had ignored the ways in which those effects materialized within Black residential space and residential life. Further, it ignored how these same communities were able to produce their own material interventions as well as a politics that came from their own understanding of their material interests. As Katherine McKittrick reminds us, "Black imaginations and mappings are evidence of the struggle over social space" (2006, 9). Residents worked to shift these spaces of confinement into a staging ground for living otherwise. Their work existed as a register of both a profound disconnect from the welfare state and a capacity to produce lifeworlds outside of and beyond welfare-state channels.

As private forces further unravel the welfare state, a discourse of "family responsibility" has emerged to shift onto private actors what in another context would be understood as social obligations (Cooper 2017). While a "family responsibility" discourse often works to discipline working- and middle-class people, pushing them to absorb increasing obligations during moments of austerity, McKinley, Barnes, and the mutual aid groups within the Murphy Homes demonstrate that these dynamics operate differently within spaces of racialized and sexualized poverty. Black women living in public housing have been expected to make up for underdevelopment throughout the history of the welfare state, from its height to its nadir.[7] This work, often carried out by people connected through kinship and sustained through intimate bonds, nevertheless is rarely read as "family responsibility" in any normative sense. As McKinley notes, the task force was incapable or unwilling to see the "family responsibility" on display among local organizers. The work of McKinley and Barnes, like others in their social groups and their extended kinship structures, existed precisely because the state had made direct material investments into urban life and also because the state and capital had failed to provide the resources sufficient to address the mounting material needs of these residents.

The "culture of poverty" myth, which has stubbornly remained at the center of liberal housing-reform efforts, asserts that direct state aid is a threat to family life. This aid, they argue, impedes resident industriousness and disincentivizes normative coupling and the production of two-parent households. McKinley, Barnes, and others demonstrate, to the contrary, that direct material aid in the form of public housing conditioned a robust social life just as intimate and just as linked by kinship as the more narrowly defined notions of family used by policy makers and normative ideologues. It would follow, then, that what was threatening about the conditions of the highrises was not the deforming effects that these housing arrangements had on family life. Rather, I take this archive of policy decisions and resident interviews to suggest that what was threatening was the myriad alternative forms of family life that emerged from those conditions, forms politicized by struggles over resources and focused on materialist political engagement. McKinley, Barnes, and others relied on extended kinship structures, mutual aid, and community that formed outside of, and independent of, the normalizing bounds of the nuclear family, made possible by direct material aid from the state to the poor. Demolishing these spaces did not solidify "family life," broadly defined. Instead, demolition foreclosed on those spatial and social forms perceived as threatening to the particular development agenda that had taken hold during this period.

Residents' critiques and the politics they put into practice enable a firmer understanding of what was meant by policy makers when they called into question high-rise public housing's ability to sustain "family life." The use of "family life" by planners brings together material, political, and symbolic concerns within an imagined domestic context (Chakravartty and da Silva 2012). Feminist scholars of political economy have long argued that the "family" names a site of uncompensated labor, necessary for the reproduction of racial capital.[8] As Coontz puts it, "family" has come to refer to that interpersonal and social space "where private and public spheres" interact (1988, 1). At a structural level, family functions as a way of "coordinating personal reproduction with social reproduction" (1). Housing within this dynamic functions as the site that stages this uncompensated labor. Within this private space–private family nexus, the labor of social reproduction necessary to racial capital is expressed and exploited.

What resident mutual aid helps to make clear is that the hegemonic form that the "family" takes within contemporary racial capitalism is not a universal form. Nor does the "family" need to name only one kind of relation. "Family" is mobilized by power in order to reproduce social relations within a dominant order, but it can also be mobilized in an effort to "try to construct a new one" (Coontz 1988, 2). In fact, as Nancy Fraser suggests, because the "social practices oriented to reproduction (as opposed to production) tend to engender ideals of care, mutual responsibility and solidarity," they lend themselves to forms of liberatory sociality (2014, 66).

## Conclusion

The tragic conclusion to this story is that the housing authority chose not to follow the task force recommendations but, instead, to far exceed them. HABC tore down the Murphy Homes development in its entirety. All 758 units were demolished, and in its place a HOPE VI project was built that contains roughly 140 privately owned homes alongside seventy-five public housing units. This vast public holding was effectively privatized. Further, the HOPE VI project was only the beginning of public housing demolition and privatization in Baltimore. Congressional investigations into "severely distressed" high-rise buildings in the 1990s turned into the wholesale "repositioning" characterizing public housing policy today.[9] Through subsequent initiatives, such as the Rental Assistance Demonstration (RAD) program, untold numbers of once de-commodified homes have been, or are scheduled to be, privatized.

Decades of underresourcing low-income housing arrangements had conditioned among residents a range of responses. While the living room meetings and courtyard soccer games of Barnes and McKinley produced relations of mutual aid and a material politics that sought to mobilize public resources in order to make improvements on, and rehabilitate, failing housing, policy makers preferred to elevate those residents willing to perform distress and preside over spectacle demolition events. The housing authority's work to shift the set of concerns into the cultural terms of "family" and child safety reframed the organizing work of residents as the calls of "vulnerable" populations, issuing from the depths of concentrated poverty, in need of help. This reframing of housing activism as a "cry for help" obscured residents' material politics and has contributed to the overall view in Baltimore and similar cities that high-rise demolition was a natural and inevitable response to the developments' disrepair. What oral histories with building organizers reveal is that the fate of these buildings was not predetermined. That the residents had perspectives beyond alienation and despair. And that the work of demolition was political work.

**Robert Thomas Choflet** is a lecturer in the Department of African American Studies at the University of Maryland, College Park. He studies the radical intellectual and political traditions that emerge from spaces of racialized poverty. He can be reached at choflet@umd.edu.

## Notes

1. As Ruth Wilson Gilmore reminds us, the most salient aspects of disinvestment are not "absolute erasure." Rather, this process is generative. What gets produced by capital and the state as it disinvests from spaces of social reproduction has immense utility within the larger political economy

(devalued labor, devalued land, and housing insecurity, where residents are displaced from public housing arrangements). But this disinvestment also conditions resistance. As Gilmore notes, "ordinary people do not abandon themselves"; rather, they produce new forms of sociality and "renovate already existing activities" (2007, 179).

2. The "new front door" was a popular motif among planners. Urban Design Associates, the Pittsburgh-based firm who would act as master planners for multiple public housing privatization projects in Baltimore, including an eight-hundred-million-dollar East Baltimore redevelopment project centered on the neighborhoods surrounding Johns Hopkins Hospital, highlighted Heritage Crossing, the neighborhood that would eventually be built in the place where the Murphy Homes once stood. Their portfolio highlights the "single family detached houses" that replaced the buildings, initiating a "transformation [that] will create a new front door for West Baltimore neighborhoods" (Urban Design Associates 2010).

3. For a discussion of high-rise towers and the notion of "disrepute," see Williams 2005.

4. Quoted in Thompson 1990b. See also Thompson 1990a; Keyser 1990a, 1990b. Other representative articles similarly highlight resident sentiment that focused on child-rearing and child safety. One resident is quoted as saying, "My children aren't safe in a place they call home" (quoted in Fletcher 1993), while another says of the Murphy Homes, "This is no place to bring up children" (quoted in Valentine 1993). Media accounts of the time aided in shaping a narrative that public housing families were in peril.

5. On "exclusionary amenities," see Tobias Armborst, Daniel D'Oca, and Georgeen Theodore, "The Dream of a Lifestyle: Planned Communities and the Tools of Exclusion," International New Town Institute, newtown-institute.org/spip.php?article1055; as well as their larger treatment of the "arsenal of exclusion," in *The Arsenal of Exclusion and Inclusion* (New York: Actar, 2017). For a history of Roland Park, see Robert Fogelson, *Bourgeois Nightmares: Suburbia, 1870–1930* (New Haven, CT: Yale University Press, 2007), in particular, 59–115. See also Roberta Moudry, "Gardens, Houses, and People: The Planning of Roland Park, Baltimore" (master's thesis, Cornell University, 1990); and James Waesche, *Crowning the Gravely Hill: A History of the Roland Park–Guilford–Homeland District* (Baltimore, MD: Maclay, 1987). A recent reinterpretation of Roland Park that emphasizes the roots of residential segregation in larger histories of racism and empire is found in Paige Glotzer's *How the Suburbs Were Segregated: Developers and the Business of Exclusionary Housing, 1890–1960* (New York: Columbia University Press, 2020).

6. For an in-depth discussion of this dynamic, see Carby 1992.

7. On this score, see for example Kornbluh 2007; Farmer 2017; Orleck 2006; Piven and Cloward 1978; and Nadasen 2004.

8. Seminal works in this tradition include Vogel (1983) 2013; Federici 2004, (2012) 2020; Folbre 1982. A good introduction to these ideas can be found in McNally and Ferguson 2015, as well as in Fraser 2014. Much of this scholarship expands on questions offered in Engels 1902.

9. Citing capital needs of over twenty-six billion dollars, with that number growing by $3.5 billion each year since 2010, HUD has since asserted a need to change course on housing policy. It debuted its "reposition" language in a letter to local housing authorities in November of 2018, encouraging new "flexibilities" and offering a raft of "tools" to help facilitate the transformation. As the National Low Income Housing Coalition notes, "the term ['repositioning'] essentially means reducing the number of homes in the public housing stock" through the processes of demolition and privatization. While this language may have been new, it crystallized a longer process that began with federal investigations into underfunded public housing in 1989. The present article argues that this long process has been animated by a cultural politics shaped by planners, which has come to displace the materialist demands for investment and renovation that came from public housing residents. On the number of demolished units to date, see Center on Budget and Policy Priorities 2021; United States Department of Housing and Urban Development, Office of Indian and Public Housing, "Repositioning Public Housing," November 14, 2018, https://nlihc.org/sites/default/files/Repositioning_ Public_Housing-PIH.pdf; United States Department of Housing and Urban Development, "Repositioning: Handouts and Frequently Asked Questions," https://www.hud.gov/program_offices/public_indian_ housing/repositioning/faqs; and National Low Income Housing Coalition, "HUD Letter to PHAs Signals Intent to Dramatically Reduce Public Housing Stock," November 18, 2018, https://nlihc.org/resource/ hud-letter-phas-signals-intent-dramatically-reduce-public-housing-stock.

## Works Cited

Baltimore Empowerment Zone Strategic Plan. 1994. Box 73, folder 2. Empower Baltimore Management Corporation Records, R0141-EBMC. Baltimore Regional Studies Archives.

Capital News Service Staff. 2008. "Heritage Crossing Fails to Make Upton Bloom." *Capital News Service*, December 19, 2008. https://cnsmaryland. org/2008/12/19/heritage-crossing-fails-to-make-upton-bloom/.

Carby, Hazel. 1992. "Policing the Black Woman's Body in an Urban Context." *Critical Inquiry* 18, no. 4 (Summer 1992): 738–55.

Cassie, Ron. 2022. "Baltimoreans Didn't Want a New Baseball Park 30 Years Ago—Then We Saw Camden Yards." *Baltimore*, April 2022. https://www.baltimoremagazine.com/section/sports/camden-yards-turns-30-how-ballpark-almost-didnt-get-built/.

Center on Budget and Policy Priorities. 2021. "Public Housing Basics." Updated 2021. https://www.cbpp.org/research/public-housing.

Chakravartty, Paula, and Denise Ferreira da Silva. 2012. "Accumulation, Dispossession, and Debt: The Racial Logic of Global Capitalism—an Introduction." *American Quarterly* 64, no. 3: 361–85.

Cohen, Charles. 2019. "Destroying a Housing Project, to Save It." *New York Times*, August 15, 2019.

Coontz, Stephanie. 1988. *The Social Origins of Private Life: A History of American Families, 1600–1900*. New York: Verso.

Cooper, Melinda. 2017. *Family Values: Between Neoliberalism and the New Social Conservatism*. New York: Zone Books.

Engels, Friedrich. 1902. *The Origin of the Family, Private Property and the State*. Chicago, IL: Charles H. Kerr & Company.

Farmer, Ashley. 2017. *Remaking Black Power: How Black Women Transformed an Era*. Chapel Hill: University of North Carolina Press.

Federici, Silvia. 2004. *Caliban and the Witch: Women, the Body and Primitive Accumulation*. Brooklyn, NY: Autonomedia.

———. (2012) 2020. *Revolution at Point Zero: Housework, Reproduction, and Feminist Struggle*. London: Palgrave Macmillan.

Fletcher, Michael. 1993. "Work Crews Follow on the Heels of Mayor's Visit to Public Housing." *Baltimore Sun*, January 31, 1993.

Folbre, Nancy. 1982. "Exploitation Comes Home: A Critique of the Marxian Theory of Family Labour." *Cambridge Journal of Economics* 6, no. 4: 317–29.

Fraser, Nancy. 2014. "Behind Marx's Hidden Abode." *New Left Review*, no. 86: 55–72.

Gilmore, Ruth Wilson. 2007. *Golden Gulag: Prisons, Surplus, Crisis, and Opposition in Globalizing California*. Berkeley: University of California Press.

Kelley, Michael J. 1991. "Letter to Hon. Kurt L. Schmoke and Robert Hearn from Michael J. Kelley." March 12, 1991. Enoch Pratt Free Library, Vertical Files: Housing-Baltimore.

Keyser, Tom. 1990a. "Troubled Housing Projects." *Baltimore Sun*, November 24, 1990.

———. 1990b. "Families in City's High-Rises Cope with Violence, Drugs, Children at Risk." *Baltimore Sun*, November 27, 1990.

Kornbluh, Felicia. 2007. *The Battle for Welfare Rights: Politics and Poverty in Modern America*. Philadelphia: University of Pennsylvania Press.

Lipsitz, George. 2011. *How Racism Takes Place*. Philadelphia: Temple University Press.

Marcuse, Peter. 1995. "Interpreting 'Public Housing' History." *Journal of Architectural and Planning Research* 12, no. 3: 240–58.

McKittrick, Katherine. 2006. *Demonic Grounds: Black Women and the Cartographies of Struggle*. Minneapolis: University of Minnesota Press.

McKormac Barron and Associates. n.d. "Biographies." Accessed January 2014. http://www.mccormackbaron.com.

McNally, David, and Sue Ferguson. 2015. "Social Reproduction beyond Intersectionality: An Interview." *Viewpoint*, October 31, 2015. https://viewpointmag.com/2015/10/31/social-reproduction-beyond-intersectionality-an-interview-with-sue-ferguson-and-david-mcnally/.

Nadasen, Premilla. 2004. *Welfare Warriors: The Welfare Rights Movement in the United States*. New York: Routledge.

NCSDPH (National Commission on Severely Distressed Public Housing). 1992. "Working Papers on Identifying and Addressing Severely Distressed Public Housing." Washington, DC: Department of Housing and Urban Development. https://www.huduser.gov/portal/Publications/pdf/HUD-11659.pdf.

Ndubuizu, Rosemary. 2021. "Faux Heads of Households and Gendered and Racialized Politics of Housing Reform." *Feminist Formations* 33, no. 1: 142–64.

Norman, Jon R. 2012. "Housing for Families but Not for People: Federal Policy and Normative Family Ideals in Mid-century California." *Sociological Focus* 44, no. 3: 210–30.

Oakes, Amy, and Tom Pelton. 1999. "Blast to Wipe Out Episodes in Public Housing History; Implosion on July 3 to Level Murphy Homes." *Baltimore Sun*, June 23, 1999.

Ollove, Michael. 1989. "Balcony Inspected after Boy's Death." *Baltimore Sun*, June 9, 1989.

Orleck, Annelise. 2006. *Storming Caesars Palace: How Black Mothers Fought Their Own War on Poverty*. New York: Beacon Press.

Pekkanen, Sarah, and Zerline A. Hughes. 1999. "After 36 Years, A Pile of Memories; Murphy Homes High-Rises, Once Home to Hundreds Imploded in W. Baltimore." *Baltimore Sun*, July 4, 1999.

Piven, Frances Fox, and Richard Cloward. 1978. *Poor People's Movements: Why They Succeed, How They Fail*. New York: Vintage.

Sies, Mary Corbin. 1997. "Paradise Retained: An Analysis of Persistence in Planned, Exclusive Suburbs, 1880–1980." *Planning Perspectives* 12, no. 2: 165–91.

Thompson, Ginger. 1990a. "No Children in High-Rise, Study Urges Baltimore Task Would Move Families." *Baltimore Sun*, November 21, 1990.

———. 1990b. "Getting Rid of High-Rise Projects." *Baltimore Sun*, December 2, 1990.

United States Department of Housing and Urban Development, Office of Indian and Public Housing. 2018. "Repositioning Public Housing." November 14, 2018. https://nlihc.org/sites/default/files/Repositioning_Public_Housing-PIH.pdf.

United States Department of Housing and Urban Development. n.d. "Repositioning: Handouts and Frequently Asked Questions." https://www.hud.gov/program_offices/public_indian_housing/repositioning/faqs.

Urban Design Associates. 2010. "Mixed-Income Urban Neighborhoods." October 10, 2010. https://issuu.com/urbandesignassociates/docs/new_mixedincm.

Valentine, Paul. 1993. "Baltimore Mayor Tours the Terrain of a Complex Crisis." *Washington Post*, January 31, 1993, B01.

Vogel, Lise. (1983) 2013. *Marxism and the Oppression of Women*. Boston: Brill.

White, Tony. 1996. "Lexington Terrace Implosion Closes Chapter on Poorly Planned Complex." *Afro-American Red Star*, June 22, 1996.

Williams, Rhonda Y. 2005. *Politics of Public Housing: Black Women's Struggles against Urban Inequality*. New York: Oxford University Press.

# Uncertainty as Statecraft:
# Family Movements Contesting Disappearance

Amina Zarrugh

**Abstract:** State violence, particularly in the form of enforced disappearance, is designed to terrorize publics and quell organized forms of dissent. Most fundamentally, however, disappearance as a form of violence operates to disrupt family and kin-based bonds. In this article, I outline how family has emerged as a mobilizing framework to contest enforced disappearance, driven largely in response to how states produce a pervasive sense of uncertainty and liminality for women and their families living in the aftermath of a relative's disappearance. Drawing on an interdisciplinary literature that foregrounds Butler's (2006) notion of "grievability," I detail how the effects of disappearance lay the groundwork for social movements to mobilize under the rubric of family to dispute state-based assertions that the disappeared are "unmournable." Family-based social movements against disappearance highlight the contradictions between the valorized position of "family" in many state ideologies and the disruptions to families wrought by state violence. **Keywords:** disappearance; family; grief; social movements; uncertainty

Enforced disappearance is a mode of state violence practiced by democratic and autocratic states, with the United Nations Working Group on Enforced and Involuntary Disappearance recognizing thousands of people as disappeared by state or state-sanctioned actors in 109 countries around the world (United Nations 2022). The term "disappearance" refers to how individuals are taken to undisclosed locations and information concerning their whereabouts is denied to family and community members. As a technique of political and social terror, the practice of disappearance is designed to instill fear in the general population and terrorize the families of disappeared

*WSQ: Women's Studies Quarterly* 51: 1 & 2 (Spring/Summer 2023)

individuals, whom state and non-state actors seek to isolate and depoliti-cize. A somewhat overlooked, but deeply critical, feature of disappearance is its totalizing disruption of familial life, which particularly and dispropor-tionately affects those left behind to manage the emotional, familial, and institutional costs of disappearance.

The absence of a disappeared relative, such as a legal spouse or crucial financial support, exacts extended punishment upon family members in state-regulated kinship relationships. Among the hardships that families face in the aftermath of a disappearance are legal struggles vis-à-vis the state to access bank accounts and inheritance, legally remarry, and possess full guardianship of children. These disruptions are produced by the absence of formal confirmation from the state of a disappeared individual's death, exacerbating the costs that families endure in the protracted wake of a disappearance.

However, contrary to the intended function of disappearance to desta-bilize family and community, this form of violence and political repression has given rise to solidarities in the form of largely women-led social move-ments demanding information about the whereabouts of disappeared men and women. Families, in particular, are key actors in these social move-ments, and they are driven by a series of uncertainties about which they seek answers: Where are their disappeared relatives? Are they alive? Are they dead? Who is responsible for the disappearances? The uncertainties surrounding what happened to their disappeared relatives, combined with the contradictory information provided to them by the state, is the very impetus for these social movements.

Forced disappearance has been a distinct strategy of state violence in political systems characterized by authoritarian governance, though disap-pearances certainly extend to democracies as well (Wright 2018). Studies of disappearance have focused extensively on the use of forced disappearance in the Americas by military dictatorships in the 1970s and 1980s—which witnessed tens of thousands of Latin Americans disappeared across multi-ple countries in the region—as well as in the Middle East and North Africa (Weld 2013; Gatti 2014; Levey 2014; Rowayheb and Ouaiss 2015; Shaery-Yazdi 2020; Cronin-Furman and Krystalli 2021). Accordingly, it is from these geographic and political contexts that I draw conclusions about the forms and configurations that social movements have taken in response to forced disappearance.

In this article, I address how uncertainty fostered by forced disappearances comes to pervade political and social life, characterizing both the social movements that arise to contest disappearance and the operations of the state itself. In particular, I examine how situations of ambiguity created by disappearance can be important points of departure for collective action. The absent bodies characteristic of forced disappearance introduce to the lives of those left behind a protracted liminality. Namely, families contend with the uncertainties regarding the whereabouts of their loved one and, painfully, whether their disappeared relative is alive or dead. In addition, uncertainty surrounds the issue of who is culpable for the disappearance. While arms of the state are often key perpetrators—through direct action or inaction—the precise individuals responsible often remain unaccounted for, and in many contexts non-state actors enact violence with impunity. These uncertainties can remain unresolved for years and decades, compelling and sustaining social movements, particularly among family members of the disappeared.

These movements draw strategically, and in culturally specific and resonant ways, on the framework of family as a strategy for contesting the state. For example, the Committee of the Parents of the Missing and Disappeared in Lebanon strategically organized road blockades and sit-ins that featured women and children participants, against whom "the Lebanese authorities [were] less inclined to use violence" lest they undermine the Lebanese state's legitimacy in the public eye (Rowayheb and Ouaiss 2015, 1013). Under the rubric of family, activists also engage in framing and repertoires of contention that make use of distinct kinship relations to lay bare the contradiction between forced disappearance as a form of violence disruptive to families and the veneration of family extolled in many state ideologies. For example, groups emphasize different kinship relations ranging from parents (like the Association of Parents of Disappeared Persons in Kashmir), to mothers and grandmothers (like the Madres de Plaza de Mayo in Argentina), to relatives more generally (like the Group of Relatives of the Detained and Disappeared in Chile) in order to communicate how disappearance radically disrupts the ability to parent, mother, and maintain familial life.

Drawing on Judith Butler's (2006, 2016) notion of "grievability," I unpack how the liminality of uncertainty surrounding disappearance compels families to mobilize and introduce alternative strategies for claiming power that cannot exclusively be regarded as appealing to a "rights frame" or an "injustice frame" as might be observed in other kinds of social movements (Snow and Benford 2000). While the modes by which activists mobilize the category of family are often gendered and differ across cultural and political contexts, the prevalence of "family" as a framework of social movement mobilization suggests that it represents both a pragmatic mode of organizing in contexts of distrust and also a powerful symbolic resource for social movements contesting power.

### Uncertainty as Statecraft

Unlike mass arrests or executions, forced disappearance is a form of violence that is characterized by the abduction of individuals, often by state authorities or by non-state actors like organized crime syndicates and drug cartels with the state's implicit cooperation, from their homes or public places to undisclosed locations. As a common mode of state violence across the world, forced disappearance has been documented by the United Nations Working Group on Enforced and Involuntary Disappearance (UN WGEID) on all continents and has been a favored form of policing political dissidence in some eras and regions, particularly in Latin America during the 1970s and 1980s (United Nations 2006). Families of disappeared men and women are commonly denied information about the whereabouts of their relatives, whom the authorities do not acknowledge or maintain are not in their custody (Sutton 2018).

As a distinct form of state violence, the power of disappearance rests in its creation of ambiguity and uncertainty as well as its abilities of erasure. In the case of political dissidence, forced disappearance functions to not only police and punish dissidence but also to extinguish from the public arena the notion that any political opposition existed at all; if someone disappears, so too does the political philosophy or lifestyle that they embraced. For example, in the context of Mexico, Pilar Calveiro argues that disappearance has long functioned to disguise the contradictions that surface when political dissent emerges in response to populist and revolutionary discourse: if "populism presupposes the representation of the people [. . .] recognizing the existence of a powerful popular dissidence [. . .] would therefore dissolve this fiction" (2015, 83). Accordingly, she writes, "it is more effective for this type of governmentality to 'disappear' dissidence at all levels: to ignore it or deny it, rather than make it visible and repress it through legal channels, which would allow it to exist in public and deligitimise [sic] the government" (83). In such contexts, disappearance functions to foster uncertainty and erasure on both physical and symbolic levels.

Thus, uncertainty is a form of statecraft, a deliberate mode of governance that troubles conventional boundaries of life and death in order to advance the power of the state. As a form of statecraft, uncertainty functions to obscure the state's violence by rendering its culpability unclear. For the family members, this form of statecraft produces a series of uncertainties that unfold on multiple levels. First and foremost, disappearance introduces uncertainties regarding whether a disappeared person remains alive. Seldom are families provided with information about the whereabouts of their disappeared relative, and often many whose relatives have been murdered by the state never receive confirmation of the death, formally or informally.

It is for this reason that Gabriel Gatti (2014) argues that disappearance escapes easy categorization as life or death and as presence or absence. Disappearance complicates our notions of identity and how we use language to describe it; as Gatti writes, "How can a death without a body be managed?" (2014, 3). Likewise, in her exploration of the meaning of absence in social life, sociologist Avery Gordon (2008) considers disappearance as representing a type of liminality between life and death. Although death may eventuate from an individual's disappearance, as many cases across South America attest, Gordon argues that disappearance cannot be properly understood as a type of death; in contrast, disappearance is a distinct form of power and repression that "transgresses the distinction between the living and the dead" (127).

In this way, Gordon argues, the state that disappears is in the business of "producing ghosts" who engage in what she terms a "haunting" that "is specifically designed to break down the distinctions between visibility and invisibility, certainty and doubt, life and death that we normally use to sustain an ongoing and more or less dependable existence" (126). This breakdown also transforms the political meaning of subjects disappeared, which, Gordon states, "have lost all social and political identity, no bureaucratic records, no funerals, no memorials, no bodies, nobody" (80). The act of disappearance radically depoliticizes an individual, which is an important means of suppressing political opposition, and destabilizes the lives of those left behind.

A second level at which uncertainty pervades the lives of those left behind after a disappearance is through a protracted ambiguity, sometimes never resolved, surrounding the precise identity of those responsible for their loved one's disappearance. How can anyone be held accountable for a crime of disappearance if the perpetrator, or perpetrators, remain unknown? It is not uncommon in cases of disappearance for perpetrators to enact a disappearance in plain clothes, rendering themselves unidentifiable as belonging to a particular arm of the state such as police, military, or internal security authorities, among others (Stevens 2010). In addition, while many discussions of forced disappearance address it as a form of state violence, there are pervasive forms of disappearance unfolding outside of the direct purview of the state but flourishing because of the state's relative apathy or, in some cases, tacit complicity. For these reasons, and owing to the clandestine nature of disappearance, commissions like Brazil's Special Commission on Political Killings and Disappearances (CEMDP) acknowledge that there are "a wide range of cases where, despite the existence of uncontested political persecution, there was not sufficient evidence to characterize a death or disappearance as a state responsibility" (Bohoslavsky and Torelly 2014, 246).

The absence of state accountability has been the case particularly in Mexico, where women have been disappeared with relative impunity in a form of gender-based violence termed *feminicidio* (Orozco Mendoza 2019). According to some scholars, impunity of violence, such as disappearances, against women is among the paradigmatic features of feminicidio that distinguish it from other forms of gender-based violence (Lagarde 2007 as cited in Orozco Mendoza 2019). Beyond the case of feminicidio and impunity, however, there are cases in which the state's role in a disappearance is itself shrouded in uncertainty, as we observe in the infamous case of Ayotzinapa, the town where forty-three students went missing in the Mexican state of Guerrero in 2014. The perpetrators remain unclear, with conflicting accounts that implicate organized crime, officials and police officers from the nearby town of Iguala, and the Mexican Army (Wright 2018). While the families assign blame to the state of Mexico, which they argue is corrupt in its complicity with crime, the ambiguity surrounding who was directly responsible for the disappearance fuels uncertainty about whether all those who are culpable have been held accountable despite numerous arrests in the case. This distrust of the state, paired with the uncertainty surrounding whether their relatives remain alive or not, means that families are suspended in a protracted state of anguish and hope (Castillo 2014; Lopez 2022).

Another important, but often overlooked, aspect of disappearance is how the uncertainty produced by the state also, in turn, comes to define the state itself. Transnational feminist scholars remind us that "the state" is not a singular, monolithic entity but, rather, is composed of multiple agencies and bureaucracies that are often defined by "messiness rather than smooth functioning" (Kim-Puri 2005, 146). Modern governance itself actually derives considerable power from its inconsistencies and contradictions, which amplify its power by rendering it unpredictable (Blom Hansen and Stepputat 2001). The uncertainty that is deliberately weaponized as part of disappearance comes to define not only the state's operations but also the state itself, as multiple offices possess conflicting, inconsistent, unclear information. Thus, when a family seeks answers about the whereabouts of a disappeared relative, they may be referred to multiple offices intentionally, as some arms of the state seek to foment uncertainty, but also because sectors of the state lack coherence: one agency of the state is likely to be uncertain about affairs of another agency. Ironically, these levels of uncertainty—as endured by families of the disappeared and as circulated at the level of the state—foster the grievances that can give rise to the very forms of resistance that the state seeks to eradicate through disappearance.

## Grievability and the Politics of Mourning

An attendant function of disappearance and the uncertainty it creates is to stigmatize disappeared persons and those around them, including a disappeared person's family, extended kin, and neighborhood. The stigmatization of the disappeared takes many forms, including state framing of those disappeared as "terrorists" (Rojas-Perez 2017). Indeed, the label of "terrorist" has functioned in some settings, such as Israel, as a justification for denying to families the body of a loved one who has been taken or killed by the state (Wahbe 2020). In such cases, the state communicates that the disappeared are unworthy of mourning by denying to their families any evidence of their death. This ambiguity suspends for families the possibility that their relatives remain alive, delaying indefinitely the prospect of commemorating the disappeared or conferring upon them funeral rites of significant spiritual and emotional import.

These experiences of the disappeared connect to the notion of grievability, the question of whose lives are worthy of mourning (Zebadúa-Yáñez 2005; Butler 2006; Cole 2015; Boudreaux 2016). For Judith Butler (2016), ungrievable life is constituted by those lives that are considered worthy of destruction, which Rojas-Perez rearticulates as any lives "deemed killable" by the state (2017, 285). In such a context, an "ungrievable life" is a life "that cannot be mourned because it has never lived, that is, it has never counted as a life at all" (Butler 2015, para. 5). Butler's notions of "ungrievable life" emerge out of her study of the post-9/11 context and the "war on terror," and her intervention has been advanced and complemented by scholars who have tracked the political production of ungrievability with regard to Muslim life the world over, such as is the case with drone warfare in Pakistan and Afghanistan (Choudhury 2006; Cole 2015; Clark 2021). The notion of "ungrievable life" has also circulated beyond the context of the war on terror to describe the disposability of numerous groups, such as migrants (Mazzara 2020), and the multiple forms of violence directed toward queer bodies as part of the everyday workings of societies (Gould 2001; Puar 2007; Haritaworn et al. 2014).

In the context of the violent disappearances and murders of young women in Ciudad Juárez, Verónica Zebadúa-Yáñez (2005) brings together Butler's (2006) notions of grievability and Giorgio Agamben's (1998) notions of "homo sacer" (one who can be killed with impunity but not sacrificed) to argue that certain lives are deemed ungrievable precisely because they are regarded as unworthy of life. For Agamben, as Zebadúa-Yáñez states, "in modern politics the sovereign is instead he who decides the value or non-value of life as such, on what is to count as a life worthy of being lived" (2005, para. 14). Extending these theoretical insights to disappearance in general, the disappeared person could be said to represent an ungrievable, unworthy life precisely because they can be subjected to state violence with relative impunity. Insofar as grievability is also deeply intertwined with formal recognition of someone's death, which often remains uniquely elusive for the disappeared, those family and friends who do find their lives grievable are suspended from being able to commemorate them as valuable and worthy.

The framing of the disappeared as unworthy of collective grief is rendered explicit when families mobilize to commemorate the disappeared and are met with repression, arrests, and prohibitions on further gatherings (Castro 2002). An emblematic example of how the state regards disappeared persons as "ungrievable" is in the context of Libya, where some families began receiving death certificates for relatives disappeared decades earlier. The certificates were accompanied with a strict prohibition on holding a funeral (Zarrugh 2016).[1] Functionally, the strict policy sanctioning unauthorized funerals prevented an opportunity for large numbers of extended family and community members to gather, thus preemptively quelling a possible protest. Symbolically, however, the prohibition communicated that the disappeared's life was not grievable and mournable. A similar interruption of grief rituals, termed *ritualcide* (LeVine 2010), has been observed in the case of political opponents of Myanmar's military rule, where families have been explicitly denied their bodies and prevented from practicing funerary rights (Thein-Lemelson 2022).

Indeed, attempts to commemorate and reframe the lives of disappeared persons have become a key feature of social movements driven by the uncertainty and grief associated with disappearance. The mobilization of grief as an emotion by social movements around disappearance echoes the importance of grief in other social movement contexts (Jasper 1998, 2011; Gould 2001; Whittier 2001). Despite the importance of grief in social movements, Bayard de Volo maintains that grief has been neglected as an important emotion in social movement mobilization largely because "of the emotional division of labor: it is women (especially noncombatant women) who are the primary bearers of grief" (2006, 464). In addition, grief has long been regarded by some social movement scholars as a good mobilizer for brief—but not necessarily protracted, robust, or sustained—collective action (Tarrow 1998; Kim 2002). According to Tarrow, "death has always been connected to an institutionalized form of collective action—the funeral—that brings people together in ceremony and solidarity" (1998, 36). However, as he continues, "the same reasoning tells us why death is seldom the source of a sustained social movement. For death's moment is brief and the ritual occasion offered by a funeral is soon over" (Tarrow 1998, 36).

The case of disappearance presents a slightly different relationship to death. Given that the death remains a possibility but is uncertain and cannot be confirmed, the rituals associated with closure are elusive. In this sense, the uncertainty surrounding death actually becomes the very source for collective action, and so long as the circumstances of a death remain uncertain and ambiguous, sustained social movement engagement is likely. For instance, the Asociación Madres de Plaza de Mayo (Association of the Mothers of the Plaza de Mayo) in Argentina mobilized for answers about the fate of their disappeared children beginning in 1977 and remained formally active until 2006—for almost forty years—at which time a sector of the organization, the Founding Line, announced that it would continue to commemorate the disappearances in weekly and annual marches.

Thus, emotions generally associated with death, such as grief and sorrow, assume new meaning and have greater salience in cases like forced disappearance where the uncertainty of death and the absence of a body produce a lack of closure. This protracted closure is legible in the practice of continued memorialization years after a disappearance has occurred (Orozco 2019; Willems 2021). For example, in Mexico, families perform ceremonies that Ohlson calls "necrographies," which include the creation of engraved street epitaphs that feature biographies of the disappeared that "speak in the first person as if those who talk were still alive" (2019, 672). For the surviving family, this is a "life-long commitment of performing protests and special rites to guard the ambiguous status of their missing as separate from those who are undoubtedly dead. They sustain the possibility that they may be alive" (Ohlson 2019, 687). It is precisely the intertwined conditions of uncertainty and grief that contribute to the development of ongoing social movements around disappearance, which are driven largely by women and the family, the very institution most interrupted and compromised by disappearance.

### Mobilizing Uncertainty: Family-Based Social Movements

The uncertainty of disappearance, paired with the framing of disappeared persons as ungrievable, has fueled protests around the world, a large number of which have been orchestrated by women and the families of the disappeared. While a wide range of constituencies perceive disappearance as an injustice and a human rights violation, families come to the fore because it is the family that is a key site of destruction when disappearances are enacted by the state or other entities. The uncertainty around disappearances fuels an attendant set of uncertainties that plague the family in particular: Who will now be the economic provider for the family? Who will parent children? Who will care for aging parents?

Given what is widely documented as a disproportionate share of men who are disappeared, the uncertainties produced by this form of violence also impart very gendered consequences for women within families (Dewhirst and Kapur 2015). These consequences are particularly acute insofar as states institutionalize rights and responsibilities in gendered ways, including at the level of the economy and family law (MacKinnon 1989). For example, Dewhirst and Kapur (2015) point out that, following the disappearances of their husbands, many women are compelled into wage-earning labor that is particularly low-paid and high-risk, such as sex work. Exploitative work environments then introduce a series of hazards, such as abuse, that can threaten the lives of the women left behind and also introduce social stigmas, which might further isolate women from extended kin (Ghazi 2021).

On a social level, because states generally deny families information about whether their disappeared loved one remains alive or is dead, families occupy a series of "half" statuses, as occurs with disappearances in Kashmir (Zia 2019). Women whose husbands are disappeared occupy a liminal status as formally married but informally widowed. Zia refers to such women as "half widows" and their children as "half orphans." The refusal of the state to afford families certainty of a loved one's death also introduces complications to pragmatic life-and-death matters such as the ability to inherit or access bank account information, which further situates many families in precarious economic circumstances in the months and years following the disappearance of a relative.

For all of these reasons, disappearance represents a profoundly disruptive force to familial life, not only in the aftermath of a disappearance but for years and decades following the act of violence. It halts the ability of the family to be reorganized or reconstituted, permanently disrupting familial and kin-based relations. Accordingly, it is women and their families as a constituency who organize collectively in protest of forced disappearance. The language of family affords social movements a strategic framing advantage (Zarrugh 2022), especially insofar as states around the world enshrine family, and its protection, as a dignified status in state constitutions (Charrad 2001). For example, Rita Noonan writes that a "maternal frame" was employed by women mobilizing in Chile "when a change in state form threatened the integrity and safety of their families" (1995, 94); with regard to disappearance, she contends that mothers, sisters, and daughters strategically and ironically drew upon a notion of traditional norms of womanhood that were promoted by Pinochet's government to "subvert the state" (82). By drawing upon family, particularly motherhood, as a framework for mobilization, social movements highlight the contradictions between the state's symbolic exaltation of family and its orchestration of violence that disrupts families (Goker 2016).

As Noonan (1995) also acknowledges, however, the pressure that movements may face to accept normative conceptions of family can also circumscribe the particular gains that groups like women can secure from the state. By extension, embracing normative models of family, including the prescription of traditional gender norms and heterosexuality, may limit the possibilities of organizing among those who cannot mobilize under these constructions of family and gender. Snow and Benford acknowledge framing constraints such as these when they state that frames may "vary in terms of how inclusive and flexible they are, and thus in their interpretive scope, and that this variability can affect the mobilization of some aggrieved groups in comparison to others" (2000, 619).

In addition to employing framing that draws upon family to highlight contradictions of the state, social movements around disappearance also mobilize grief and mourning during protest. Protestors make grief legible through what Tilly (2006) refers to as "repertoires of contention," which include protestors adopting garments associated with mourning and mobilizing mock empty coffins to communicate the ambiguity surrounding whether a loved one remains alive. As it is often families that gather for funerals, the mobilization of family also connects intimately to the notion of collective mourning, a defiant act in light of the framing of the disappeared as "ungrievable."

In numerous cultures, it is the rituals of women that make grief most legible in public space (Rojas-Perez 2017). Humphrey and Valverde refer to these gestures as forms of "political mourning" that "make grief public in order to demand accountability from the state" (2007, 181). Athanasiou (2005) discusses the role of mourning in the context of the transnational organization Women in Black, which she refers to as an "activism of mourning." The protests, led and orchestrated by women, contest the human rights abuses and deaths of civilians in wars and conflicts, an activism that Athanasiou argues are "public and collective formations by which trauma is addressed in all its affective, social, and political or biopolitical implications, intimacies, and limits" (2005, 42).

In the case of disappearance, women, particularly mothers, in multiple contexts publicly mourn, sometimes donning black garments to connote funeral rituals, and mobilize photographs of their disappeared relatives to assert the grievability of the disappeared (Navarro 1989; Schirmer 1989; Taylor 2001; Castro 2002; Burchianti 2004; Abou Assi 2010; Goker 2016; Zarrugh 2016; Zia 2019). In Latin America, multiple family-based groups have exalted photographs of the disappeared or mobilized religious iconography, including affixing carpenter's nails to their bodies to emulate Christ's suffering, to confer an honored status to their disappeared relatives (Schirmer 1989; Taylor 2001; Adams 2002). In Argentina, women also walked in pairs to evade state prohibitions on group demonstrations and wore white scarves, sometimes embroidered with the name of their disappeared relative, around the Plaza de Mayo in the capital city of Buenos Aires. In the case of Sri Lanka, Malathi de Alwis (2009) offers examples of women mobilizing the garments of the disappeared during protest to simultaneously assert the ongoing absence of their disappeared relative and the state-orchestrated interruption of their abilities to parent in light of the disappearance of a child. Thus, family mobilizations effectively communicate how disappearance not only creates uncertainties but also fundamentally disrupts the right to family and its protection. It is in this way that families, as those directly experiencing the absence in the most intimate of ways, come to the fore to contest forced disappearance.

## Conclusion

Movements around forced disappearance highlight the ways by which uncertainty drives social movements contesting state violence. For families, the forms of uncertainty produced by disappearance are multiple, including uncertainty surrounding whether disappeared relatives are dead or alive, the whereabouts of their bodies, and who precisely is culpable for the disappearances. In addition, the weaponization of uncertainty by the state comes to characterize the operations of the state itself as the actions of multiple bureaucracies and agencies become uncertain and illegible to one another, only further depriving families from being able to manage their lives in the wake of a disappearance. Paired with a state framing of the disappeared as "ungrievable" and unworthy of social mourning, forced disappearance represents a state-orchestrated or state-sanctioned attempt to upend familial and kin-based bonds, which extend to community bonds in contexts where family and local community are deeply intertwined.

The wide-ranging number of social movements that have emerged in response to forced disappearance, however, suggests that families experience uncertainty and ungrievability in a way that also facilitates powerful, sustained social movements that challenge the state-orchestrated (or state-sanctioned) destruction of the family. Given the well-documented disproportionate effects of disappearance on families, particularly women left behind following the disappearance of a spouse, it is women who often come to the fore to strategically mobilize their kin-based relations. By asserting that the lives of the disappeared are indeed "grievable," they simultaneously resist the destruction of the family while also making demands that lay the groundwork for reconstituting the family again.

Moving forward, this article invites scholars to examine social movements with attention toward the roles that uncertainty might play within a movement and how forms of state violence or injustice impact kin-based relations. By acknowledging these dimensions of state violence, scholars are poised to illuminate heretofore overlooked dimensions of the myriad roles of constituencies like women and their families in a range of cases where state violence interrupts and disrupts family life, as we observe in cases like police brutality, incarceration, and immigrant detention, among others.

**Amina Zarrugh** is an associate professor of sociology at Texas Christian University. Her research focuses on politics and forced disappearance in North Africa as well as race and ethnicity in the United States. Her work has appeared in journals such as *Ethnic and Racial Studies*, *Critical Sociology*, *Middle East Critique*, *Teaching Sociology*, and *Contexts*, among others. She can be reached at amina.zarrugh@tcu.edu.

## Notes

1. The prohibition on funerals is a compelling example of how states frame particular lives as ungrievable, because funerals and public pronouncements of a death are important commemorative gestures that indicate a life is worth mourning. As Judith Butler states of an obituary, "It functions as the instrument by which grievability is publicly distributed. It is the means by which a life becomes, or fails to become, a publicly grievable life" (2006, 34).

## Works Cited

Abou Assi, E. 2010. "Collective Memory and Management of the Past: The Entrepreneurs of Civil War Memory in Post-War Lebanon." *International Social Science Journal* 61, no. 202: 399–409.

Adams, Jacqueline. 2002. "Art in Social Movements: Shantytown Women's Protest in Pinochet's Chile." *Sociological Forum* 17, no. 1: 21–56.

Agamben, Giorgio. 1998. *Homo Sacer: Sovereign Power and Bare Life*. Stanford, CA: Stanford University Press.

Athanasiou, Athena. 2005. "Reflections on the Politics of Mourning: Feminist Ethics and Politics in the Age of Empire." *Historein*, no. 5: 40–57.

Bayard de Volo, Lorraine. 2006. "The Dynamics of Emotion and Activism: Grief, Gender, and Collective Identity in Revolutionary Nicaragua." *Mobilization* 11, no. 4: 461–74.

Blom Hansen, Thomas, and Finn Stepputat. 2001. *Sovereign Bodies: Citizens, Migrants, and States in the Postcolonial World*. New Brunswick, NJ: Princeton University Press.

Bohoslavsky, Juan Pablo, and Marcelo D. Torelly. 2014. "Financial Complicity: The Brazilian Dictatorship under the 'Macroscope.'" In *Justice and Economic Violence in Transition*, edited by D. N. Sharp, 233–62. New York: Springer.

Boudreaux, Corrie. 2016. "Public Memorialization and the Grievability of Victims in Ciudad Juárez." *Social Research* 83, no. 2: 391–417.

Burchianti, Margaret E. 2004. "Building Bridges of Memory: The Mothers of the Plaza de Mayo and the Cultural Politics of Maternal Memories." *History and Anthropology* 15, no. 2: 133–50.

Butler, Judith. 2006. *Precarious Life: The Powers of Mourning and Violence*. New York: Verso.

———. 2015. "Precariousness and Grievability—When Is Life Grievable?" Verso (blog). November 16. https://www.versobooks.com/blogs/2339-judith-butler-precariousness-and-grievability-when-is-life-grievable.

———. 2016. *Frames of War: When Is Life Grievable?* New York: Verso.

Calveiro, Pilar. 2015. "Disappearance and Governmentality in Mexico." In *Disappearances in Mexico: From the 'Dirty War' to the 'War on Drugs,'* edited by Silvana Mandolessi and Katia Olalde, 75–96. New York: Routledge.

Castillo, Mariano. 2014. "Remains Could Be Those of 43 Missing Mexican Students." *CNN*, November 11, 2014. https://www.cnn.com/2014/11/07/world/americas/mexico-missing-students/.

Castro, Antonio García. 2002. "The Third Party: Power, Disappearances, Performances." *Diogenes* 49, no. 1: 66–76.

Charrad, Mounira M. 2001. *States and Women's Rights: The Making of Postcolonial Tunisia, Algeria, and Morocco*. Berkeley: University of California Press.

Choudhury, Cyra A. 2006. "Comprehending 'Our' Violence: Reflections on the Liberal Universalist Tradition, National Identity and the War on Iraq." *Muslim World Journal of Human Rights* 3, no. 1: 1–20.

Clark, Lindsay. 2021. *Gender and Drone Warfare: A Hauntological Perspective*. New York: Routledge.

Cole, Teju. 2015. "Unmournable Bodies." *New Yorker*, January 9, 2015. https://www.newyorker.com/culture/cultural-comment/unmournable-bodies.

Cronin-Furman, Kate, and Roxani Krystalli. 2021. "The Things They Carry: Victims' Documentation of Forced Disappearance in Colombia and Sri Lanka." *European Journal of International Relations* 27, no. 1: 79–101.

de Alwis, Malathi. 2009. "'Disappearance' and 'Displacement' in Sri Lanka." *Journal of Refugee Studies* 22, no. 3: 378–91.

Dewhirst, Polly, and Amrita Kapur. 2015. *The Disappeared and the Invisible: Revealing the Enduring Impact of Enforced Disappearances on Women*. New

York: International Center for Transitional Justice. https://www.ictj.org/sites/default/files/ICTJ-Global-Gender-Disappearances-2015.pdf.

Gatti, Gabriel. 2014. *Surviving Forced Disappearance in Argentina and Uruguay: Identity and Meaning.* New York: Palgrave MacMillan.

Ghazi, Noura. 2021. "Wives of the Detainees and Disappeared: Women under Suspended Sentences." The Tahir Institute for Middle East Policy. https://timep.org/commentary/analysis/wives-of-the-detainees-and-disappeared-women-under-suspended-sentences/.

Goker, Zeynep Gulru. 2016. "The Mourning Mother: Rhetorical Figure or a Political Actor?" In *The Making of Neoliberal Turkey,* edited by C. Ozbay, M. Erol, A. Terzioglu, and Z. Umut Turem, 141–58. New York: Routledge.

Gordon, Avery F. 2008. *Ghostly Matters: Haunting and the Sociological Imagination.* Minneapolis: University of Minnesota Press.

Gould, Deborah. 2001. "Rock the Boat, Don't Rock the Boat, Baby: Ambivalence and the Emergence of Militant AIDS Activism." In *Passionate Politics: Emotions and Social Movements,* edited by J. Goodwin, J. M. Jasper, and F. Polletta, 135–57. Chicago: University of Chicago Press.

Haritaworn, Jim, Adi Kuntsman, and Silva Posocco. 2014. *Queer Necropolitics.* New York: Routledge.

Humphrey, Michael, and Estela Valverde. 2007. "Human Rights, Victimhood, and Impunity: An Anthropology of Democracy in Argentina." *Social Analysis: The International Journal of Anthropology* 41, no. 1: 179–97.

Jasper, James M. 1998. "The Emotions of Protest: Affective and Reactive Emotions in and around Social Movements." *Sociological Forum* 13, no. 3: 397–424.

———. 2011. "Emotions and Social Movements: Twenty Years of Theory and Research." *Annual Review of Sociology* 37, no. 1: 285–303.

Kim, Hyoyoung. 2002. "Shame, Anger, and Love in Collective Action: Emotional Consequence of Suicide Protest in South Korea, 1991." *Mobilization* 7, no. 2: 159–76.

Kim-Puri, H. J. 2005. "Conceptualizing Gender-Sexuality-State-Nation: An Introduction." *Gender & Society* 19, no. 2: 137–59.

Lagarde, Marcela. 2007. "Por los Derechos Humanos de las Mujeres: La Ley General de Acceso de las Mujeres a un Vida Libre de Violencia." *Revista Mexicana de Ciencias Politicas y Sociales,* no. 49: 143–65.

Levey, Cara. 2014. "Of HIJOS and Niños: Revisiting Postmemory in Post-Dictatorship Uruguay." *History & Memory* 26, no. 2: 5–39.

LeVine, Peg. 2010. *Love and Dread in Cambodia: Weddings, Births and Ritual Harm under the Khmer Rouge.* Singapore: National University of Singapore Press.

Lopez, Oscar. 2022. "Mexico Arrests Top Prosecutor in Case of Missing Students and Issues 80 Warrants." *New York Times*, August 20, 2022. https://www.nytimes.com/2022/08/20/world/americas/mexico-arrests-jesus-murillo-karam.html.

MacKinnon, Catherine A. 1989. *Toward a Feminist Theory of the State.* Cambridge, MA: Harvard University Press.

Mazzara, Federica. 2020. "Subverting the 'Ungrievability' of Migrant Lives." *PARSE*, no. 10: 1–18.

Navarro, Marysa. 1989. "The Personal Is Political: Las Madres de Plaza de Mayo." In *Power and Popular Protest: Latin American Social Movements*, edited by S. Eckstein, 241–58. Berkeley: University of California Press.

Noonan, Rita K. 1995. "Women against the State: Political Opportunities and Collective Action Frames in Chile's Transition to Democracy." *Sociological Forum* 10, no. 1: 81–111.

Orozco, Elva F. 2019. "Mapping the Trail of Violence: The Memorialization of Public Space as a Counter-Geography of Violence in Ciudad Juárez." *Journal of Latin American Geography* 18, no. 3: 132–57.

Orozco Mendoza, Elva F. 2019. "*Las Madres De Chihuahua*: Maternal Activism, Public Disclosure, and the Politics of Visibility." *New Political Science* 41, no. 2: 211–33.

Puar, Jasbir. 2007. *Terrorist Assemblages: Homonationalism in Queer Times.* Durham, NC: Duke University Press.

Rojas-Perez, Isaias. 2017. *Mourning Remains: State Atrocity, Exhumations, and Governing the Disappeared in Peru's Postwar Andes.* Stanford, CA: Stanford University Press.

Rowayheb, Marwan G., and Makram Ouaiss. 2015. "The Committee of the Parents of the Missing and Disappeared: 30 Years of Struggle and Protest." *Middle Eastern Studies* 51, no. 6: 1010–26.

Schirmer, Jennifer. 1989. "'Those Who Die for Life Cannot Be Called Dead': Women and Human Rights Protest in Latin America." *Feminist Review*, no. 32: 3–29.

Shaery-Yazdi, Roschanack. 2020. "Search and Sovereignty: The Relatives of the Lebanese Disappeared in Syria." *British Journal of Middle Eastern Studies* 48, no. 5: 1016–32.

Snow, David A., and Robert D. Benford. 2000. "Framing Processes and Social Movements: An Overview and Assessment." *Annual Review of Sociology*, no. 26: 611–39.

Stevens, Philip. 2010. "The International Convention for the Protection of All Persons from Enforced Disappearance—A Welcoming Response to a Worldwide Phenomenon with Limited Relief." *THRHR*, no. 73: 368.

Sutton, Barbara. 2018. *Surviving State Terror: Women's Testimonies of Repression and Resistance in Argentina.* New York: New York University Press.

Tarrow, Sidney. 1998. *Power in Movement: Social Movements and Contentious Politics.* Cambridge, UK: Cambridge University Press.

Taylor, Diana. 2001. "Making a Spectacle: The Mothers of the Plaza de Mayo." *Journal of the Association for Research on Mothering,* no. 3: 97–109.

Thein-Lemelson, Seinenu M. 2022. "Killing the Funeral in Myanmar." *Anthropology News,* September 2, 2022. https://www.anthropology-news.org/articles/killing-the-funeral-in-myanmar/.

Tilly, Charles. 2006. *Regimes and Repertoires of Contention.* Chicago: University of Chicago Press.

United Nations. 2006. "International Convention for the Protection of All Persons from Enforced Disappearance." December 20, 2006. Accessed May 24, 2015. http://www.ohchr.org/Documents/ProfessionalInterest/disappearance-convention.pdf.

———. 2022. "About Enforced Disappearance." Accessed March 15, 2022. http://www.ohchr.org/en/special-procedures/wg-disappearances/about-enforced-disappearance.

Wahbe, Randa May. 2020. "The Politics of *Karameh*: Palestinian Burial Rites under the Gun." *Critique of Anthropology* 40, no. 2: 323–40.

Weld, Kirsten. 2013. "Because They Were Taken Alive." *ReVista* 13, no. 1: 8–11.

Whittier, Nancy E. 2001. "Emotional Strategies: The Collective Reconstruction and Display of Oppositional Emotions in the Movement against Child Sexual Abuse." In *Passionate Politics: Emotions and Social Movements,* edited by J. Goodwin, J. M. Jasper, and F. Polletta, 233–50. Chicago: University of Chicago Press.

Willems, Eva. 2021. "Absent Bodies, Present Pasts: Forced Disappearance as Historical Injustice in the Peruvian Highlands." In *Post-Conflict Memorialization: Missing Memories, Absent Bodies,* edited by Olivette Otele, Luisa Gandolfo, and Yoav Galai, 171–93. Cham, Switzerland: Palgrave Macmillan.

Wright, Melissa W. 2018. "Against the Evils of Democracy: Fighting Forced Disappearance and Neoliberal Terror in Mexico." *Annals of the American Association of Geographers* 108, no. 2: 327–36.

Zarrugh, Amina. 2016. "'Only God Knows': The Emergence of a Family Movement against State Violence in Libya." PhD diss., University of Texas at Austin.

———. 2022. "Toward a Sociology of Family Movements: Lessons from the Global South." *Sociology Compass* 16, no. 5: e12976.

Zebadúa-Yáñez, Verónica. 2005. "Killing as Performance: Violence and the Shaping of Community." *E-misférica* 2, no. 2. https://hemisphericinstitute. org/en/emisferica-2-2/2-2-essays/killing-as-performance-violence-and-the-shaping-of-community.html.

Zia, Ather. 2019. *Resisting Disappearance: Military Occupation and Women's Activism in Kashmir.* Seattle: University of Washington Press.

# After *Roe*: Race, Reproduction, and Life at the Limit of Law

Sara Clarke Kaplan

**Abstract:** This article examines media portrayals of reproductive health care from the summer of 2022 as an entry point to reconsider liberal reproductive politics after the *Dobbs* decision. It argues that these commonsense narratives of medical and legal crisis reflect and reproduce long-standing liberal approaches to reproductive rights, mystifying contemporary reproductive coercion's origins in the management and exploitation of raced reproductivity. Greater attention to the historical racialized structures of reproductive unfreedom, I argue, would enable deeper understandings of the expansion of state control over physical and social reproduction. **Keywords:** Black reproductivity; abortion; liberal politics; reproductive justice; reproductive health

On June 24, 2022, after months of rumors and leaked information, the U.S. Supreme Court issued its long-awaited official decision in the abortion-rights case of *Dobbs v. Jackson Women's Health Organization*. In a reversal of the 1973 landmark decision in *Roe v. Wade*, a court majority declared that the right to an abortion is not constitutionally protected, thus returning to individual states the power to regulate all aspects of abortion not governed by federal law. In the wake of *Dobbs*, the national legal landscape for abortion underwent a rapid transformation: by the end of that summer, twelve states had begun enforcing preexisting "trigger laws"—abortion bans or restrictions already passed by state governments but held in abeyance by *Roe*. Two states had approved new abortion regulations, and nearly a dozen others' existing or new abortion bans had returned to local courts for judicial review under the new legal precedent (*New York Times* 2022).

*WSQ: Women's Studies Quarterly* 51: 1 & 2 (Spring/Summer 2023)

Within days, the first reports of reproductive policy run amok in *Dobbs*'s wake began to appear in major news venues. In midwestern states from Missouri to Wisconsin, patients with ruptured fallopian tubes, uterine infections, or life-threatening placental hemorrhages were experiencing unheard-of delays in treatment while hospital administrators parsed unclear legal codes to determine questions of criminal and civil liability. People with lupus, rheumatoid arthritis, or multiple sclerosis reported that national pharmacy chains CVS and Walgreens were denying them refills for necessary chemotherapeutics because the same medications are used to eradicate potentially fatal ectopic or molar pregnancies. Across Texas, expectant parents mourned nonviable pregnancies while simultaneously navigating the obstacles that the state's so-called heartbeat law placed in the way of medical terminations after six weeks of gestation. And in Ohio, a pregnant ten-year-old survivor of sexualized and gendered violence was required to travel to Indiana to escape her home state's abortion ban with no exceptions for rape or incest (Ducharme and Law 2022; Feibel 2022; Goldhill 2022; Stern 2022).

The reports trickled in at first, soon to be followed by a flood of similar stories. Shared anecdotally on social media, invoked by protesters at summer rallies and marches on the Supreme Court, and referenced in the speeches of Democratic politicians—most famously by President Joseph Biden as evidence of the need for an executive order to protect abortion access—they quickly coalesced into a nationwide, collective narrative of state-organized medical abandonment and legal chaos that became iconic of the seismic shift in reproductive politics initiated by *Dobbs*.

The rapidity with and extent to which these cases of extreme medical and legal crisis seized the popular political imagination was, in no small part, due to their resonance with a broader perception of the current political moment as a crisis of liberal governance. Elected officials from the president to city council members decried *Dobbs* as "a tragic step backwards for equal rights" that foreshadowed a national reversion to pre-*Roe* "back alleys," even as Planned Parenthood, the ACLU, and even the Young Democrats of America warned it was the first step in a forward march toward a post-*Dobbs* dystopian future in which "reproductive rights are under attack like never before" (ACLU New Mexico 2022; Action Network 2022; Sweet 2022). Within this narrative, the *Dobbs* decision was depicted as a wormhole in the linear progression of liberal governance through which the nation would be simultaneously dragged back to an earlier, less enlightened era and propelled into a draconian dystopian future.

By the time of the court's official release of the *Dobbs* decision, it had become a truism that the case's likely outcome—state prohibitions on abortion in approximately half of the country—would have a disproportionate effect on women and other pregnant people of color, on the poor, and on gender-non-conforming people. Activists, reporters, and armchair pundits alike cited the well-known statistics: nearly 40 percent of people receiving abortion care in the United States are Black, over 65 percent are non-white or Indigenous, and nearly half live below the poverty line—a category in which women-identified people of color and Indigenous people have among the highest rates of representation (Jagannathan 2019; Kaiser Family Foundation 2020). Others noted that lack of access to abortions would exacerbate the already extreme national crisis of Black maternal mortality.[1] Not only are Black people 3.5 times more likely to die of pregnancy- or childbirth-related causes, but the vast majority of these are preventable deaths from conditions that could be treated with access to adequate and attentive reproductive health care (Goodwin 2022; MacDorman et al. 2021).

Despite these frequent explications of the disproportionately severe impact that abortion's criminalization would have on the lives and economic well-being of poor women and other childbearing people of color in the months leading up to the final decision, post-decision reporting on *Dobbs*'s cataclysmic impact on reproductive health care remained conspicuously silent on such questions. Indeed, the iterative depictions of escalating medical and legal crises were largely evacuated of any analysis of racialized power and difference at all. Marked only by medical condition, reproductive status, and state of residence, the protagonists in these cautionary tales of *Dobbs*-ian catastrophe were represented as iconic reproductive subjects, unfettered by the material specificities of race or class, citizenship, or language. Their deracination enabled them to serve as empathetic representatives of universal womanhood in crisis, a category that feminists of color have long argued is implicitly synonymous with whiteness. At the same time, the oft-repeated assertion that these incidents of legal overstep and medical impotence constituted a level of reproductive coercion "like never before" served to efface the long and well-documented history of forced reproduction, coerced sterilization, and medical and state surveillance and criminalization that have shaped the reproductive experiences of Black, Indigenous, and other reproducing people of color for centuries.

The framing of post-*Roe* reproductive politics as a moment of liberal governance in crisis and the foreclosure of race as a structuring element of reproductive politics are not coincidental. Rather, their conjuncture is symptomatic of the ways in which, embedded as it is in liberal ideologies and lexicons, dominant abortion rights discourse both leverages and effaces the co-constitution of race and reproduction in the United States, enabling an ongoing disavowal of what Dorothy Roberts has described as the dependence of white, middle-class women's reproductive liberty on the wide-scale reproductive control of Black people and other people of color (Roberts 1997). What follows, then, uses this moment of extremity as an entry point to reconsider the broader discursive field of post-*Roe* reproductive politics. I start by considering how the adopted discourse around the medical and legal crisis precipitated by *Dobbs* reflects and reproduces long-standing liberal approaches to reproductive rights in general, and abortion access in particular. By invoking racialized difference while simultaneously disavowing the constitutive role of race in U.S. reproductive politics, I argue, dominant liberal discourses on reproductive rights mystify contemporary reproductive coercion's origins in the management and exploitation of raced reproductivity as a necessary condition for the creation, growth, and maintenance of the U.S. racial capitalist state.[2] I end by considering how situating the current moment more broadly and deeply within the racialized structures of reproductive unfreedom, past and present, that constitute what I call Black reproductivity might generate new ways of understanding the current expansion of state control over physical and social reproduction, and how we might respond to it.

### The Embodied Crisis of Liberal Governance

In the popular narrative of post-*Dobbs* crisis, the medical and legal emergencies of individual reproductive bodies indexed a broader crisis of the U.S. body politic itself, in which juridical law had overrun all rational limits and had been reduced to an exercise of domination enacted through the spectacular display of arbitrary authority over individual reproductive bodies. In turn, the ensuing legal and medical chaos was decried as signaling a systemic breakdown of liberalism's key tenets, in which scientific knowledge, reason, and the ethical imperative of individual rights were laid to waste by vague laws crafted with less attention to jurisprudence than to Christian beliefs around procreation and conception. Even as they issued an apocalyptic warning of liberal governance in crisis, these accounts of national legal and medical state of emergency implicitly retrenched the very tenets of liberal political ideology ostensibly under siege: the "truth" of medical science, the inextricability of rights and reason, and the positing of an alternative, secular morality in the place of Christian theology.

Tales of medical and ethical crises precipitated by *Dobbs* have served as cautionary tales of the unplanned consequences when politically interested laws meet their limit in the embodied realities of medical science: the chronically ill body or the errantly implanted embryo, the physical capacities of a barely pubescent child, or the unpredictability of human genetics. Anecdote after anecdote laid out how, in the imminent head-on collision between errant and authoritarian laws and the material complexities of biomedical science, reproductive rights were quickly approaching a critical crisis. This depiction of *Dobbs* as precipitating a crisis of liberal ideals in which arbitrary laws threaten to undermine scientific truths illustrates what L. H. Stallings has described as the primacy given in mainstream reproductive politics to scientific discourse as the appropriate site for the production of knowledge and negotiation of power (2019, 106). Since the original *Roe* decision, liberal efforts to defend the legal right to abortion against a widespread grassroots and legislative anti-abortion campaign have relied on scientific discourse to create cultural and political meaning around abortion. For half a century, defenders of abortion access have relied on notions of scientific truth to underscore the fallaciousness of the anti-abortion movement's claims regarding fetal life, inextricably linking scientific knowledge production, rational choice, and individual rights as the ideological and epistemological undergirding of liberal reproductive politics. Medical science's claim to empirical truth has become a vital tool for defining and delimiting the meaning of life and death, rights and personhood within liberal political discourse around abortion access. Not only have reproductive rights organizers relied on medical science to challenge anti-abortion advocates' mystification of the biological processes of human reproduction through the religious rhetoric of "unborn lives" and the characterization of abortion as murder, but they have employed the logics and lexicons of medical science to construct alternative algorithms for calculating the meaning and value of life and the attendant apportionment of rights. From complex assessments and explanations of fetal viability as a measure of personhood to clear and consistent emphases on abortion as health care, the scientific parsing of the biological limit of life has been an integral part of the mainstream abortion rights movement's arguments regarding relative rights of the pregnant person versus the fetus.

Amid the medical and legal crises precipitated by *Dobbs*, the relative calculation of life was rearticulated once again: each well-publicized medical emergency demonstrated how, rather than saving or protecting fetal lives, the new prohibitions on medical treatment devalued and endangered existing lives through their draconian implementation and potentially deathly effects.

These narratives of physical lives and individual rights endangered by religious irrationality and legal overreach rearticulated the relationship between scientific empiricism, personal rights, and the primacy of reason, offering an alternative, explicitly secular model of liberal morality. In a counterdiscourse to the religious right's anti-abortion polemics of innocence and guilt, sacrifice and sin, Biden and his compatriots held up the "sacred" individual rights that are "foundational" to U.S. liberal democracy, and castigated anti-abortion legislators and judges for an "extremism" that is "antithetical to everything we believe as Americans." Juxtaposed with the dogmatic and uncaring politicians who had unleashed a "flood of cruelty" were those innocent victims caught in the deluge: bleeding and feverish patients at risk, traumatized and violated children, grieving would-be parents dreading the delivery of a stillborn child (Stern 2022).

Yet in the secular moral code of mainstream reproductive politics, it was not only right-wing political leadership that was condemned. With their emphasis on medical emergencies, nonviable pregnancies, and non-gestating people caught up as collateral damage in *Dobbs*'s aftermath, these stories collectively made a concomitant, implicit distinction between the unwitting victims of reproductive abandonment depicted in these stories of medical and legal extremity and the ostensibly less-innocent pregnant people who "simply" seek to terminate their pregnancy in the interests of their own quotidian well-being. In the words of one desperate "victim" of Texas's six-week abortion ban, "you know, they paint this woman into being this individual that doesn't care about her life, doesn't care about the life of the children she creates or whatever. And she just recklessly and negligently goes out and gets abortions all willy-nilly, left and right. [ . . . ] Abortions are sometimes needed out of an act of an emergency, out of an act of saving a woman's life" (Feibel 2022). Disturbingly like the right-wing lawmakers critiqued in these *Dobbs*-era medical morality tales for drafting laws without attention to reason or rights, these other(ed) abortion seekers are deemed guilty of irrationality, recklessness, and negligence. Who are these women for whom the position of empathetic victim is foreclosed? Statistics would suggest they are Black, Indigenous, or people of color, likely to be living at or below the poverty line.

Deciphering the implications of this distinction between the deracinated women whose *lives need saving* and implicitly racialized reckless abortion seekers who *don't care about life* requires attending to how white liberal subjecthood has long relied on Blackness as the embodiment of a subjugated and less-than-fully-human status against which (white) personhood and liberty are measured. As I have argued elsewhere, Blackness as a category and a subject position operates as and at the limit of the human against which liberal humanism itself has been constructed. The hegemonic discourse of liberal humanism through which the United States imagines itself and through which the attendant vocabulary of natural rights and personal liberty are articulated is transmuted in the case of the Black subject into imminent criminality, "individual . . . blameworthiness," articulated through the lexicon of sexual and reproductive deviance (Hartman 1997, 6; Kaplan 2021). This ontological problem of Black humanity is all the more vexing in the political context of abortion, in which the question of personal liberty and the juridical recognition of personhood under the law—both inextricable from the racialized construction of the human—has long been the staging ground for legal debates over fetal rights. Historically, Blackness has functioned as the juridical name for property without personhood and obligations without rights; Black subjects have embodied the imagined social category of dependent, non-autonomous subjecthood. In this sense, the default terms of the abortion debate within liberal Western political discourse—the moral and legal parsing of rights, personhood, bodily autonomy, and the boundaries of human life—makes little distinction between the Black reproductive subject and the fetus they carry.

To emphasize this concomitant articulation of (white) medical and legal humanity alongside (Black) sexual and legal rightlessness is not to argue for an expansion of the category of reproductive (or human) rights. Rather, it is to highlight how both liberal humanism itself and the reproductive rights that white women have achieved through the tools and avenues of liberal governance have required and rationalized the deprivation, containment, and criminalization of women of color's reproductive freedom in general, and Black reproductive freedom in particular. In short, it is to underscore that the current logics underpinning mainstream reproductive politics still require rigorous rethinking to imagine new frameworks of racialized, classed, and gendered freedom.

## Raced Reproduction at the Boundary of Life and Death

The remainder of this article seeks to provide an alternative reading of the vexed relationship between Western liberalism and raced reproductivity that might contribute to just such a rethinking. It is built on three key premises. First, race and reproduction have been inextricably entangled technologies of power and knowledge since the origins of the U.S. as a settler and racial state. In the context of U.S. racial capitalism, reproduction is always already a "racial project," structured by and interpreted through systems of racial meaning-making. And vice versa, modern racial categories and logics of race rely upon notions of reproduction—biological or otherwise—for their coherence. Second, and more specifically, the creation, expansion, and maintenance of the U.S. racial state has relied on the administration, expropriation, and production of knowledge around Black procreation, domestic labor, and sexual labor and leisure as a crucial part of the state and extra-legal administration of Black life and death. It is this assemblage of racial imaginaries and social policies, systems of labor and bodies of knowledge, that I refer to, here and elsewhere, as *Black reproductivity* (Kaplan 2021). Third, and finally, the maintenance of white liberal subjecthood, with its idealization of individual sovereignty and self-sufficiency, has required the disavowal and denegation of its collective dependence on Black people and other people of color for the material and discursive reproduction of the necessary conditions for white liberty.

As Stallings reminds us, biomedical discourses around reproduction are no less a form of cultural meaning-making simply because they are presented in the lexicon of empiricism (2019, 106). In the context of Black reproductivity, scientific knowledge production has never been a tool for reproductive freedom or autonomy; rather, historically it has been inseparable from the regulation and exploitation of the raced and gendered body. In the antebellum context, the expansion of cash-crop plantation economies and the shift to the scientific management of slave populations coincided and converged with the professionalization of medical care and the emergence of women's health as an area of scientific inquiry and debate, inextricably entangling the surveillance and management of Black women's reproduction, and the production of scientific knowledge about the female body, with the maintenance and expansion of U.S. racial capitalism (Goodwin 2022; Ivy 2016; Schwartz 2006). Indeed, it bears remembering that, thanks to the multi-year experimentation of Dr. J. Marion Sims on the captive and enslaved Betsey and Anarcha, gynecology's emergence as a scientific field is indelibly indebted to the ongoing surgical torture of enslaved Black women's bodies in the interest of restoring their reproductive viability. Concomitantly, the "mastery" of the slaveholder also became a science—one in which existing tools of terror and brutality and strategies of negotiation were joined by the extensive biopolitical management of enslaved labor and discipline, of their domestic relationships and familial structures, their bodies and behaviors, their reproductive functions, and even their desires. This management of Black life in the service of white wealth demanded the control of enslaved females' reproductive functions and labor via the disciplinary and regulatory exercise of power and knowledge through which to "administer, optimize, and multiply" Black reproductive life, "subjecting it to precise controls and comprehensive regulations" (Schwartz 2006).

In emancipation's wake, the ostensible incorporation of new Black citizens into liberal democracy was conditional, built on stringent systems for the regulation, subordination, and containment of Black bodies and populations. In the transformation from slavery's punitive systems of captivity, coercion, and dispossession to the delimited nominal freedom of slavery's afterlife, the scientific and social rationalization of Black life via the surveillance, organization, and regulation of Black reproductivity remained crucial, requiring the creation and institutionalization of new modes of social and biological scientific knowledge. Feminist of color activists and scholars have long documented how in the century and a half since Black emancipation, the creation and implementation of ostensibly progressive reproductive technologies for family planning such as contraception, abortion, or surgical sterilization have been imbricated with and implemented through a eugenic logic of social engineering intended to disproportionately control and delimit reproduction by poor people, white ethnic immigrants, and people of color (Davis 1983; Roberts 1997; Ross 1990). This heightened focus on Black procreation and domesticity conjoined with mid-century Keynesian social welfare policies and social management programs to make the management of Black reproductive life an integral part of U.S. projects of modernization, industrialization, and rationalization.

Given this history, reproductive coercion cannot be characterized as the singular domain of the late twentieth-century religious right. Rather, the biopolitical management of raced life and death through modes of reproductive control is inextricable from the birth and evolution of Western liberalism in the U.S. Whether it be the religious right's exhortation to "protect the lives of the unborn," or the defense of abortion as health care with the claim to "save women's lives," the purported protection and increased valuation of life emerges as an oft-repeated rationale for the surveillance, control, and production of knowledge around Black reproductivity. What is elided in anti-abortion propagandists' and family planning advocates' opposing claims to valorize, preserve, or protect life, however, is the extent to which reproductive politics remain a primary terrain for the biopolitical management of racialized populations and disciplining of individual and collective non-white bodies. In this sense, both contemporary state policies of reproductive control and the mainstream political project of reproductive rights are forms of what Grace Hong has described as the contemporary neoliberal management of racial life (2015).

What political possibilities, then, can be found in marking how contemporary systems of reproductive coercion position reproductive subjects at the precipice of life and death? One approach would be to see it as a mode of what Michel Foucault dubs sovereign power—that is, the "subjugation of life to the power of death" (1990, 137). There is much to be appreciated in contemporary critiques of state reproductive control as inextricable from other death-dealing structures including mass incarceration and detention, post-Keynesian abandonment, and environmental destruction. Within this framing, the widespread criminalization of abortion, codified in law at the end of the nineteenth century, can be situated within the *longue durée* of the "age of human sacrifice," and the management of procreation can be seen as part of the same national project as segregation, lynching, and malign medical neglect and intervention (Holland 2020; Gilmore 2002).

Too narrow a consideration of sovereign power runs the risk of overlooking the intimate modalities of raced reproductive power, however. Indeed, attending to reproductive politics and racialized subjection as inextricable demands a profound rethinking of how the politics of life and death—making *live* and making *die*—are theorized. It is not solely through medical crises or the withholding of emergency care that the violence of reproductive control will be most profoundly felt by women and other pregnant people of color. Rather, quotidian sites and scales of social and biological reproduction, from the intimate places of body or home to the public offices of disaffected social workers and watchful welfare officers, are primary contested terrains upon and through which the U.S. racial state coordinates the regulation and surveillance of the national body. Material and ideological geographies of reproductivity, then, function as central nodes for entailment to state power. Just as racial difference has always been articulated through gendered and sexualized notions of nonnormativity, immorality, and excess, tropes of failed, unfit, and pathological maternity have naturalized the subjection of reproductive subjects of color to the spectacular and banal technologies of policing and surveillance that make up the structures of reproductive carcerality.

It is through this quotidian management and coordination of relations of reproduction that *Roe*'s reversal will be most extensively felt. On the one hand, the criminalization of abortion will function as a system of malign abandonment, disproportionately impacting people of color in midwestern and southern states and other places where people of color are more likely to have restricted access to affordable contraceptives. A lack of resources for travel, access to sick leave and childcare provision, and other raced and classed barriers are already rendering abortion inaccessible to poor people of color in these regions—places where Black women have the highest rates of maternal mortality and pregnancy complications. On the other hand, the criminalization of abortion will magnify existing structures of reproductive carcerality, expanding state capacities to surveil, control, and punish the bodies and lives of reproductive subjects of color.

Accordingly, this meditation concludes by revisiting the language of life as a provocative point of potential intervention in contemporary reproductive justice organizing. Rather than arguing that the goals of the anti-abortion movement are diametrically opposed or constitutively foreign to a terminology of life, I want to suggest that the anti-abortion movement is a necropolitical exercise of power, simultaneously death-dealing and life-regulating, that gains its greatest purchase not through the nurturance of individual life but through the surveillance, regulation, and criminalization of raced, gendered, and sexualized life. In the face of polemical claims that the so-called pro-life movement's fascination with life begins with the fetus and ends with birth, I would argue that the fetus is, at most, a tool for the real work of power: the entailment of raced and gendered populations through the management of physical bodies, social identities, and sexual practices.

In this framework, the past four decades of political mobilization around the recriminalization of abortion can be seen as part of a broader state project of white heteropatriarchal revanchism underpinned by a punitive logic of gendered and sexual control. In that context, even as it operates in the name of "protecting life," the state-sanctioned denial of access to reproductive health care is best understood as the state organization of medicalized violence that makes those subjects of improperly raced, gendered, and sexualized reproduction vulnerable to premature death (Gilmore 2002). These recent reiterated accounts of pregnant and potentially pregnant bodies pushed to the brink of death, children foreclosed from the life they imagined, or would-be parents mandated to carry to term a fetus predestined to die, represent contemporary state modes of reproductive coercion not only as an exercise in *making die* masquerading under the façade of "life" but as a process of both *making die* and *making live*. It marks not simply the religious right's attack on dominant liberal norms and ideals but the emergence of a new historical bloc, rooted in white nationalism's willingness to sacrifice white nonnormative sexual and gendered subjects in the service of reproducing the racial capitalist, heteropatriarchal state. Such an approach, capable of addressing reproductive coercion as emerging from long-standing structures of racial management and dispossession, but not limited in their enactment to people of color, might allow us to reject long-standing algorithms of scientific reason, personal rights, and liberal morality along with their racial shadows: blameworthiness, deviance, and obligation. Such an approach might enable organizers for racial and sexual justice to approach this post-*Dobbs* moment not as a state of exception but as a critical pressure point in the broader politics of race and reproductivity on which contemporary U.S. racial capitalism relies—not from a Klaxon call of liberalism in crisis, but from a counter movement aligned with raced, gendered, and sexualized freedom.

**Sara Clarke Kaplan** is an associate professor of literature and critical race, gender, and culture studies and executive director of the Antiracist Research and Policy Center at American University. She is the author of *The Black Reproductive: Feminism and Insurgent Motherhood*, and can be reached at skaplan@american.edu.

## Notes

1. The collected data on the disproportionate morbidity and mortality of Black pregnant people and their offspring use the gendered terminology of "maternity" and "women"; for statistical consistency, I refer to the data accordingly.

2. The conspicuous exception to this general categorization of dominant liberal discourse around reproductive politics is the work of legal scholar Michele Goodwin. Outside of liberal discourse, the ongoing theory and praxis of reproductive justice thinkers, organizers, and advocates clearly offers a much-needed remedy to the violent foreclosures tracked in this article. My own thinking owes much to their work.

## Works Cited

ACLU New Mexico. 2022. "ACLU Repro Rights Community Engagement Strategist Talks about the Status of Repro Rights in New Mexico." June 13, 2022. Accessed September 10, 2022. https://www.aclu-nm.org/en/news/aclu-repro-rights-community-engagement-strategist-talks-about-status-repro-rights-new-mexico.

Biden, Joseph. 2022. "Remarks by President Biden on Protecting Access to Reproductive Health Care Services." July 8, 2022. Accessed July 24, 2022. https://www.whitehouse.gov/briefing-room/speeches-remarks/2022/07/08/remarks-by-president-biden-on-protecting-access-to-reproductive-health-care-services/.

Davis, Angela Y. 1983. *Women, Race & Class*. New York: Vintage Books.

Ducharme, Jaime, and Tara Law. 2022. "When Is an Abortion Lifesaving? It's Not Always Clear." *Time*, July 7, 2022. Accessed September 10, 2022. https://time.com/6194397/abortions-lifesaving-ectopic-pregnancy/.

Feibel, Carrie. 2022. "How Abortion Bans Complicated One Woman's Problematic Pregnancy." *National Public Radio*, July 26, 2022. https://www.wbur.org/hereandnow/2022/07/26/abortion-bans-pregnancy.

Foucault, Michel. 1990. *The History of Sexuality: An Introduction*. New York: Vintage.

Gilmore, Ruth Wilson. 2002. "Fatal Couplings of Power and Difference: Notes on Racism and Geography." *The Professional Geographer* 54, no. 1: 15–24.

Goldhill, Olivia. 2022. "'A Scary Time': Fear of Prosecution Forces Doctors to Choose between Protecting Themselves or Their Patients." *Stat*, July 5, 2022. Accessed September 12, 2022. https://www.statnews.com/2022/07/05/a-scary-time-fear-of-prosecution-forces-doctors-to-choose-between-protecting-themselves-or-their-patients/.

Goodwin, Michelle. 2022. "The Urgency for Reproductive Freedom: From Slavery to the New Jane Crow." *Ms.*, May 24, 2022. Accessed July 24, 2022. https://msmagazine.com/2022/05/24/abortion-slavery-reproductive-freedom-13th-amendment-constitution-black-women-history/.

Hartman, Saidiya V. 1997. *Scenes of Subjection: Terror, Slavery, and Self-Making in Nineteenth-Century America*. Oxford, UK: Oxford University Press.

Holland, Jennifer L. 2020. *Tiny You: A Western History of the Anti-abortion Movement*. Oakland: University of California Press.

Hong, Grace Kyungwon. 2015. *Death beyond Disavowal: The Impossible Politics of Difference*. Minneapolis: University of Minnesota Press.

Ivy, Nicole. 2016. "Bodies of Work: A Meditation on Medical Imaginaries and Enslaved Women." *Souls: A Critical Journal of Black Politics, Culture, and Society* 18, no. 1: 11–31.

Jagannathan, Meera. 2019. "Nearly half of women who have abortions live below the federal poverty level." *MarketWatch*, October 4, 2019. https://www.

marketwatch.com/story/nearly-half-of-women-who-have-abortions-live-below-in-the-federal-poverty-level-2019-05-17.

Kaiser Family Foundation. 2020. "Reported Legal Abortions by Race of Women Who Obtained Abortion by the State of Occurrence." Accessed September 14, 2022. https://www.kff.org/womens-health-policy/state-indicator/abortions-by-race/.

Kaplan, Sara Clarke. 2021. *The Black Reproductive: Unfree Labor and Insurgent Motherhood*. Minneapolis: University of Minnesota Press, 2021.

MacDorman, Marian F., et al. 2021. "Racial and Ethnic Disparities in Maternal Mortality in the United States Using Enhanced Vital Records, 2016–2017." *American Journal of Public Health* 111: 1673–81.

*New York Times*. 2022. "Tracking States Where Abortion Is Now Banned." Accessed September 14, 2022. https://www.nytimes.com/interactive/2022/us/abortion-laws-roe-v-wade.html.

Roberts, Dorothy. 1997. *Killing the Black Body: Race, Reproduction, and the Meaning of Liberty*. New York: Pantheon.

Ross, Loretta. 1990. "Raising Our Voices." In *From Abortion to Reproductive Freedom: Transforming a Movement*, edited by Marlene Gerber Fried. Boston: South End Press.

Schwartz, Marie Jenkins. 2006. *Birthing a Slave: Motherhood and Medicine in the Antebellum South*. Cambridge, MA: Harvard University Press.

Stallings, L. H. 2020. *A Dirty South Manifesto: Sexual Resistance and Imagination in the New South*. Oakland: University of California Press.

Stern, Mark Joseph. 2022. "The Real Reason Why the GOP Is Rushing to Pass Abortion Bans without Exceptions for Rape." *Slate*, July 19, 2022.

Sweet, Lynn. 2022. "Chicago-area reaction to pending Roe v. Wade Supreme Court decision striking down abortion rights." *Chicago Sun-Times*, May 3, 2022. Accessed September 22, 2022. https://chicago.suntimes.com/2022/5/2/23054627/chicago-area-react-pending-roe-v-wade-supreme-court-decision-striking-down-abortion-rights.

Young Democrats of America. 2022. "Restore *Roe*: We Will Not Go Back." Accessed July 24, 2022. https://actionnetwork.org/petitions/protect-roe-v-wade-save-reproductive-rights.

# PART II. STATE OF THE FIELD: NEW AND FORTHCOMING WORKS ON STATE/POWER

# How to Make Revolution

Christina Heatherton

**Abstract:** Christina Heatherton reflects on lessons from her new book, *Arise! Global Radicalism in the Era of the Mexican Revolution* (University of California Press, 2022) to describe how to avoid the traps of revolutionary nostalgia and engage in the collective process of making radical struggle. **Keywords:** internationalism; nostalgia; radicalism; solidarity

In September 2022, two hundred years after her birth, a statue of Harriet Tubman was installed at the entrance to CIA headquarters. The statue was meant to celebrate Tubman's history as a spy for the Union army during the U.S. Civil War. It also reflected CIA ambitions to develop greater "minority representation" in its ranks, a goal less likely hindered by a lack of Black statues and more likely by the agency's record of coups, torture, assassinations, racist violence, and sabotage. A similar irony imbues Treasury Department plans to place Tubman's face on the twenty-dollar bill. The transformation of Tubman—a formerly enslaved woman—into legal tender is a jarring way to commemorate her subversion of the slave economy, to say the least. Tubman, of course, freed herself from slavery and then courageously enabled others to do the same. Her name graces parks, museums, landmarks, and street signs along routes of the Underground Railroad, paths she forged to freedom and from bondage. In upstate New York, where she lived for over half a century, her name now unironically adorns a state prison. During the Civil War, Tubman facilitated movements of "contraband," the name given to fugitive slaves who crossed over Union lines and "stole themselves" into freedom. In 2020, George Floyd lost his life for possession of a different

*WSQ: Women's Studies Quarterly* 51: 1 & 2 (Spring/Summer 2023)

kind of contraband, an allegedly forged twenty-dollar bill. Had the bill in question possessed Tubman's face, it would have represented contraband twice over: first in the state's murderous classification and second in the grim enlistment of its radical legacy (Sernett 2007, 85–86; House 2017; Brockell 2022).

The year 2022 also marked a century since the death of Ricardo Flores Magón, an unrepentant anarchist and key agitator of the Mexican Revolution. Mexican President Andrés Manuel López Obrador declared this centennial the "Year of Ricardo Flores Magón." The commemorative banner unfurled at his January press conference depicts Flores Magón in a brown suit, looking rumpled but studious against a royal maroon backdrop. Glasses perched above his nose, the tips of his mustache slightly twirled, he looks up expectantly, pen in hand. Next to him is his name and a title announcing him as "precursor to the Mexican Revolution." Below him is the seal of the Mexican government, the very state he had devoted his life to overthrowing (Contreras 2022).

Flores Magón's first arrest came in 1892, during a student protest against President Porfirio Díaz's increasingly dictatorial regime. There, he gave his first political speech to fellow students, igniting his life's work of radical agitation and incurring a lifetime of state repression. Were Flores Magón able to peer out into the present world from within the banner, he would see an increasingly militarized Mexican state. A recent leak of government documents confirms a vast expansion of military power in domestic arenas, ramped-up surveillance against journalists, repression against dissidents, and scandalous state complicity with drug cartels. It further implicates government officials in the 2014 murder and disappearance of forty-three students from the rural town of Ayotzinapa. Those students had been headed to Mexico City to commemorate the Tlatelolco massacre, a 1968 event where protesting students had been viciously murdered by government forces. On their way to the commemoration, students were stopped and kidnapped by local state forces and later disappeared. Seeking justice, the classmates of the forty-three have organized alongside the parents into a "Ricardo Flores Magón Committee." As an official investigation declares the loss of the Ayotzinapa students a "crime of the state," the Ricardo Flores Magón of the official government banner awkwardly confronts his namesake in a radical anti-government organizing effort (Lomnitz 2014, 57–59; Abi-Habib 2022; Lopez 2022; Pinto 2022; Kitroeff, Bergman, and Lopez 2022).

Revolutionary enemies of the state are often quaintly refashioned into its gentle mascots. Tubman and Flores Magón offer two recent examples of how radical nostalgia can be deployed toward reactionary aims. "Not even the dead," wrote Walter Benjamin, "will be safe from the enemy if he is victorious." As Benjamin depressingly rejoined, "This enemy has not ceased to be victorious" (2007, 255). Nostalgia often reveals less about the era it recalls and more about the longings of the moment in which it is invoked. In the uncertainty of our present era, glutted as it is with radical nostalgia, revolutionary heroes of the past seem to be tapped for an otherwise unavailable moral authority. How does such refashioning impair our conceptions of history and struggle? How might we wrest revolutionary traditions from such antithetical fates? Can such reckoning afford us alternative approaches to the questions of state power and revolution? In what follows, I reflect on these questions and on my experience grappling with them in my new book, *Arise! Global Radicalism in the Era of the Mexican Revolution* (University of California Press, 2022).

*Arise!* is a study of internationalism, a recognition of the ways that people have been unevenly waylaid by the global capitalist system and developed forms of revolutionary solidarity in spite of social and spatial divisions, including national boundaries, in order to confront it. The book takes its title from the first word of "The Internationale" (1888), the definitive anthem to internationalism. "Arise ye prisoners of starvation," the song begins. In this way, *Arise!* self-consciously joins a long tradition of authors who have plumbed the song's lyrics to grapple with the legacy of internationalism in their own times. Melvin Dubovsky borrowed the lyric "we have been naught, we shall be all," to title his study of the anarcho-syndicalist Industrial Workers of the World *We Shall Be All*. Famously, Frantz Fanon took the second line of the song, "Arise ye wretched of the earth," to title his indictment of colonialism in and beyond French Algeria, *Wretched of the Earth*. After she left the Communist Party, Dorothy Healey wanted to title her memoir *Tradition's Chains Have Bound Us*, a reconfiguration of the lyrics "No more tradition's chains shall bind us." Healey argued that unless a radical tradition was "able to constantly keep alive that challenging, questioning and probing of the real scene around it," it would only ever be a mere shadow of itself, a snare of revolutionary nostalgia where hope is trapped and strangled, rather than a living, breathing tradition that might allow us to survive (Healey and Isserman 1993, 13–14). This is perhaps the central lesson of my book.

To make its case, *Arise!* approaches the question of internationalism from a somewhat unusual route. It traces the legacy of internationalism related to the Mexican Revolution of 1910–1920 and its afterlives persisting into the 1940s. While the Mexican Revolution is often narrated as a contained nationalist event sparked by a revolt against President Díaz's dictatorial reign and the vastly uneven forms of modernization and dispossession developed under his over three-decade-long rule, my book contends that the revolution was a decisively global event in its origins and influence. *Arise!* tracks the currents of abolition which influenced Mexico's anti-colonial revolts and subsequently, its definition of freedom. It also considers the movement of global capital which inspired the uprising, noting, for example, that at the outbreak of the revolution, U.S. investors owned over one-quarter of Mexico's surface and over 80 percent of its mineral rights. The book charts how the revolution became a crucible of internationalism for the world's "rebels." Some of the historical figures I highlight include Okinawan organizer Paul Kōchi, who discovered internationalism while crossing through revolutionary Mexico; Indian anticolonial activist M. N. Roy, who transformed a fight against British colonialism into an internationalist struggle and cofounded the Mexican Communist Party; and radical African American artist Elizabeth Catlett, who brought together internationalist traditions rooted in Black radicalism and the Mexican Revolution. The book tracks the making of radical thought through what I call "convergence spaces," sites within which disparate revolutionary traditions were compressed together, producing new articulations of struggle. From farm worker strikes at the U.S.-Mexico border; art collectives in Chicago, Harlem, and Mexico City; and a prison "university" in Leavenworth Federal Penitentiary, where Ricardo Flores Magón would spend his final years among a motley crew of global radicals, the book observes how the Mexican Revolution staged a significant set of convergences within which internationalism was "made."

To confront the nostalgia that often accompanies histories of revolution, the book emphasizes the open and contingent process of *making*. This process is reflected in the chapter titles, which include "How to Make a Flag," "How to Make a University," "How to Make Love," and "How to Make a Dress." The introduction, "How to Make a Rope," explains the making of a lynch rope at the turn of the twentieth century. As a commodity-chain story, it first traces the cultivation of various component fibers, including manila from U.S. imperial control over the Philippines, cotton or domestically produced hemp from U.S. Jim Crow sharecropping regimes, and henequen or sisal from the southernmost Mexican state of Yucatán, a product of dispossessed Indigenous Yaqui and Huastec people and indentured workers hailing from Spain, China, Cuba, the Canary Islands, and Korea. Such an exposition reveals coterminous regimes of accumulation, a world tied together in the production of the commodity and, subsequently, in the racist terror wrought through it. At the same time, by unbraiding the strands and tracing the forms of revolt found in each space, I contend, we can begin to observe a history of shared struggle. From the revolts of Mexican people during the revolution, to the rebellion of Filipinos to imperial rule and Chicago organizers against labor exploitation, to Indigenous resistance to dispossession, one gains a sense of a world connected in struggle through the making and unmaking of the rope. Such a charting illustrates how the movement of global capital has produced its own unintended negations. By beginning with these contradictions rather than with the more familiar history of the most well-known revolutionary heroes, I maintain that we can discover an overlooked form of internationalism from below.

I came to this study by accident. Many of my Okinawan relatives, including one great-uncle, came to the United States via Mexico. That relative, Morisei Yamashiro, became a farmworker and labor organizer in the fields of the Imperial Valley in Southern California. There, Okinawan, Japanese, Chinese, Black, Filipino, South Asian, Indigenous, poor white, and Mexican workers labored together. Before Okinawan and Japanese Americans were forcibly relocated to internment camps during World War II, there were early FBI raids on their communities. Labor organizers were among the first to be targeted. When federal agents showed up at Yamashiro's door in 1942, he allegedly fought back ("F.B.I. Removes" 1942). According to his son, Yamashiro "had been down in Mexico fighting with Pancho Villa, so he knew how to take care of business!" This reflection was provocative. Could the radical resistance of Okinawans and Japanese in the United States been forged through their affinity with Mexican peasants during the Mexican Revolution? To answer, I was forced to confront gaps in my own family's history as well as shibboleths I had inherited about Asian American and labor history.

I examined the reflections of another Okinawan migrant, Paul Shinsei Kōchi, who had known my relatives in Southern California and traveled a similar path at the same time. The second chapter of my book examines Kōchi through his memoir *Imin no Aiwa* (An Immigrant's Sorrowful Tale), which describes how he found internationalism in Mexico. It describes his escape from Okinawa and from the surveillance of imperialist Japan; his solidarity with Indigenous Kanaka Maoli in Hawaiʻi, with Tongva people in California, and with Yaqui in northern Mexico as well as with Indian, Chinese, and other Asian immigrants and with Mexican peasants in the revolution; and his subsequent position of internationalism. As I write:

> Paul Kōchi's story demonstrates how the uprooted, dispossessed, and despised of the world came to know each other in shadows, in the tangled spaces of expulsion, extraction, transportation, debt, exploitation, and destruction: the garroting circuits of modern capital. Whether crammed in tight ship quarters; knocking together over the rails; sweating and swaying in the relentless tempo of industrial agriculture; inhaling the dank air of mine shafts; hearing each other breathing, coughing, fighting, singing, snoring, and sighing through thin walls; or corralled like livestock in jails and prisons, the contradictions of modern capital were shared in its intimate spaces. Within such sites, people discovered that the circuits of revolution, like the countervailing circuits of capital, were realizable in motion, often through unplanned assemblages. Roaring at their backs were the revolutionary currents of the late nineteenth and early twentieth centuries, currents that howled from the metropolitan hearts of empire and wailed across the peripheries of the global world system. Standing before them, in the middle of its own revolution, was Mexico. From the vantage point of these struggles, the new century did not simply portend the inevitability of urban revolts and insurgencies at the point of production, but an epoch of peasant wars, rural uprisings, anti-colonial movements, and, of course, the Mexican Revolution. Mexico, as both a real country and an imagined space of revolution, would become a crucible of internationalism for the world's "rebels" like Paul Kōchi. (Heatherton 2022, 51–52)

In focusing less on individuals and more on the movements of poor, working-class, and marginalized people—those often excluded in official archives and nostalgic historical narratives—*Arise!* is inspired by the principles of social history, or history from below. This tradition is most firmly linked to E. P. Thompson's (1963) *The Making of the English Working Class.* In my own trajectory, this tradition has been guided by the work of theorists like W. E. B. Du Bois (1962) and C. L. R. James (1989). Their work traces internationalist traditions cultivated along abolitionist routes, what historian Julius Scott has named *A Common Wind* (2020).

I came to this historical tradition through another unusual journey. In 2007, I was a member of the Bristol Radical History Group in Bristol, England. We were a random mix of elementary school teachers, cancan dancers, contractors, painters, engineers, and one talented but underemployed web designer. That year the British government celebrated the two-hundredth anniversary of the abolition of the British slave trade. Official events hailed politicians like William Wilberforce and the legislation that abolished the slave trade in order to contrive redemptive nationalist narratives of the British state. In response, our group highlighted an alternative history. In free lectures, we discussed the resistance of enslaved African people and global abolitionist currents whose actions made the trade untenable and impossible. In art exhibits, film screenings, and concerts we celebrated abolition as a jubilant history. We organized walking tours to show people where reparations had been dispensed; not to formerly enslaved people but to former slaveowners, who subsequently invested state compensation for their lost "property" into industries, transportation hubs, and Bristol's built environment.

A statue in the city center, for example, commemorated Edward Colston, a town father of the late seventeenth and early eighteenth centuries. Colston was a leader in the local Bristol Merchant Venturers Society and an executive of the Royal African Company who had massively profited from the slave trade. Our tours reconsidered Colston's legacy, and the seeming amelioration of the past represented by his statue. Years later, in the global Black Lives Matter protests of 2020, while people in the United States were confronting the ties between racist violence and racist history by toppling statues of Confederate soldiers, the people of Bristol engaged in their own powerful reckoning. A jubilant crowd brought down the statue of Colston. With a dramatic collective heave, they threw it off a bridge into the waters of the River Avon, sinking the man into the same global waterways that had once ferried his own monstrous wealth.

Internationalism, as I argue in *Arise!*, is a practice that is collectively forged and never simply found. By casting off cynical nostalgia, I believe we can be emboldened by histories from below to critically engage the radical traditions we find we have inherited. Perhaps by enlivening these histories, we can topple the consecrated monuments that confine our political imaginations and arise together towards something more just.

**Christina Heatherton** is the Elting Associate Professor of American Studies and Human Rights at Trinity College. She is the author of *Arise! Global Radicalism in the Era of the Mexican Revolution*. She coedited *Policing the Planet: Why the Policing Crisis Led to Black Lives Matter* with Jordan T. Camp. She currently codirects the Trinity Social Justice Initiative. She can be reached at christina.heatherton@trincoll.edu.

## Works Cited

Abi-Habib, Maria. 2022. "Mexico Military Is Hacked, Exposing Abuse and Efforts to Evade Oversight." *New York Times*, October 6, 2022.

Benjamin, Walter. 2007. "Theses in the Philosophy of History." In *Illuminations: Essays and Reflections*, edited by Hannah Arendt, 196–209. New York: Schocken Books.

Brockell, Gillian. 2022. "A Statue of Legendary Spy Harriet Tubman Now Stands at the CIA." *Washington Post*, September 20, 2022.

Contreras, Ezequiel Flores. 2022. "Gobierno de AMLO declara el 2022 como el año de Ricardo Flores Magón, precursor revolucionario." *Proceso*, January 3, 2022.

Du Bois, W. E. B. (1935) 1962. *Black Reconstruction in America: An Essay toward a History of the Part Which Black Folk Played in the Attempt to Reconstruct Democracy in America, 1860–1880*. New York: Atheneum.

"FBI Removes 46 Japs." *Imperial Valley Press*, February 20, 1942.

Healey, Dorothy Ray, and Maurice Isserman. 1993. *California Red: A Life in the American Communist Party*. Urbana: University of Illinois Press.

Heatherton, Christina. 2022. *Arise! Global Radicalism in the Era of the Mexican Revolution*. Oakland: University of California Press.

House, Samantha. 2017. "After $12 Million Update, Former Cayuga County Center Will Again House Youth Offenders." *Syracuse.com*, September 22, 2017.

James, C. L. R. 1989. *The Black Jacobins: Toussaint L'Ouverture and the San Domingo Revolution*. New York: Vintage Books.

Kitroeff, Natalie, Ronen Bergman, and Oscar Lopez. 2022. "Evidence 'Invalidated' in Explosive Report on Mexico's 43 Missing Students." *New York Times*, October 26, 2022.

Lomnitz, Claudio. 2014. *The Return of Comrade Ricardo Flores Magón*. New York: Zone Books.

Lopez, Oscar. 2022. "Mexico Says Disappearance of 43 Students Was a 'Crime of the State.'" *New York Times*, August 20, 2022.

Pinto, Ñaní. 2022. "Mexico's Military Knew Ayotzinapa 43 Were Kidnapped, Then Covered It Up." *NACLA*, April 2, 2022.

Scott, Julius. 2020. *The Common Wind: Afro-American Currents in the Age of the Haitian Revolution*. New York: Verso.

Sernett, Milton C. 2007. *Harriet Tubman: Myth, Memory, and History*. Durham, NC: Duke University Press.

Thompson, E. P. 1963. *The Making of the English Working Class*. London: IICA.

# Trans of Color Entrapments and Carceral Coalitions

Ren-yo Hwang

**Abstract:** An introduction to my book project currently titled "Trans of Color Entrapments and Carceral Coalitions," this short essay demonstrates how mainstream protrans identity politics have become influenced by procarceral politics. This piece introduces the concept of *carceral coalitions* in order to spotlight how and when coalition-building might perform a cross-identity, multi-issue, multicultural politics while also reinforcing ongoing carceral agendas and carceral futures. The manuscript attends to how 1980s Los Angeles charted a new era in which minoritarian social movement and civil rights organizing under the banner of "antiviolence" became dutifully tracked into a vision of winnable goals by way of law and order, and the endless multiplications of anti-Black criminalization and punishment that have followed. With brief examples such as the 1985 Los Angeles–founded K6G (formerly K-11), considered the first official self-segregated gay and transgender jailing unit in the U.S., the essay demonstrates how state-based gender-responsive entrapments have only further carved out penal pathways as models for securing trans "safety," and how abolitionist feminist interventions might be possible in revisioning safety altogether. **Keywords:** trans-of-color politics; transgender imprisonment; gender-responsive policing; hate crimes; coalition-building; carceral reform; transformative justice

In 1985 Los Angeles founded K6G (formerly K-11), considered the first self-segregated gay and transgender jailing unit, within the largest jail in the world, Los Angeles County's Men's Central Jail (MCJ). K6G was established following a 1982 class action legal suit filed by lawyers in association with the ACLU of Southern California (*Robertson v. Block* 1985; Dolovich 2012, 978).[1] The legal suit sought to highlight how "homosexual inmates" are at higher risk of sexual violence when placed in general population with

*WSQ: Women's Studies Quarterly* 51: 1 & 2 (Spring/Summer 2023)

nonhomosexual inmates. Mainstream lesbian, gay, bisexual, and transgender (LGBT) organizations and affiliates, such as the Los Angeles Gay and Lesbian Center, the West Hollywood Gay Pride Parade, and the West Hollywood Public Safety Commission, have hailed the jailing unit as a critical and progressive jail reform measure that offers precedent, and a model, for safer and more humane custodial practices (Robinson 2011, 1320).

In 2014 *LA Weekly* produced a video and article entitled "In the Gay Wing of L.A. Men's Central Jail, It's Not Shanks and Muggings but Hand-Sewn Gowns and Tears" (Ucar 2014). The video opens with the message "The sights and sounds you are about to witness are an inside look at the culture of the Gay Wing inside Men's Central Jail in Downtown Los Angeles." After the video opens with a shot of a heavy institutional green door slamming shut, next the viewer is dropped into a scene within K6G, where an incarcerated person, using a plastic fork and empty soda bottle, plays makeshift percussions in a fast tempo atop a steel top bunk. The video cuts to an improvised catwalk down the middle of two tightly stacked rows of bunk beds. Two feminine figures are seen walking the ad hoc runway in DIY white dresses converted from institutional garb. Yah Yah, one of the main subjects of the video, is a Black trans woman sporting a white halter dress styled with elbow-length white gloves. Yah Yah's voice narrates the runway scene, stating:

> Over there [referring to the general population of the jail] is more organized, more politics, you know . . . you do . . . or you get . . . disciplined. Whereas over here, it's more freedom. And you are more allowed to say what you feel and how you feel. As opposed to being in line or living in fear. You don't have to live that way in here.

Filmed as a kind of exposé-meets-PSA, this three-minute video aims to "humanize" trans and gay subjects behind the confines of a jail cell by placing a spotlight on the experiences of those housed in the supposedly haven-esque dormitory of K6G, saved from the otherwise predatory and homophobic environment of the general population (GP).[2] Yah Yah's description of her ability to survive beyond a male-designated jail is marked by her naming of an "over there" versus an "over here"—that is, the organized politics of GP, where discipline and punishment comes by way of both violent power grabs and infighting by inmates, but also from the institutional infrastructure and correctional officers themselves. The space of K6G as an "over here," as that which provides "more freedom," is still far from the reality of actually being free. To be able to say "what you feel and how you feel," as Yah Yah testifies, is indeed some kind of alleviation from the institutionalization of patriarchal violence that underlies the logic and practices of carceral facilities everywhere. However, the measure of freedom remains proportionate to the unfreedom of locked institutional doors and the various scales of enforced enclosures throughout the jail. Free-ness constituted by an inescapable "in here" is predetermined by the institutional walls and psychological warfare of being caged as a means of state-based justice and "safekeeping," even if providing the possibility of a kind of temporary palliation for some.[3]

To remedy sexual violence in a prison or jail by way of a logic of individualism, or carceral reform via litigation-based activism—one that roots out the bad actors by uplifting the incarcerated individual to the level of a protectable subject under the tenets of civil rights—too often distracts from alternative organizing efforts that aim to confront the very material conditions that provoke and reproduce such cultures of violence in the first place.[4] In carceral facilities, sexual violence is largely dealt with as rooted in heterogenous circumstances specific to a perpetrator and, too, the deliberation of whether there is blame to share upon the survivor. The fear of "arbitrary violence" remains the rationale for the unbridled exertion of state power via law, order, and punishment, and thus constricts any real possibility of anti-violence and violence prevention outside of the state's capacity to legislate and predetermine safety. The trap of K6G is in its ability to be an absolute diversion from attending to the mechanics of sexual and gendered violence that undergird the very inception and cultures of perpetual domination that are the mainstay of carceral institutions.

The founding of K6G relied on levying the constitutional clause of "cruel and unusual punishment" to demand more humane conditions of confinement for a targeted population. Such strategies of allaying violence for singular identities ("homosexual inmates" or "gay prisoners" in the case of *Robertson v. Block*) has only entrapped us further. In 2020 California adopted the Transgender Respect, Agency, and Dignity Act (SB-132) which "allow[s] incarcerated transgender, non-binary and intersex people to be housed and searched in a manner consistent with their gender identity."[5] Though SB-132 was long fought for by incarcerated transgender communities and allies inside and outside California prisons, those who have been able to advocate for successful transfer to a gender-affirming facility have only attested to widespread harassment, transphobia, medical neglect, and the use of secure housing units (SHU, essentially solitary confinement by another name) for "safekeeping." The invocation of "respect, agency and dignity" are perhaps euphemistically used to paint a picture of gender-responsive imprisonment while continuing a long legacy in which selective safekeeping within penal institutions allows for the lowest bar by which "safety" can be conceived of—that is, the ability to abundantly expose certain persons to more or less harm, or to penalize certain persons and groups over others. In other words, there is no safety within and by way of carceral institutions; there is simply a redirection, temporary withholding, or postponement of certain kinds of punishment in exchange for others considered perhaps less lethal. Gender-elective jailing as an end goal only reifies a vision of a world promising more policing, prosecution, prisons.

The advent of K6G, like the failed $3.5 billion plan to revamp the MCJ and build a "mental health center," was intended to make existing jails and prisons "better and safer." JusticeLA (est. 2017), an unapologetically anti-carceral coalition made up of over forty organizations across California and Los Angeles (such as Californians United for a Responsible Budget [CURB] and the Stop LAPD Spying Coalition), successfully strategized the shut-down of this colossal jail reform expansion plan in 2019 (JusticeLA, n.d. a). The coalition made national headlines in fall of 2017 with the carefully coordinated direct action involving one hundred steel-frame jail beds staged in front of an L.A. County Board of Supervisors crucial budget meeting, blocking traffic downtown in order to hold a community press conference featuring organizers in orange T-shirts reading "I am not the property of L.A. County jail" (Agrawal 2017). Paired with art-based activism (#JailBed-Drop) and strategic endorsements and pressures to uphold resentencing efforts at early release (penal nonreformist reforms such as Prop. 57 or the Public Safety and Rehabilitation Act of 2016), JusticeLA continues to put pressure on county officials to invest in community-centered alternatives to incarceration. The coalitional work has since developed into the Los Angeles County Alternatives to Incarceration (ATI) Work Group, seeding a final report of 114 anticarceral pro–community care recommendations.[6] To date, these recommendations have been largely unheeded by the county,[7] even with the resulting founding of an Alternatives to Incarceration Office within Los Angeles County and the Justice Care and Opportunities Department (JCOD), "the County's new central agency unifying LA County's efforts to serve vulnerable justice-impacted people and communities and drive forward the Board of Supervisors' vision of Care First, Jails Last" (JCOD, n.d.).

In my book manuscript, "Trans of Color Entrapments: Carceral Coalitions and Accounting for Violence," I demonstrate how mainstream protrans identity politics have become influenced by procarceral practices, arresting our shared political imaginaries and analysis through the formation of what I term *carceral coalitions*, as well as how activists have developed alternative visions. Unpacking the contradictory pairing of the adjective *carceral* with *coalition*, such a concept spotlights the tendency in which coalition-building might perform a cross-identity, multi-issue, multicultural politics while also reinforcing ongoing carceral agendas and carceral futures. Further, *carceral coalitions* names the ways in which even social justice–oriented goals and outcomes, organized across minority and marginalized identity groups via coalition-building, have become so deftly oriented toward carceral outcomes (even when the outcome is to reform and amend the deteriorative impact of carceral systems). In order to demonstrate how trans-of-color and anti-violence politics continues to be trapped within the haunting legacies of the past, the book attends to how 1980s Los Angeles charted a new era in which minoritarian social movement and civil rights organizing, under the banner of antiviolence, became so dutifully tracked into a vision of winna-ble goals by way of law and order, and thus the endless multiplications of anti-Black criminalization and punishment that has followed.

"Trans of Color Entrapments" demonstrates how state-based gender-responsive entrapments, such as trans safekeeping in the example of K6G, have carved out the various penal pathways by which we have arrived at the critical juncture where carceral enforcement against anti-trans violence continues to be rewarded and celebrated as a viable model for practicing and securing trans "safety." Such carceral pathways have emerged from, and become particularly entrenched in, the rhetoric of state "antiviolence" over the last few decades. A trans politics that is produced by way of carceral coalitions is one in which the inclusion of the identity marker of "trans" is reduced to all things considered gender-responsive, gender-affirming, or gender-inclusive. The death-wielding trap here promises a one-dimensional politics that need only affirm and offer inclusion into preexisting carceral logics and institutions. State-mediated and penalty-first gender affirma-tion practices produce only more asymmetry of violence, especially for trans-of-color communities. The book manuscript overall investigates how coalitional strategies centering justice-based remediation have, often unintentionally, prioritized the outcome of law, order, and punishment *as* accountability, diminishing the possibility for more investments in holis-tic, preventative, antipunitive, and community-based solutions to address the root causes of antiminoritarian violence.

Following the wake of the landmark Civil Rights Act of 1964, and the radical international, anti-imperialist, antiwar multicultural and revolution-ary coalitions of the 1970s (locally, for example, the Coalition Against Police Abuse or CAPA, est. 1976), the focus on the 1980s in Los Angeles demon-strates how "model minoritarian" identity politics became institutionalized through a curation of community partnerships strong-armed into collabo-ration with state agencies such as the Los Angeles County Commission on Human Relations (LACCHR), Los Angeles Police Department (LAPD), and Los Angeles Sheriff's Department (LASD). For instance, in the case of K6G, the ACLU Foundation of Southern California brought this class action forward as influenced by ACLU's historic jail reform wins via the Orange County Jail Project, the Gay Prisoners Committee of the ACLU National Gay Rights Project, and the ACLU Rights of Homosexuals Committee (eventually becoming ACLU of Southern California Gay Rights Chapter in 1975 and then the Lesbian and Gay Rights Project in 1986). Working along-side renowned gay community leaders such as Morris Kight (cofounder of the Gay Liberation Front and the Gay Community Center in 1971 [now known as the Los Angeles LGBT Center], Kight served as a member of the LACCHR for two decades), the commission is most known for devel-oping cross-cultural coalitional building strategies, in cooperation with the LAPD, to address violence targeting historically marginalized minori-tarian communities (e.g., Network Against Hate Crimes, est. 1984). The invocation of "community" by institutions such as LACCHR has meant selectively partnering with minority-based civil rights organizations such as the Anti-Defamation League of B'nai B'rith, the Asian Pacific American Legal Center, and the Los Angeles LGBT Center to participate in the collec-tive labor of identifying violence through *identificatory inclusion* into systems of carcerality. Such inclusion into carceral systems and logics has come to model a kind of depoliticization and deradicalization of a critical identity politics that otherwise is expressly meant to shed light on how power is abused by the elite.[8] Conscription into coalitional labor of "identifying violence" for and on behalf of policing has only reproduced a penalty-first ideology resulting from a multiculturalist endorsement of state-based antivi-olence strategies, requiring only the constant reform of carceral technologies for improving practices toward *counting* violence.

Over the last three decades, Los Angeles has continued to chart a legacy for itself as a model city and county for progressive LGBT-friendly social services, and as led by the Los Angeles LGBT Center, the larg-est service-providing LGBT center in the world. The center, like the LACCHR, is built upon tenets of community safety as requiring some form of community policing and thus constant deferral to the power of agencies such as the LAPD, West Hollywood Police Department, and LASD to lead the way in gay- and transgender-affirming reforms in policing, arrest, and imprisonment. Yet, even with such incremental LGBT-inclusive and progressive police and jail reforms, Los Angeles continues to destabilize queer and trans anticarceral antiviolence coalitions through efforts to secure transgender-sensitive policing and imprisonment using models of community-police partnerships, or "relation-based" policing. The strategy of relation-based policing, as part of a multipronged effort to rebrand community policing, relies on the tactic of selectively designating a set of cooperative community stakeholders to form community-police partnerships. Such efforts result in law enforcing and state agencies exerting power via the domineering momentum of the criminal punishment system, keeping community organizations, social service agencies, civil rights associations, human relations commissions, and academic researchers in alignment with their priorities. Though many of these community-centered entities might in fact remain well-intentioned in the shared endeavor to address civil rights violations and injustice at the level of bias-motivated violence, such coalitional efforts are often misspent in the arena of speculating, tracking, managing, and inoculating "social risk" through existing penal technologies such as "community inclusive" crime reporting and data.

A key example of carceral coalition-building was showcased when LAPD Chief Charlie Beck unveiled the new and improved LAPD transgender policing guidelines entitled "Office of the Chief of Police: Police Interaction with Transgender Individuals" on April 12, 2012, to a celebratory crowd at the Lesbian, Gay, Bisexual, and Transgender Community Forum.[9] The three-page memo was crafted as a collaboration between the Los Angeles mayor's office, members of the LAPD, legal advocates, academics, as well as transgender community members selected by the City of Los Angeles Human Relations Commission's official "Transgender Working Group." The memo opens with the stated purpose of "establish[ing] procedures that create mutual understanding, prevent discrimination and conflict, and ensure the appropriate treatment of transgender individuals" (Beck 2012). LAPD's collaboration with entities such as the City of Los Angeles Human Relations Commission (HRC) is customary, given that one of HRC's central aims is to foster "meaningful engagement and trust-building between Los Angeles law enforcement and communities around complex neighborhood problems—especially those related to race, gender, culture, and social status—and ultimately translate this trust into sustained and systemic policy or programs that transform police-community relations" (HRC, n.d.). HRC's Transgender Working Group, now renamed Transgender Advisory Council (TAC), is tasked as a liaison between transgender communities and law enforcement, through initiatives such as LAPD's memo on improving transgender interactions. Antiviolence initiatives, as hosted by TAC, are predetermined through a model of "coalition building" through hand-selected working groups and "community stakeholders" vetted by law-enforcing institutions.

An example of the carceral continuum of gender-affirmation within the LAPD memo is perfectly summarized in one of the opening recommendations, stating, "non-traditional gender identities and gender expressions do not constitute reasonable suspicion or prima facie evidence that an individual is or has engaged in prostitution or any other crime" (Beck 2012, 2). This guideline gestures to the century-long legacy in which LAPD has outright criminalized sexual and or gender nonconformity (from the Anti-Masquerading Ordinance of 1889 to Rule No. 9 in 1967), and in the present, transgender and cisgender women of color in or suspected of working in the sex economy. The memo does not take issue with the criminalization of sex work itself, nor does it advise against the hypersurveillance of gendered forms of racialization. Rather, the memo simply suggests that "gender identity" in itself should not "constitute reasonable suspicion or prima facie evidence." Such a singular-identity-based proclamation disassembles and dematerializes the inextricability of race with gender—that is, gender as always already racialized and race as always already gendered. In other words, gender presentation should not rise to the level of constituting reasonable suspicion, yet the constancy of LAPD's racial profiling and racially motivated violence continues to be rejected by the agency itself as unfounded (Queally and Poston 2020).

Replying to a question from the audience concerning the persisting police discrimination against trans communities, and in reference to future disciplinary action for failure to adhere to the memo guidelines set forth, then LAPD Chief Beck stated proudly, "*This* [LAPD] *is a para-military organization. Following rules is part of what we base our core values on*" (Ocamb 2012). Paramilitary values for Beck is likely a nod to the hierarchical obedience within fraternal order organizations such as the LAPD. However, police accountability and disciplinary action in response to offenses by individual officers rely on evidence of wrongdoing in the first place, wrongdoing that is far too often rebuffed and mitigated by claims of discretionary judgment by police. Police accountability as a genre of performative accountability is at best a symbolic slap on the wrist, wholly disaggregated from the violent institutions and structures that condition, perpetuate, and organize the possibility of antiqueer and anti-trans violence in the first place. Beck's self-congratulatory claim of being a "para-military organization" is accordingly substantiated by the ongoing efforts by LAPD to intensify police relations internationally between "progressive" militarized law-enforcement agencies across the globe. LAPD's transnational policing and counterterrorism efforts alongside LGBT-progressive police reforms remain two sides of the same carceral coin—co-constitutive efforts to advance carceral technologies for targeting and criminalizing poverty and racialized embodiment.[10] Yet the constancy of state-based and interpersonal violence and premature death faced by queer, trans, Black, and Indigenous people of color (QTBIPoC) persists.

Over the span of just five months in Los Angeles from 2014 to 2015, the premature and brutal deaths of three transgender women of color resurfaced long-standing political rifts in the QTBIPoC community along the lines of either divestment or reinvestment in criminal policy and legislation via a call for prosecution of "anti-trans hate crimes." Zoraida Ale Reyes was a well-admired twenty-eight-year-old Latinx queer/trans immigrant undocumented activist who was often described as "fearless," someone who was "making the biggest sacrifices and dreaming the biggest dreams";[11] Aniya Knee "Asia" Parker, a fifty-four-year-old Black femme elder, was described by her family as "with a heart of gold, befriending everybody, and a good heart. A giver with a sense of humor";[12] Deshawnda Ta-ta Sanchez was a twenty-one-year-old aspiring fashion design student who was known for her creative passion and participation in the Los Angeles LGBT Center's youth programs (Ryan and Cheng 2014; Santa Cruz 2015). In each of their cases, their transgender identity was debated by presiding law enforcement and mainstream journalists alike, as to whether or not it was a leading factor that led to their demise. However, for QTBIPoC communities mourning these three women, the somber reality was that anti-trans and antiqueer violence remains a constant under racial capitalism. QTBIPoC communities in Los Angeles and the surrounding areas, along with the women's families of origin, hosted direct action marches, vigils, and memorials in order to raise both ruckus and awareness of the persistent climate of unsafety faced by trans women of color. With collective grief and rage funneled into collective action following the stolen lives of Zoraida, Aniya, and Deshawnda, the long-standing political tensions concerning the strategy and demand for police to "do their jobs" resurfaced.

Breaking free from patriarchy's progeny of penalization, transformative justice, and abolition feminism asks us what might be possible in terms of truly disrupting cyclical harm and violence if we choose instead to center the needs of those who have suffered violence directly, endured nonconsensual and uninvited pain, and whose bodies have become the archive of routinized harm. In other words, what is made possible when antiviolence requires an engagement with community and survivor-centered strategies that seek to both deter and interrupt violence beyond the coercive practices of producing quantifiable evidence from one's body to induce a level of support and accountability? What would it have looked like if Zoraida, Aniya, or Deshawnda knew that robust and unwavering community support would have descended upon them, without question, if they were ever in need of a ride share, a communal safety plan when left feeling vulnerable, and the ability to locate all the desired and necessary resources for their health, housing, food, embodied joy, and rest? What mechanisms of community safety could be possible if it did not require the surveilling and interrogating of a survivor to prove the harm they endured, furnishing acceptable identification or proof of citizenship, or being criminalized for their mode of economic survival? What could be possible if we would dare to ask that their lives mean something before death, before violence, and beyond being counted as data points?

In sum, by focusing on three particular strands of state-based "gender-responsive" carceral strategies in Los Angeles that have been revered as progressive wins—trans imprisonment, trans protection, and trans policing—the concept of *carceral coalitions* aims to narrate how racial liberalism, or liberal law-and-order strategies of organizing community coalitions, has only stealthily strong-armed select representatives (a rainbow coalition of model minoritized subjects) from their respective communities to both form and reform minoritized political identities within the spaces and logics of carcerality. In the end, the book manuscript is a story of how even a "trans-of-color politics," one that is intersectional, coalitional, and touts antiviolence, is no less susceptible to the encroachment and ever-pervasive will of the state: law, order, and carcerality. In other words, when coalitional antiviolence politics are not rooted in a kind of prefigurative politics that centers visionary world-making outside of systems of punishment, then carceral systems of punishment of the state will continue to prefigure coalitional politics to no end.

## Acknowledgments

Brief sections from this short piece have been taken from my full-length, peer-reviewed article entitled "Don't Count on Us Dying: Carceral Accuracy and Trans-of-Color Life Beyond Hate Crimes," which is featured in *QED: A Journal in GLBTQ Worldmaking* 9, no. 3, special issue, "Queer Healing and Transformative Justice" (Spring 2023).

**Ren-yo Hwang** (they/them) is an assistant professor in gender studies and critical social thought at Mount Holyoke College. Their scholarship examines late twentieth-century carceral technologies, abolition, transformative justice, and QTBIPoC antiviolence activism and visual cultures of resistance. Their scholarship is published or forthcoming in *Abolition Feminisms Vol. 2*, *QED: Journal of GLBTQ Worldmaking*, *Foucault Studies*, *Transgender Studies Quarterly*, and *Critical Ethnic Studies Journal*. They currently serve on the board of Dignity Power Now and are a member of the anticarceral support network Trans Advocacy Group (TAG). They can be reached at rhwang@mtholyoke.edu.

## Notes

1. For more on K6G, see Dolovich 2011, 2012; Robinson 2011; and Spade 2012.
2. The article states, "The gay wing is a far less dangerous, more humane place to be. Unlike the angry, racially polarized culture of Men's Central Jail, in K6G many of the inmates help one another face their days, and sometimes their years, together" (Ucar 2014).
3. I use the concept of *palliation* alongside Louise Tam's (2022) work on *palliative states*.
4. The Los Angeles Sheriff's Department's "Custody Division Manual" explains the connection of litigation activism in establishing the classification-based housing system used internally, stating, "The classification and housing of gay, gender non-conforming, intersex, and transgender inmates is also established in connection with, and shall adhere to, the legal settlement of Robertson, Belisle, and Rumph v. Sherman Block et al. (1985) 82 1442 WPG" (189).
5. K6G is argued in the book project as an early iteration of SB-132. See State of California 2020.
6. For a complete look at the recommendations, please see Los Angeles County 2021.
7. For more, see JusticeLA, n.d. b. Also see Los Angeles County, n.d.
8. For more on identity politics and elitism, see Táíwò 2022.
9. Sociologist and professor of criminology and law Valerie Jenness, a contributor to shaping the guidelines, describes the event: "Los Angeles Police Department (LAPD) rolled out to the community new guidelines governing

police interactions with transgender individuals, with Chief Charlie Beck there to help usher in a new era in community relations. I was gratified to help write this historic policy, watch LA's 'top cop' affirm its importance, and celebrate the adoption of this policy with the very community that stands to benefit from it." She continues, adding to her quote given to the Associated Press, "Policies like this codify an organization's values and express them to the community. The LAPD is trying to commit to respecting the transgender community with its policies. I wish policies like this had been in place a long time ago" (Jenness 2014, 8).

10. "The Los Angeles Police Department is one of the largest and most innovative law enforcement agencies in the world. It is responsible for providing police service to an area encompassing 468 square miles and 21 community areas, representing approximately over 4 million residents as of 2016." Los Angeles Police Foundation, n.d., "Organization Flow Chart."

11. Alexa Vasquez of FAMILIA: Trans Queer Liberation Movement, as quoted in Quezada 2014. Reyes, once a student of the University of California, Santa Barbara, could not remain so due to her undocumented status. She would later re-enroll in school through a local community college. She worked on undocumented student issues with organizations such as El Movimiento Estudiantil Chicanos de Aztlan (MEChA), 50 Orange County Dream Team, and De Colores Queer Orange County. For more, see Silvestre 2017. See also Boster 2022.

12. This quote is taken from the family's fundraising page, "Aniya Parker Funeral Fund" (https://www.gofundme.com/f/aniyaparker) to raise money to transport Aniya's body back to Arkansas for burial. The deadname and the nickname "Ballie" is used by the family, but I have opted to omit this since the queer Los Angeles community has insisted that Aniya and or her nickname of Asia be used when addressing her in life and posthumously.

## Works Cited

Agrawal, Nina. 2017. "Black Lives Matter, Other Activists Protest to Stop Jail Expansion." *Los Angeles Times*, September 26, 2017. https://www.latimes.com/local/lanow/la-me-ln-black-lives-matter-protests-jail-expansion-20170926-story.html.

Beck, Charlie. 2012. "Office of the Chief of Police: Police Interaction with Transgender Individuals." Office of the Chief of Police, Los Angeles Police Department, April 10, 2012. http://lapd-assets.lapdonline.org/assets/pdf/OCOP_04-10-12.pdf.

Boster, Mark. 2014. "Zoraida Reyes Remembered." *Los Angeles Times,* June 24, 2014. https://www.latimes.com/local/lanow/la-me-ln-zoraida-reyes-photos-photogallery.html.

Dolovich, Sharon. 2011. "Strategic Segregation in the Modern Prison." *American Criminal Law Review* 48, no. 1: 1–110.

———. 2012. "Two Models of the Prison: Accidental Humanity and Hypermasculinity in the L.A. County Jail." *Journal of Criminal Law & Criminology* 102, no. 4: 965–1117.

HRC. n.d. "The Human Relations Commission: Who Are We?" Human Relations Commission, City of Los Angeles. Accessed January 22, 2022. https://housing.lacity.org/community-resources/human-relations-commission.

Jenness, Valerie. 2014. "Pesticides, Prisoners, and Policy: Complexity and Praxis in Research on Transgender Prisoners and Beyond." *Sociological Perspectives* 57, no. 1 (March): 8.

Justice Care and Opportunities Department (JCOD). n.d. "About Us." Accessed November 15, 2022. https://jcod.lacounty.gov/about-us/.

JusticeLA Coalition (JLA). n.d. a. "Who We Are." JusticeLA. Accessed November 15, 2022. https://justicelanow.org/about/.

———. n.d. b. "2022 ATI Report Card." JusticeLA. Accessed November 15, 2022. https://justicelanow.org/2022-ati-reportcard/.

Los Angeles County Alternative to Incarceration (ATI) Work Group. 2020. "Care First, Jails Last: Health and Racial Justice Strategies for Safer Communities." March 2020. https://ceo.lacounty.gov/wp content/uploads/2020/10/1077045_AlternativestoIncarcerationWorkGroupFinalReport.pdf.

———. n.d. Los Angeles County, Chief Executive Office Alternatives to Incarceration (CEO-ATI). Accessed November 15, 2022. https://ceo.lacounty.gov/ati/.

Los Angeles Police Foundation and the Los Angeles Police Department. n.d. "LAPD Organization Chart." Accessed January 13, 2023. https://www.lapdonline.org/lapd-organization-chart/.

Los Angeles Sheriff's Department. 2021. *Custody Division Manual,* vol. 5, "Line Procedures," section 5-02/050.00, "Classification, Screening, and Housing of Gay, Gender Non-Conforming, Intersex, and Transgender Inmates." July 22, 2021. https://pars.lasd.org/Viewer/Manuals/14249.

Ocamb, Karen. 2012. "LAPD Announces Historic New Trans Guidelines & Policies." *Bilerico Project,* April 14, 2012. https://bilerico.lgbtqnation.com/2012/04/lapd_announces_historic_new_trans_guidelines_polic.php.

Queally, Ames, and Ben Poston. 2020. "For Years, California Police Agencies Have Rejected Almost Every Racial Profiling Complaint They Received." *Los Angeles Times*, December 14, 2020.

Quezada, Janet Arelis. "Local Activists Mourn Slain Transgender and Immigrant Rights Warrior, Zoraida 'Ale' Reyes." *GLAAD*. June 13, 2014. https://www.glaad.org/blog/local-activists-mourn-slain-transgender-and-immigrant-rights-warrior-zoraida-ale-reyes.

Robinson, Russell K. 2011. "Masculinity as Prison: Sexual Identity, Race, and Incarceration." *California Law Review* 99, no. 5: 1309–1408.

Ryan, Kennedy, and Kimberly Cheng. 2014. "Transgender Woman Shot, Killed while Pounding on Door of South L.A. Home for Help." *KTLA*, December 4, 2014. http://ktla.com/2014/12/04/transgender-woman-shot-killed-while-pounding-on-door-of-compton-home-for-help.

Santa Cruz, Nicole. 2015. "Last Words of Transgender Woman Killed in South L.A. Key to Probe, Police Say." *Los Angeles Times*, February 26, 2015. http://www.latimes.com/local/lanow/la-me-ln-arrest-death-transgender-woman-20150226-story.html.

Silvestre, Adriana. 2017. "Whispers of Joy: Undocumented Trans Narratives." MA thesis, University of California, Los Angeles.

Spade, Dean. 2012. "The Only Way to End Racialized Gender Violence in Prisons Is to End Prisons: A Response to Russell Robinson's 'Masculinity as Prison.'" *California Law Review Circuit*, no. 3: 182–93.

State of California, Senate. 2020. *An Act to Add Sections 2605 and 2606 to the Penal Code, Relating to Corrections*, Senate Bill no. 132, chapter 182, filed with the Secretary of State, September 26, 2020, approved by Governor, September 26, 2020. https://leginfo.legislature.ca.gov/faces/billTextClient.xhtml?bill_id=201920200SB132.

Táíwò, Olúfẹ́mi O. 2022. *Elite Capture: How the Powerful Took Over Identity Politics (and Everything Else)*. Chicago: Haymarket Books.

Tam, Louise. 2022. "Palliative States: Migrant Advocacy and Necrocapitalistic Care in Canadian Mental Health Services." PhD diss., Rutgers University.

Ucar, Ani. 2014. "In the Gay Wing of L.A. Men's Central Jail, It's Not Shanks and Muggings but Hand-Sewn Gowns and Tears." *LA Weekly*, November 18, 2014. https://www.laweekly.com/in-the-gay-wing-of-l-a-mens-central-jail-its-not-shanks-and-muggings-but-hand-sewn-gowns-and-tears/.

# Black Liberals, the Cold War Straight State, and the Politics of Ambivalence

Jennifer Dominique Jones

**Abstract:** This essay recounts how two civil rights organizations—the National Association for the Advancement of Colored People and the National Urban League—encountered and responded to antiqueer state practices and policies during the Cold War era. It draws upon my forthcoming monograph *Ambivalent Affinities: A Political History of Blackness and Homosexuality after World War II* (University of North Carolina Press), which contends that the modern civil rights movement and the white supremacist backlash to it were crucial arenas in which ideas about Blackness and homosexuality (often defined as same-sex intimacy and gender dissidence) were discursively linked. In this essay, I argue that Black liberals not only encountered politicized concepts of homosexuality, but that their responses, at times, were ambivalent and responsive to a heteronormative state that increasingly criminalized and penalized queer subjects. A work of Black feminist and queer history, this article contributes to a rich interdisciplinary literature that interrogates how anti-Black violence (interpersonal and structural) occurred in gendered and sexual realms with legacies that reverberate into the twenty-first century. **Keywords:** Black Freedom Struggle; civil rights; queer history; Black liberalism; the state

During the waning days of August 1963, activists Anne "Essie Mae" Moody, Joan Trumpauer, the Reverend Ed King, and Jeanette King returned to Canton, Mississippi, after attending the historic March on Washington for Jobs and Freedom. They joined over 250,000 Americans of various backgrounds in the nation's capital to articulate their support for federal civil rights legislation. The dangers of traveling as an interracial party in the South prompted them to spend a night sleeping in Rev. King's vehicle at a "federal park in the Tennessee mountains." Upon waking, Moody, who was Black,

*WSQ: Women's Studies Quarterly* 51: 1 & 2 (Spring/Summer 2023)

and Trumpauer, who was white, decided to use the public showers and changing rooms to wash away the proverbial dust of the road. However, two white female travelers—"from Georgia"—thwarted their efforts to travel unmolested. Upon entering the space, the two white travelers encountered the interracial pair nude and drying each other off with paper towels. Moody remembered their shocked and disgusted response to this public display of interracial same-sex intimacy. She recounted:

> They didn't know how to react. It was a shock to them. Here we were, a black girl and a white girl, standing in a Southern Public shower naked. I guess they thought we were having a "nude-in" or "wash-in" or something. Anyway, they didn't stay around to watch the demonstration. (Moody 1968, 332)

According to Moody, their presence in a public shower functioned as an unintentional political demonstration that challenged the anti-Blackness that so often marked interstate travel nationwide and especially in the South. However, her comments also suggest that their nudity and intimacy transgressed not only racial norms but sexual norms as well. The possible assumption that the two were civil rights activists engaged in a sexual encounter was timely. Days before the March on Washington, segregationist South Carolina Senator Strom Thurmond sought to undermine the moral character of the civil rights movement by publicizing the morals charge conviction of Bayard Rustin, the deputy director of the march, a decade earlier. The charge proved effective, not only because many Americans viewed same-sex intimacy as nonnormative, but because homosexuality was stigmatized and criminalized by the various laws, policies, and political narratives that suffused the Cold War United States. This context may have shaped the encounter in the Tennessee washroom that August day, and what occurred next. As Moody and Trumpauer waited for the Kings in their vehicle, the two women approached the pair. Accompanied by several other white women, the group gestured towards the interracial duo, seemingly trying to discern their relationship to each other. After several minutes, Rev. and Mrs. King returned from the restrooms, got into the vehicle, and the party drove away. Trumpauer and Moody laughed as they peered at the confused bystanders out of their rear window. Moody shared her friend's conclusion that "at that point it dawned on them that we were, in their language, professional agitators" (Moody 1968, 332–34).

I begin with this relatively minor anecdote in Moody's memoir *Coming of Age in Mississippi* because it illustrates the ways in which civil rights organizers encountered narratives that linked their activism with sexual deviancy and transgression. A rich historiography documents long-standing characterizations of Black intimacies and interracial sex as deviant (Brown 1996; Morgan 2004; Rosen 2009; Haley 2016). Moreover, participants within the civil rights movement and the ideologically broader Black Freedom Struggle navigated material forms of sexual and gender-based violence as well as discourses of sexual immorality (Romano 2003; Dailey 2004, 119–44; McGuire 2010). However, the response of the white travelers from Georgia indexes a particular variation of this discourse—namely, that support for civil rights and homosexual behavior were fellow travelers (Howard 1999; Leighton 2013).

My forthcoming monograph *Ambivalent Affinities: A Political History of Blackness and Homosexuality after World War II* (University of North Carolina Press) attends to a broader set of ideological, material, and political crossings, namely how the postwar Black Freedom Struggle, and challenges to it, served as important arenas where ideas about Blackness and homosexuality were linked together. In *Ambivalent Affinities* I argue that particular articulations of Blackness and homosexuality as political identities were mutually referential and, to a degree, co-constitutive. Not in the language of shared or intersecting identities, but rather in the rhetoric of what Nayan Shah calls *estrangements*—that is, the processes through which certain individuals are marked by differentiation, subjected to policing, and excluded from social, political, and economic privileges (Shah 2018, 262–63). While these linked articulations of Blackness and homosexuality emerged largely outside the realm of state action, they were profoundly undergirded by the anti-Blackness and heteronormativity of law, policy, and state practices. Indeed, this book attends to a critical moment of simultaneity during the five decades after World War II—namely, that at the same time that the multifaceted, polyvocal Black Freedom Struggle labored to dismantle the variegated tentacles of white supremacy at the federal, state, and local levels, entities and individuals in all three arenas helped forge a powerful (if incomplete) binary between homosexuality and heterosexuality, in which the former was criminalized, pathologized, and stigmatized and the later promoted, protected, and privileged.

Like Moody and her companions, Black liberals encountered intersecting forms of policing and disparagement at the height of the Cold War era, in which support for civil rights was linked to communist sympathies and sexual immorality. Like Moody and her companions, Black liberals responded in profoundly context-specific ways when homosexuality (as a set of behaviors and as a positionality policed by the state) crossed paths with their pursuits of racial equality and Black political empowerment. When this occurred, Black liberal activists, political organizations, and later, elected officials enacted a series of context-specific and, at times, ambivalent responses to state-sponsored forms of heteronormative and white supremacist action. The context of these encounters shifted between the 1950s and 1960s and the 1970s and 1980s.

As this brief article suggests, during the two decades after the Second World War, Black liberals encountered homosexuality in the particular context of Cold War politics and homophobia. In the 1970s and 1980s, these engagements shifted as gay and lesbian activists sought access generally to municipal levers of power. These activists and some Black elected officials developed a sense of similar marginalization and shared political adversaries, nurturing at times fragile alliances (Hanhardt 2013; Stewart-Winter 2017). Across these periods, I characterize their approach to (homo)sexual matters as largely pragmatic. While this approach created opportunities to challenge homophobia reflected in law, policy, and politics, I argue that, in general, collective and individual action tended to align with the heteronormativity of the broader society. This is due, in part, to the long-standing historic vulnerability of Black communities to narratives of sexual and gender deviance, in part through state involvement within family life and marriage. Crucially, their actions responded to the heteronormativity of the state (Roberts 1997; Hunter 2019; Kadaswamy 2021). In what follows, I offer a brief analysis of two moments in which Black liberal organizations encountered the heteronormative power of the state and adopted two differential strategies in response.

### The NAACP Encounters the Sexual Exclusion of the State

The National Association for the Advancement of Colored People (NAACP) encountered the anti-homosexual apparatus of the state during its advocacy to expand African American access to military service and social welfare programs in the 1940s. Founded in 1909, the NAACP emerged from the Second World War as one of the most important political organizations advancing racial equality and the inclusion of African

Americans in mainstream life. While the NAACP acted as a vocal proponent of Black service members throughout the war, it was the creation of its
Veterans Affairs Bureau in January 1945 that institutionalized their advocacy
on behalf of African Americans currently and formerly enlisted in the military. Attorney and former trial judge advocate Jesse O. Dedmon Jr. served
as the first (and only) secretary of the organization.[1] Under his leadership
from 1945 to 1949, the bureau addressed thousands of allegations of racial
discrimination in the army and navy and sought to assist individual veterans seeking medical care, GI benefits, and employment opportunities.

The NAACP's Veterans Affairs Bureau spent a significant amount
of time and energy challenging undesirable discharges, also known as
blue discharges for the colored paper upon which they were printed.
These removals from service technically existed as an intermediate form
of discharge between an honorable discharge (for good or exemplary
service) and a dishonorable discharge (for a conviction in military court).
However, blue discharges were often punitive in that they targeted those
who exhibited behavior understood to be deficiencies of character, including alcoholism, drug addiction, chronic lying, and sexual psychopathy
(which included homosexuality) (Bérubé 2010, 139–40). Two groups
disproportionately received this discharge: African Americans and alleged
homosexuals. Black military personnel who challenged discriminatory
treatment were often targeted with removals from service by racist officers.
African Americans—who constituted less than 10 percent of those serv-
ing in the armed forces—received 22 percent of blue discharges (Bérubé
2010, 139–40).[2] However, it was the second group—those removed for
alleged homosexual behavior—that became most publicly associated
with blue discharges. While the military had long prosecuted sodomy and
buccal coitus (oral sex) under the Articles of War, the adoption of the blue
discharge was, at first, an act of reform during the interwar years meant to
avoid overly penalizing those diagnosed with homosexuality, which was
pathologized as a mental illness (Bérubé 2010, 128–48). However, the association between homosexuality and blue discharges deepened during the
war, creating the taint of sexual deviancy even on veterans removed for
other offences.

In the NAACP's records of their advocacy work, the vast majority of
veterans' correspondence does not specify the cause of the undesirable
removal from service. However, a handful of documents do indicate homosexuality as the cause for removal. In these instances, individual veterans and

their advocates brought their petitions to the bureau.[3] And, in these cases, it seems that Dedmon and his associates challenged their discharges and thus the homophobic military and social welfare policies of the state. They did so in two ways. First, it appears that the Veterans Affairs Bureau sought to overturn removals from service that emerged from allegations of homosexual behavior. In doing so, they were one of the few organizations that supported veterans of any background who challenged the legality of punitive federal measures against those accused of homosexuality (Canaday 2009, 157–58). Second, in seeking to revoke Black veterans' blue discharges, they sought to increase the number of African Americans who could receive the benefits associated with the Servicemen's Readjustment Act of 1944. Popularly known as the GI Bill of Rights, this legislation bestowed an array of benefits to veterans and their families, including job training, subsidized life insurance, and access to health care, as well as loans to attend college, create small businesses, and purchase homes or farms (Bérubé 2010, 139–40). However, the state's administering bureaucracy, the Veterans Administration, regularly denied benefits to those removed for alleged homosexual behavior and, in the South especially, to African American veterans (Woods 2013).[4] In helping Black veterans removed for homosexuality, the NAACP's Veterans Affairs Bureau challenged the state's anti-Black and anti-homosexual policies as well as offered critical support to a doubly marginalized group of former service members.

Notably, this moment of challenge by Black veterans and their advocates in the NAACP was short-lived. In 1948, three years after the creation of the bureau, the NAACP's national leadership believed that the auxiliary was no longer necessary. In a letter dated August 10, NAACP Executive Secretary Walter White informed Dedmon that "the question which has been raised on several occasions by members of the Board [is] whether or not the necessity of a Veterans' Bureau has not about ended."[5] Despite Dedmon's protests that the need for the department's efforts continued to be great, the bureau closed the following year. While the integration of the military seemed to spur the push to close this entity, it is more than likely that the narrowing political vision of the NAACP during the deepening hold of Cold War conservatism discouraged its continuing operation. The moderating influence of anti-communist sentiments within and outside of the NAACP resulted in its espousal of anti-left rhetoric by the early 1950s.[6] The related rise of the Lavender Scare during the late 1940s, in which the federal government increasingly sought to remove alleged homosexuals from civilian and military employment, combined with the prominent tendency to associate political subversion with same-sex desire, more than likely inhibited any challenges to the homophobic apparatus of the state (Dean 2001; Johnson 2004).

### The National Urban League and Politically Efficacious Uses of Homophobic Policing

Several years after the NAACP's Veterans Affairs Bureau closed, another civil rights organization, the National Urban League (NUL), encountered the state's efforts to police sexual dissidence. Notably, the NUL encountered this policing through the arrest and conviction of a white supremacist adversary, John W. Hamilton—an arrest and conviction the organization was able to use to their political advantage. Hamilton was a St. Louis–based demagogue whose anti-NUL rhetoric threatened many of the organization's chapters. A Boston native who moved to Missouri to follow radical right and anti-communist warrior Gerald L. K. Smith, Hamilton formed an anti-communist and explicitly white supremacist organization, the National Citizens Protective Association (NCPA), in the early 1950s. The group targeted the NUL for their largely moderate stance on civil rights and philanthropic work. More pointedly, these segregationists characterized the organization as promoting not only integration but interracial sex that might result in mixed-race offspring.[7] In 1956, the NCPA initiated a series of boycott campaigns of Urban League chapters across the South. This campaign proved highly effective, with five municipal chapters of the Urban League barred from participating in local philanthropic drives associated with another organization, the Community Chest, including chapters in Jacksonville, Florida, and Norfolk, Virginia.[8] The national leadership of the Urban League crafted a coordinated response, including working with local Community Chest chapters and press outlets to clarify the aims of the League. However, none of these strategies proved particularly effective.[9]

It was, instead, the arrest of Hamilton on a morals charge that provided the League with a powerful weapon to undermine this adversary. On October 13, 1956, Hamilton was arrested and charged with having sex with a male minor. News of the arrest quickly reached the national leadership of the Urban League, who decided to share the news clipping with Southern chapters, the national Community Chest leadership, and key press outlets. NUL leaders only issued one public statement about Hamilton's arrest.[10]

Executive Secretary Lester B. Granger mentioned Hamilton's sexual as well as political misdeeds in his *New York Amsterdam News* column in November 1956. He characterized the charges as "impairing the morals of a male minor—sex perversion, to put it bluntly."[11]

The NUL, then, did not simply publicize the arrest of an opponent for a sexual crime. Instead, the organization engaged in a contemporary, common, and highly effective offensive strategy used across the political spectrum, namely alleging that a political opponent engaged in homosexual behavior and (in this instance) publicizing their arrest on a morals charge. In publicizing Hamilton's arrest, the NUL demonstrated a keen understanding of the role of sexuality in Cold War domestic politics, wherein the allegedly sexually nonnormative and predatory nature of various types of radicals (communists, antiracists) could be mapped onto the bodies of specific individuals (Freedman 1987, 83–106; Chauncey 1993, 160–79; Jenkins 1998; Dean 2001, 63–168). While it is likely that the leadership of the NUL publicized Hamilton's arrest out of genuine moral censure, that alone does not explain the deliberate way in which they sought to promulgate and profit from this incident by widely sharing information about the arrest with mainstream and Black newspapers, local Community Chest chapters, and their own membership. The campaign, it seems, proved effective, preventing further grassroots attacks on Urban League chapters.

### Conclusion

In centering Cold War–era Black liberal encounters with sites of anti-homosexual policing and punishment, I argue that a kind of ambivalence marked their efforts. On the one hand, these individuals and organizations regularly prioritized specific objectives rather than embrace respectability (with its claims to sexual and gender normativity) for its own sake. These challenges were varied and included challenging heteronormative (and homophobic) law, policy, and custom and, in a later moment not addressed here, forging alliances with gay and lesbian political communities as well as embracing a more expansive vision of Black intimate life beyond respectability. On the other hand, the power of normative gender and sexual definitions continued to exert influence over Black liberal decision-making. Black liberals possessed a keen understanding of the centrality of grammars of deviance to white supremacist articulations of anti-Blackness. More broadly, they understood how the state's power to police, punish, and exclude unfolded across varied forms of marginalized positionalities, including sexual and gender dissidence. Understanding their responses to such harm—whether propagated by state actors or implicitly supported via state policies and practices—allows for a fuller understanding of the complicated legacies of Black liberal engagements with heteronormativity during the middle of the twentieth century and beyond.

## Acknowledgments

I would like to thank Dayo F. Gore and Christina B. Hanhardt for the invitation to submit this piece and their incredibly helpful feedback, as well as the *Women's Studies Quarterly* editorial staff for their efforts.

**Jennifer Dominique Jones** is an assistant professor of history and women's and gender studies at the University of Michigan. A Black feminist historian, her work centers Black queer communities and histories of gender, sexuality, and race in the twentieth-century United States. Her book *Ambivalent Affinities: A Political History of Blackness and Homosexuality after World War II* is forthcoming in the Justice, Power, and Politics Series at the University of North Carolina Press. She can be reached at jonejenn@umich.edu.

## Notes

1. For more on Veterans Affairs, see "Capt. Dedmon Named NAACP Vet's Secretary," *New York Amsterdam News*, December 30, 1944, 5A; "Veterans Secretary Named by NAACP," *New Journal and Guide*, January 6, 1945, 3; "Named Vets' Secretary," *Chicago Defender*, January 6, 1945, 9; and "NAACP Veterans' Secretary Named," *Baltimore Afro-American*, January 6, 1945, 3.
2. The one most often leveled at Black servicemen was the Section VIII discharge (especially 615-360, and 615-368/369). The navy did not have specific regulations but issued directives that urged for the discharge of "habitual homosexuals." For more on this, see Bérubé 2010.
3. For examples, see Elon Bruce to Jesse Dedmon, June 27, 1947, fol. Discharge Reviews "B" 1945–50, II: G6, National Association for the Advancement of Colored People Records, LC; Attar T. Gibson to Judge Advocate General's Office, May 7, 1947, fol. Discharge Reviews "G" 1945–50, II: G7, National Association for the Advancement of Colored People Records, LC; Case of Alfred Harrison, fol. Discharge Reviews "H" 1945–50, II: G7; and Case of James Perkins, fol. Discharge Review Perkins, James 1947, II: G8, National Association for the Advancement of Colored People Records, LC.

4. For more about the Veterans Affairs Bureau and their work to challenge residential segregation, see Woods 2013. Also see Minutes of the Meeting of the Board of Directors, October 9, 1944, fol. Board of Directors: Inauguration of Veterans' Affairs, I: A-148, National Association for the Advancement of Colored People Records, LC.

5. Walter White to Jesse O. Dedmon, August 10, 1948; Jesse O. Dedmon to Walter White, September 10, 1948, fol. General Correspondence cont. July–December 1948, II: G11, National Association for the Advancement of Colored People Records, LC.

6. For an account of the winnowing political vision of the NAACP during the early Cold War years, see Anderson 2003. The literature on Black radicalism during the 1930s, 1940s, and 1950s is large. For some key works on this period, see Horne 1986, Kelley 1990, Kelley 2003, Ransby 2003, Gore 2011, McDuffie 2011, and Harris 2012.

7. For more on the NAACP's engagement with interracial couples and miscegenation as well as general histories of interracial marriage and miscegenation law, see Romano 2003, Pascoe 2009, Stein 2010. Pascoe's text has the most complete discussion of the NAACP's engagement with miscegenation law.

8. For example, see Flier, n.d., "Where Does Your Money Go: 58 Chests- Funds Support Anti-White Urban League," in United Community Funds and Councils of American memorandum dated February 19, 1958, fol. United Community and Councils 1956–1959, I:B14, National Urban League Records, Manuscript Division, Library of Congress, Washington, DC.

9. For specific mention of NUL strategies for organizing with social work and organized labor, see Nelson C. Jackson, memorandum, "Southern Trip February 28–March 21, 1956," to Urban League Executives, April 16, 1956, fol. United Community Funds and Councils 1956–1959, I: B14, National Urban League Records, Manuscript Division, LC.; Nelson C. Jackson, memorandum, "Attacks against the Urban League for Use at St. Louis Meeting," to Lester B. Granger, May 16, 1956, fol. Subversion and the UL Memoranda General 1956, I: A49, National Urban League Records; "Negro-Aid Group Will Lose Funds," *New York Times*, September 15, 1956, 6; "States Rights Group Would Bar League Aid," *Norfolk Journal and Guide*, October 27, 1956, box 4, Urban League of St. Louis, WUSL.

10. The account of the alleged molestation is contained in a copy of the police report obtained by the National Urban League. Police Report of John Hamilton, October 13, 1956, fol. Subversion and the UL Miscellaneous, I:A50, National Urban League Records, Manuscript Division, Library of Congress,

Washington, DC. In Atlanta Urban League Papers, box 24 Administrative
Files, 1943–1961, series 6 Grace Hamilton, 1942–1961 (1967), subgroup
II Presidents' Files, 1922–1990, Atlanta Urban League Papers, ARC.
11. Lester Granger, "Manhattan and Beyond," *New York Amsterdam News*, November 24, 1956, 8.

## Works Cited

Anderson, Carol. 2003. *Eyes Off the Prize: The United Nations and the African American Struggle for Human Rights, 1944–1955.* Cambridge, UK: Cambridge University Press.

Bérubé, Allan. 2010. *Coming Out Under Fire: The History of Gay Men and Women in World War II.* 20th anniv. ed. Chapel Hill: University of North Carolina.

Brown, Kathleen M. 1996. *Good Wives, Nasty Wenches, and Anxious Patriarchs: Gender, Race and Power in Colonial Virginia.* Chapel Hill: University of North Carolina Press.

Canaday, Margot. 2009. *The Straight State: Sexuality and Citizenship in Twentieth Century America.* Princeton, NJ: Princeton University Press.

Chauncey, George. 1993. "The Postwar Sex Crime Panic." In *True Stories from the American Past,* edited by William Graebner, 160–79. New York: McGraw Hill.

Dailey, Jane. 2004. "Sex, Segregation, and the Sacred after Brown." *The Journal of American History* 91, no. 1: 119–44.

Dean, Robert D. 2001. *Imperial Brotherhood: Gender and the Making of Cold War Foreign Policy.* Amherst: University of Massachusetts Press.

Freedman, Estelle B. 1987. "'Uncontrollable Desires': The Response to the Sexual Psychopath, 1920–1960." *Journal of American History* 74, no. 1 (June): 83–106.

Gore, Dayo F. 2011. *Radicalism at the Crossroads: African American Women Activists in the Cold War.* New York: New York University Press.

Haley, Sarah. 2016. *No Mercy Here: Gender, Punishment, and the Making of Jim Crow Modernity.* Chapel Hill: University of North Carolina.

Hanhardt, Christina B. 2013. *Safe Space: Gay Neighborhood History and the Politics of Violence.* Durham, NC: Duke University Press.

Harris, LaShawn. 2012. "Marvel Cooke: Investigative Journalist, Communist and Black Radical Subject." *Journal for the Study of Radicalism* 6, no. 2 (Fall): 91–126.

Horne, Gerald. 1986. *Black and Red: W. E. B. DuBois and the Afro-American Response to the Cold War, 1944–1963.* Albany: State University of New York Press.

Howard, John. 1999. *Men Like That: A Southern Queer History*. Chicago, IL: University of Chicago Press.

Hunter, Tera W. 2019. *Bound in Wedlock: Slave and Free Black Marriage in the Nineteenth Century*. Cambridge, MA: Harvard University Press.

Jenkins, Philip. 1998. *Moral Panic: Changing Concepts of the Child Molester in Modern America*. New Haven, CT: Yale University Press.

Johnson, David K. 2004. *The Lavender Scare: The Cold War Persecution of Gays and Lesbians in the Federal Government*. Chicago, IL: University of Chicago Press.

Kandaswamy, Priya. 2021. *Domestic Contradictions: Race and Gendered Citizenship from Reconstruction to Welfare Reform*. Durham, NC: Duke University Press.

Kelley, Robin D. G. 1990. *Hammer and Hoe: Alabama Communists during the Great Depression*. Chapel Hill: University of North Carolina, 1990.

———. 2003. *Freedom Dreams: The Black Radical Imagination*. Boston, MA: Beacon Press.

Leighton, Jared E. 2013. "Freedom Indivisible: Gays and Lesbians in the African American Civil Rights Movement." PhD diss., University of Nebraska.

McDuffie, Erick S. 2011. *Sojourning for Freedom: Black Women, American Communism, and the Making of Black Left Feminism*. Durham, NC: Duke University Press.

McGuire, Danielle L. 2010. *At the Dark End of the Street: Black Women, Rape, and Resistance—A New History of the Civil Rights Movement from Rosa Parks to the Rise of Black Power*. New York: Alfred A. Knopf.

Moody, Anne. 1968. *Coming of Age in Mississippi: The Classic Autobiography of Growing Up Poor and Black in the South*. New York: Bantam Dell.

Morgan, Jennifer L. 2004. *Reproduction and Gender in New World Slavery*. Philadelphia: University of Pennsylvania Press.

Pascoe, Peggy. 2009. *What Comes Naturally: Miscegenation Law and the Making of Race in America*. Oxford, UK: Oxford University Press.

Ransby, Barbara. 2003 *Ella J. Baker and the Black Radical Tradition*. Chapel Hill: University of North Carolina Press.

Roberts, Dorothy. 1997. *Killing the Black Body: Race, Reproduction, and the Meaning of Liberty*. New York: Vintage Books.

Romano, Renee C. 2003. *Race Mixing: Black-White Marriage in Post-War America*. Cambridge, UK: Cambridge University Press.

Rosen, Hannah. 2009. *Terror in the Heart of Freedom: Citizenship, Sexual Violence, and the Meaning of Race in the Postemancipation South*. Chapel Hill: University of North Carolina Press.

Shah, Nayan. 2018. "Queer of Color Estrangement and Belonging." In *The Routledge History of Queer America*, edited by Don Romesburg, 262–75. New York: Routledge Press.

Stein, Marc. 2010. *Sexual Injustice: Supreme Court Decisions from* Griswold *to* Roe. Chapel Hill: University of North Carolina Press.

Stewart-Winter, Timothy. 2017. *Queer Clout: Chicago and the Rise of Gay Politics.* Philadelphia: University of Pennsylvania Press.

Woods, Louis Lee. 2013. "Almost 'No Negro Veteran . . . Could Get a Loan': African Americans, the GI Bill, and the NAACP Campaign Against Residential Segregation, 1917–1960." *Journal of African American History* 98, no. 3: 392–417.

# Gendering the Politics of Black Displacement

Rosemary Ndubuizu

**Abstract:** Historians, sociologists, and critical urbanists have long argued race and racial discourse are critical cultural levers used to validate contemporary gentrification schemes in urban centers. Applying a Black feminist materialist analysis to the case study of the recent gentrification wave in Washington, DC, this article adds and deepens this literature, tracing the definitive role gender plays in facilitating displacement and affordable housing inequities in gentrifying urban centers. **Keywords:** gender; welfare reform; public housing politics; Black feminist materialism; racial state; displacement; uneven development

In my book manuscript, *The Undesirable Many: Black Women and Their Struggles against Displacement and Housing Insecurity in the Nation's Capital* (under contract with University of North Carolina Press), I argue that low-wage Black women and their families endure marginalization because the state, often in conjunction with private interests, leverages long-standing stereotypes about low-wage Black families, particularly those headed by single mothers, to rationalize the excessive exposure to displacement and housing insecurity these families face. While masking these stereotypes in coded language, representatives of the United States racial state use these stereotypes to implement what I call *disciplinary housing governance*. Disciplinary housing governance is the racially gendered and hegemonic ideology that draws on negative stereotypes about low-wage Black families to validate state-sponsored efforts to tie low-wage Black families' access to improved housing to the evaluation or surveillance of their domestic lives. Families who resist or fail to comply with these conditional measures often find

*WSQ: Women's Studies Quarterly* 51: 1 & 2 (Spring/Summer 2023)

themselves trapped in the city's oldest and declining housing stock, or worse, subjected to eviction, suffering (often serial) displacement.

By examining the post-1960s history of DC's affordable housing politics, I reveal how gender remains a critical means to depoliticize and obscure housing officials' role in reproducing racialized housing inequities. As cities pursue gentrification as their central economic and social revitalization strategy, DC provides an excellent case study for examining the intersection of local and federal government's racial politics since DC often serves as a laboratory for national policies. An analysis of DC's local debate about how to apply Housing Opportunities for People Everywhere (HOPE) VI to Ellen Wilson Dwellings, a fifty-year-old public housing community located a stone's throw from the federal government, in DC's Capitol Hill neighborhood, is a noteworthy example of the limiting effects of disciplinary housing governance. With the state's focus on Black tenants' alleged cultural deficiencies, disciplinary housing governance has enabled housing officials to accord differential state protection while protecting capital's enduring forms of extractive and discriminatory treatment and perpetuating the United States' racialized uneven development more broadly. Lastly, this ideology reveals the constitutive role gender plays in the United States' racial politics and the importance of a Black feminist materialist approach.

I adopt a methodological approach I call Black feminist materialism. I extend Black feminists' intersectional emphasis and trace the constitutive role that culture and meaning-making play in areas of the American political economy such as finance and housing.[1] Toward this end, I study affordable housing because, as an industry, it is loaded with intersectional, historical, and cultural meanings, all of which shape the politics and policy outcomes taken by different U.S. regulatory regimes. With this theoretical framework, I demonstrate how political authority figures regularly leverage gender (gender ideologies, that is) to promote the U.S. racial state's democratic aspects while also obscuring and depoliticizing its despotism, like displacement, dispossession, or other forms of state violence (Omi and Winant 2014).

### From State Failure to State Innovation

Public housing was one of the many means-tested welfare programs that solicited growing national rebuke in the 1990s. While welfare scholars have rightly noted how the political elite preferred a color-blind defense of welfare reform, the political elite relied heavily on visual performance to communicate racial appeals in the public housing reform debates. In the post–civil rights era, political elites across the political spectrum understood that successful welfare reform politics required the strategic incorporation of different public housing stakeholders. This political incorporation extended to Black public housing residents and managers, especially since public housing was popularly racialized as shelter for low-wage Black families. From the 1980s until the early 1990s, conservative leaders like the former congressman who became the secretary of Housing and Urban Development (HUD), Jack Kemp, called on Black women public housing tenant activists to stand with them and condemn local and federal politicians for failing to grant mainly Black public housing tenants the chance to attain civil society's privileged position of a homeowner. Following conservatives, moderate Democrats like HUD Secretary Henry Cisneros built upon Kemp's stakeholder incorporation strategy by calling on Black male public housing executives to validate the state's call to change its approach to public housing policy (Ndubuizu 2021). In congressional hearings and the press, Black male public housing executives like Vincent Lane and Robert Armstrong artfully appropriated the civil rights discourse of Black victimization. They then rearticulated public housing and welfare's racist origins to justify a policy call for federal deregulation that would grant local public housing authorities more discretionary power in setting admission and eviction standards for public housing. With both examples, elites' visual fusion of racial appeals and pro-market policy aims evinced a public housing politics hinged on gender performance.

To be sure, Black public housing tenant activists and Black male public housing executives were often instrumentally used by political elites to justify their political push for reducing federal expenditures on public housing. Nevertheless, their willingness to participate in the country's broader austerity politics gave the U.S. racial state the imprimatur of racial progressivism. But even as Black stakeholders, particularly Black women public housing activists, gained greater political influence, it did not change the widely circulated political perception that low-wage Black mothers living in public housing were assumed to be incompetent parents and irresponsible tenants. Since public housing's inception, its opponents, including the private real estate industry, had stressed that low-wage Black parents' poor parenting and allegedly lax morals directly contributed to their overexposure to the city's worst housing stock. Some public housing advocates shared this anti-Black racial anxiety while insisting that public housing, through selec-tive tenant selection and rigorous character education, could correct these character deficiencies. These advocates were some of disciplinary housing governance's first architects.

Over time, this disparaging depiction of low-wage Black families took a deeper and covert hold in the public housing debates. In the 1990s, during the congressional hearings on how best to reform largely majority-Black public housing, politicians and witnesses often used single Black motherhood as a proxy for public housing's decline. Take, for example, the congressional hearing on severely distressed public housing held in 1992. Single Black motherhood operated as a metonym for public housing's trou-bles (U.S. Congress 1992). Circulating as common sense, the fact that single Black motherhood was conflated with public housing decline rested on a problematic stereotypical discussion about Black public housing residents' social reproduction, a narrative that indirectly disconnected these mothers from the broader shifts in the American economy and culture that led to a rising number of single-parent households (Statista Search Department 2020). Nevertheless, Black women's seeming disregard for the heteropatri-archal family formation, and their primary reliance on welfare as a medium for survival, was emblematic of state failure. A bipartisan political consen-sus emerged and argued that state failure could only be reversed if there were sweeping changes to public housing's development, management, and resident engagement practices. These broad changes were finally legislated when the 103rd Congress created the HOPE VI program, which granted HUD and public housing authorities the power to demolish public housing marked as severely distressed, relocate displaced residents, and redevelop public housing into mixed-income communities.

### Gendering the Racial Pragmatic Politics of HOPE VI

To implement this vision, HUD and local public housing executives moved to reform its admittance policy, a key medium to control Black public housing residents' social reproduction. On its face, this policy appealed to color-blind and technocratic values, but it would have disparate and devasting consequences for low-wage Black women and their families. Ellen Wilson Dwellings, which also happened to be the nation's capital's first HOPE VI redevelopment, served as DC's first attempt to test out a new eligibility protocol for redeveloped public housing. Opened in 1940, Ellen

Wilson Dwellings was first only open to white families until 1953, when the city led the nation with a planned desegregation of its public housing units. Ellen Wilson Dwellings' 134 units eventually fell into extensive despair due to state neglect. Vice markets grew in a vacuum left by state disinvestment (and private capital abandonment), leaving Ellen Wilson Dwellings residents to intimately endure the lived realities of an expanding underground economy that used public housing as a critical node for illicit product distribution. By the late 1980s, DC housing officials saw the rising crime rates and high vacant rates at Ellen Wilson Dwellings as a chance to implement this reform to its eligibility criterion. In 1988, DC housing officials notified Ellen Wilson Dwellings residents that their community would be demolished and residents would be able to return once they submitted to a new tenant selection criterion. Touted as a privileged right accorded to those who could afford expensive private homes, DC housing officials believed public housing residents should also be able to select their neighbors. Even with this exclusionary provision reframed as a public housing tenant's right to public safety, DC housing officials were limited in the pool of eligible tenants. At that time, federal law required every public housing unit be replaced with another one, and authorities had to prioritize the unhoused and applicants earning less than 50 percent of the region's area median income.

By the 1990s, the political climate changed. Federal officials demanded aggressive reforms to public housing's operation. In DC's case, the city's public housing agency was in shambles and thus too weak to make these changes without a massive internal revamp. In one of the city's last-ditch efforts to prevent a local judge's call for receivership, DC housing officials blamed their failing management grades on the overwhelmingly Black elderly and on single Black mothers. To this end, in 1994 these housing officials pushed for tougher admission and easier eviction policy, insisting that tenant irresponsibility can only be countered with these measures. As Jasper F. Burnette, DC's public housing executive at the time, said, "We want people who can show us before they move into the building that they will pay the rent, tend to their children, and avoid the drug issue" (Kovaleski 1994). The DC public housing department's policy move was a little too late, and a local judge appointed David I. Gilmore, a white public housing executive with Boston roots, to oversee DC public housing for at least three years to implement sweeping reform, which included Ellen Wilson Dwellings' redevelopment.

Embracing a public housing reform culture that was increasingly carceral and punitive, Gilmore backed his predecessor's call to change admissions standards for public housing. Making no note of this policy's gendered and racialized effects, Gilmore defended the policy, arguing that needs-based admission did not give enough weight to tenants' parental and domestic practices, both of which he submitted were critical to improved public housing. He supported an eligibility standard that would empower public housing staff to "check criminal and credit records," determine if "applicants have a history of eviction," and "talk to former landlords or homeless shelter operators to get an idea of an applicant's behavior and housekeeping habits" (Kovaleski 1994). Gilmore's embrace of state evaluation and surveillance of public housing residents' domestic lives illustrated the enduring widespread support for disciplinary housing governance. Deployed alongside the expanding investment in the carceral state of Presidents Ronald Reagan, George H. W. Bush, and William Clinton, disciplinary housing governance empowered housing officials to once again treat public housing residents' homes as a public site of surveillance, where mainly low-wage Black women had to prove themselves deserving of improved housing conditions through adherence to evolving standards of domestic upkeep and parental care.

Gilmore, as a state representative, saw these behavior-based conditional measures as critical to the innovative and reformed welfare state, even if Black women tenant activists cried foul. For Gilmore, conditional access meant that the welfare state reinforced the obligatory (and historically explicit) citizenship expectations for the Black working class. In the eyes of some public housing residents, this conditional access to public housing meant Black families would be unfairly locked out of public housing. In the mid-1990s, when Gilmore pressed for half of the vacant units to go to the working poor and for banning those with criminal records, longtime public housing activist Jacqueline Massey resisted such a move. She feared the public housing executive's focus on tenant behavior absolved the state of its historical neglect when it came to public housing. And the criminal ban left residents who have served their time to serve another unspoken sentence in civil society through the denial of welfare via public housing. She commented, "If you're going to re-try people for something they did in the past, that's not good business. All should be forgiven, and they should go on the waiting list" (Loeb 1997).

However, the DC public housing agency's covert gendered and racialized politics of public housing reform meant that city officials preferred to work with those who agreed with the state's disciplinary approach. Such was the case at Ellen Wilson Dwellings. Once HUD implemented HOPE VI in 1993, Ellen Wilson Dwellings was the first public housing community in DC to receive funding, but by the time local officials received these funds, Ellen Wilson Dwellings' redevelopment team relied on a decision-making apparatus that prioritized and elevated the desires of wealthier residents over public housing residents. The major community-based push for HOPE VI at Ellen Wilson Dwellings came from a group of local residents in DC's Capitol Hill neighborhood who formed Ellen Wilson Neighborhood Redevelopment Corp., a thirteen-member board comprised of mainly business executives, local homeowners, and two former Ellen Wilson Dwellings residents. Working with a Georgetown-based developer tapped to lead the HOPE VI redevelopment, coalition participants openly discussed who should be allowed to live on the redeveloped site. Gender emerged as a critical reason for the coalition-backed, privately led site redevelopment to involve a strict protocol on who would be permitted to live there. As one of the active coalition members noted at the time, "single-parent families . . . are less capable of controlling their circumstances" and, as such, require the stabilizing force of wealthier homeowners to counter this reality and anchor these redeveloped communities (Powers 1992, E1). Through these ad hoc local grassroots groups, the DC public housing agency could practice stakeholder incorporation that solicited popular support for its call for public housing residents to meet state-enforced behavioral standards before they could gain admittance to the redeveloped site. In this embrace of disciplinary reform, representatives from DC's public housing agency could use gender to obscure the fact that private finance still ascribes high (capital) risk and low value to Black and poor neighborhoods.

With HOPE VI advancing the view that middle-class families and homeownership should anchor redeveloped neighborhoods, local state representatives like Gilmore implemented eligibility reforms that favored middle-class and marginalized most low-wage public housing residents. Because HOPE VI required localities to develop a self-sustaining rent structure (like public housing originally did), middle-class families were considered the primary base needed to cross-subsidize low-wage renters, with the hope HUD would no longer need to give operating subsidies to sustain public housing renters' living conditions. In exchange for this cost-saving measure, localities could determine their own eligibility rules and not be forced to admit residents living in homeless shelters or other public housing communities—a reform measure that most public housing communities not undergoing redevelopment could implement (which also meant that the concentration of poverty these officials so often lambasted continued relatively unabated, because multifamily public and privately owned rent-assisted housing was still the primary way the city could house those who could not afford rents in the private market). With this new rent structure, it made it nearly impossible for the city to rehouse public housing residents.[2] Instead, HOPE VI enabled DC to expand the income eligibility for public housing redevelopments to include HUD's broader affordable housing definition, which included households who earned up to 115 percent of the DC metropolitan median income (Loeb 1996).[3]

In a metropolitan area with one of the country's highest concentrations of wealth, the state's enforcement of this technocratic, region-based approach to eligibility for HOPE VI redevelopments meant that low-wage Black public housing residents would be disadvantaged and marginalized. Former Ellen Wilson Dwellings residents' income was only 12 percent of the DC's metropolitan income. The income-tiered units also meant former Ellen Wilson Dwellings residents could only qualify for up to fifty redeveloped units (Haggerty 1995). Their access to these units was curtailed even more, because state neglect followed the displaced tenants in more ways than one. The DC public housing agency failed to keep up-to-date records on most displaced tenants. Only twenty-nine Ellen Wilson Dwellings families expressed interest in the right to return, but they quickly learned that they needed to submit to disciplinary housing governance. If former Ellen Wilson Dwellings and other public housing residents did not pass a credit check, criminal report, and home visit at their present residences and save enough money to buy into the redevelopment's limited equity cooperative, they did not qualify to live there. Gilmore reasoned, "No, we don't want violent criminals. And we are excluding people who aren't credit-worthy and don't pay their bills" (Deane 1999, G1). Gilmore's casual statement spoke volumes about the state's disregard for the disparate impact this eligibility measure would have on low-wage Black women and their families (Duryea 2006). Since low-wage Black women and their families living in public housing were more vulnerable to police surveillance and arrest, they were disproportionally marginalized in a housing market that prohibited access to the newest units based on a household's financial or physical entanglement with the carceral state. For welfare-assisted Black women who were forced to work in temporary jobs (through the federal government's recently passed Temporary Assistance for Needy Families) and those who chose to financially struggle while doing unpaid care labor in their homes, they would also be seen by the state and private capital as undesirable tenants and would be unwelcome in the redeveloped communities.

Furthermore, these reforms indirectly regulated Black women's social reproduction of their household configuration by disincentivizing tenants from housing family members with criminal records or unemployed or credit-poor family members who could not contribute to (higher) rents. Gilmore's policy stance naturalized the U.S. racial state's ongoing differential treatment of public housing tenants and reinforced societal marginalization of returning citizens. A state difference was institutionalized through HOPE VI's introduction of homeownership options that allowed mainly middle-class and wealthier residents to exchange information (e.g., financial records) to gain access to this redeveloped site, while public housing residents had to submit to state examination of their domestic lives through HOPE VI's enforcement of character-based eligibility standards in conjunction with the character surveillance implemented through its welfare services.

Nevertheless, renamed the Townhomes at Capitol Hill and opened in 1998, the redeveloped Ellen Wilson Dwellings community became a shin-ing example for the political elite of what the reformed welfare state can do. Again, this analysis ignored how the state leveraged gender tropes to justify its color-blind valorization of free-market principles. By emphasizing house-keeping as a condition for acceptance, DC's public housing agency helped to reinscribe a racist and gendered belief about why urban public housing residents, who are overwhelmingly Black women, remain in poor hous-ing conditions, by leveraging the assumption that they are domestically and parentally irresponsible. In the wake of HOPE VI, DC officials often denied more maintenance funding for existing multifamily public housing, which inevitably worsened housing conditions and later prompted future officials to call for demolition as the primary strategy to deal with the social and political consequences of public housing disinvestment.

To be sure, while the state may have legitimized disciplinary housing governance, private landlords have embraced it too. With affordability covenants expiring, landlords with project-based, rent-assisted properties are adapting the playbook of HOPE VI officials, leveraging accusations of tenant irresponsibility to demolish and convert these homes into primarily market-rate developments. In addition, many of these landlords implement HUD's broad eligibility standards of affordable housing to privilege middle-class tenants and lock out public housing or other rent-assisted tenants with color-blind instruments like credit checks, criminal background checks, or even smaller unit sizes. In this country's post–civil rights racial regime, these instruments get overlooked as biased, because state officials, developers, and private landlords work with the finance industry to institutionally privilege homeownership (and in more recent cases, luxury rentals) as the ideal form of urban residency. This has indirectly worked to incentivize and enlist wealthier residents and sometimes other public housing residents to police mainly low-wage Black women and their families in these redevelopments in the hopes that homeowners and wealthier tenants protect their interest in a building's rising property values or social prestige (Arena 2012; Pattillo 2008; Vale 2020). While not always captured in the press coverage or government hearings, but circulated in local anti-displacement campaigns, many low-wage public housing residents have regularly decried disciplinary housing governance because it provided ideological cover for the U.S. racial state, finance, private landlords, and middle-class residents in these redeveloped sites to control and minimize the number of public housing residents who gain access to these spaces. Nevertheless, the differential treatment continues, because the U.S. racial state and (private) capital always allow for a few, among the Black poor, to be considered exceptional and deserving of inclusion in these new sites.

## Conclusion

In the post–civil rights era, the U.S. racial state has repeatedly exalted market-based solutions that perpetuate the discriminatory treatment low-wage Black families continue to face in the rental market. Instead of demanding universal improvement of the housing stock, U.S. housing policy has allowed misogynoir cultural tropes to circulate in order to justify the state's despotic practice of displacement and dispossession. It is a cultural stereotype that is increasingly obscured as private actors and a wide variety of state housing programs rely on technocratic policy measures to achieve the illusion of racial progress while perpetuating the long-standing racist idea that low-wage Black families are largely responsible for their poor housing conditions. As such, former public housing residents remain trapped in the city's worst housing stock and most likely await displacement and new disciplinary housing governance experiments once representatives from the U.S. racial state arrive with plans to bring "hope" through demolition, displacement, and dispossession.

**Rosemary Ndubuizu** is an assistant professor of African American studies at Georgetown University. Her research interests include welfare policies, post–civil rights urban politics, social movements, (Black) feminisms, and the Black radical tradition. She is currently completing her first manuscript, entitled *The Undesirable Many: Black Women and Their Struggles against Displacement and Housing Insecurity in the Nation's Capital.* She can be reached at rnn7@georgetown.edu.

## Notes

1. There is a long tradition of (Black) feminist materialists who theorize the role gender and patriarchy plays in the political economy. My methodology continues this genealogy. Black feminist materialists include Angela Davis, Rose Brewer, M Adams, Sara Clarke Kaplan, and Barbara Ransby.

2. It was a new approach to public housing that President Bill Clinton, Congress, and HUD backed when they advocated and passed the Quality Housing and Work Responsibility Act of 1998, which, among other measures, repealed the federal law that mandated one-for-one public housing replacement.

3. To be sure, at the time, public housing was available for those who earned up to 80 percent of a region's area median income. But most of these families who could afford rents higher than public housing typically remained in the private rental market.

## Works Cited

Arena, John. 2012. *Driven from New Orleans: How Nonprofits Betray Public Housing and Promote Privatization.* Minneapolis: University of Minnesota Press.

Deane, Daniela. 1999. "A New Face for Public Housing." *Washington Post*, May 8, 1999.

Duryea, Daniella Pelfrey. 2006. "Gendering the Gentrification of Public Housing: HOPE VI's Disparate Impact on Lowest-Income African American Women." *Georgetown Journal on Poverty Law & Policy* XIII, no. 3: 567–94.

Haggerty, Maryann. 1995. "Public Housing Renewal Plan Strikes a Nerve: Opposition Strong to Blueprint for Rebuilding Ellen Wilson Dwellings." *Washington Post*, September 23, 1995.

Kovaleski, Serge. 1994. "Tougher Admission Standards Pushed for DC Public Housing." *Washington Post*, October 28, 1994.

Loeb, Vernon. 1996. "Public Housing Concept Hinges on the Right Mix: Planned Complex Won't Make It without Middle-Class Families." *Washington Post*, April 25, 1996.

———. 1997. "Public Housing Proposal Would Bar Criminals: DC Screening Favors Working Poor." *Washington Post*, October 28, 1997.

Ndubuizu, Rosemary. 2021. "Faux Heads of Households and the Gendered and Racialized Politics of Housing Reform." *Feminist Formations* 33, no. 1: 142–64.

Omi, Michael, and Howard Winant. 2014. *Racial Formation in the United States*. New York: Routledge.

Pattillo, Mary. 2008. *Black on the Block: The Politics of Race and Class in the City*. Chicago, IL: University of Chicago Press.

Powers, William. 1992. "A Housing Complex DC Forgot: Group Seeks to Transform Abandoned Ellen Wilson Dwellings." *Washington Post*, August 22, 1992.

Statista Search Department. 2020. *Number of Children Living with Single Mother or Single Father from 1970 to 2020*. Statista. file:///Users/rnn7/Downloads/statistic_id252847_number-of-us-children-living-in-a-single-parent-family-1970-2020.pdf.

U.S. Congress. Senate. 1992. *Distressed Public Housing, Hearings before the Subcommittee on Housing and Urban Affairs*. 102nd Congress, 2nd Sess., March 25.

Vale, Lawrence. 2020. *After the Projects: Public Housing Redevelopment and the Poorest Americans*. Oxford, UK: Oxford University Press.

# PART III. CLASSICS REVISITED

Selections from *Triple Jeopardy* 1, no. 1
(September–October 1971)

**Fig. 1.** *Triple Jeopardy* 1, no. 1 (September–October 1971), 1. Inaugural cover. Third World Women's Alliance, Bay Area chapter records, Sophia Smith Collection, Smith College Special Collections, Northampton, MA.

THIRD WORLD WOMEN'S ALLIANCE TUESDAY SCHEDULE

| | |
|---|---|
| SEPTEMBER 21 | HOSPITAL WORKERS |
| | —Working conditions |
| | ——Management & Labor Relations |

SEPTEMBER 28        CONCEPTS OF LOVE & SEX

——Bourgeois and Revolutionary Attitudes

THIS SESSION OPEN TO MEN

OCTOBER 5        NUTRITION

——General Information

—— Food Industry, Additives, Food Lobbies

OCTOBER 12        "ONLY THE BEGINNING"

——Film and Discussion of Anti—War Movement

THIS SESSION OPEN TO MEN

OCTOBER 19        GUERRILLA THEATRE

——Short Skits about third world women and the war

OCTOBER 26        THE PARTICIPATION OF THIRD WORLD PEOPLE IN THE ANTI— WAR DEMONSTRATION

THIS SESSION OPEN TO MEN

PLACE: 346 West 20th Street, N.Y.C.        TIME: 7:30 P.M. Sharp

*Third World People Welcome.*

**Fig. 2.** *Triple Jeopardy* 1, no. 1 (September–October 1971), 17. TWWA "Tuesday Schedule." Third World Women's Alliance, Bay Area chapter records, Sophia Smith Collection, Smith College Special Collections, Northampton, MA.

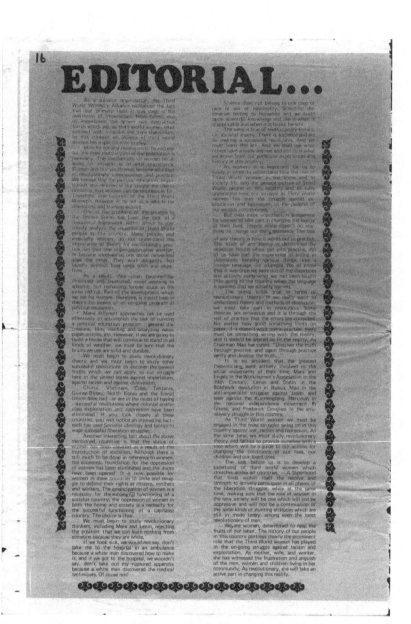

**Fig. 3.** *Triple Jeopardy* 1, no. 1 (September–October 1971), 16. "Editorial . . ." Third World Women's Alliance, Bay Area chapter records, Sophia Smith Collection, Smith College Special Collections, Northampton, MA.

# Political Education "in the Belly of the Monster": The Third World Women's Alliance's "Tuesday Schedule"

Vani Kannan

The back cover of the Third World Women's Alliance's first issue of *Triple Jeopardy* introduces readers to the group's "Tuesday Schedule" of political education events, held weekly at 346 West Twentieth Street, New York, and starting at "7:30 sharp." Topics covered in political education sessions included a broad range of domestic and international issues: hospital working conditions and management-labor relations; "bourgeois and revolutionary attitudes" toward love and sex; a critical introduction to nutrition focusing on the food industry, additives, and food lobbies; a film screening and discussion on the anti-war movement; guerrilla theater skits on Third World women and the war; and a discussion of Third World people in anti-war demonstrations. Every other week, the sessions were open to men.

This first "Tuesday Schedule" demonstrates how the Alliance's political objectives and anti-racist, anti-sexist, anti-capitalist framing deconstruct the local/global binary and refuse to draw stark divides between different scales of struggle. A critique of capitalist labor relations in the U.S. flows seamlessly into a larger discussion of the war in Vietnam; a discussion of intimate partner relations moves into a critique of the corporatization of food. The articles in the first issue of the paper demonstrate the group's adeptness at fleshing out the material interconnections among these scales: articles transport the reader from the perspectives of incarcerated revolutionaries in the U.S., to surveillance on public transportation, to a demonstration for universal day care, to the Vietnam War, to reproductive justice, to book reviews, poetry, and first-person interviews with women workers. Protest report-backs highlight the vibrant cross-section of New York City organizing that comprised the Alliance's political community. This first issue of the paper also offers a public report-back on the group's internal work,

*WSQ: Women's Studies Quarterly* 51: 1 & 2 (Spring/Summer 2023)

principles, and philosophy of organizing, demonstrating a commitment to transparency with its base.

The paper was understood as the Alliance's official news organ. As Linda Burnham puts it, the intention of the paper was as follows:

> to really speak to the ways in which women of color experience the world, and speak to the issues that were not at that time being addressed by the white women's movement, or the mainstream women's movement. And it was the early side of the recognition that women of color faced issues and discrimination and marginalization, not only as women, but as people of color, as people with particular class background, et cetera. (2005, 20)

*Triple Jeopardy* was directed toward an audience of Third World working-class women and men, and an internal criticism of the early papers addresses the need to refine this audience further to "the unpolitical sister," rather than those who were already connected to political struggles ("Dear Cheryl" 1972). The paper's editorial staff were entirely volunteer, and in early issues of the paper like this one, bylines were typically not attributed to individual authors; collective authorship served as a method of protecting members from state surveillance (Romney 2021, 109). The Alliance maintained a principled stance of not including advertisements in the paper. For example, the Alliance received a letter from someone conducting a study on survivors of sexual assault who asked whether they could advertise in *TJ*, and the Alliance said no, redirecting them to the group Bay Area Women Against Rape ("Dear Friend" 1973, 1). Because *Triple Jeopardy* was understood to be deeply connected with the Alliance's political organizing and organization-building goals, anyone who expressed interest in joining the paper was asked to join the organization itself. Frances Beal saw writing and organizing as inextricable, and "thought knowing the Alliance and being part of its activity were necessary prerequisites to writing for the paper" (Romney 2021, 108). For the Alliance, writing was embedded in organizational work, rather than existing alone or adjacent to grassroots organizing. For those of us who are writers, teach writing, or are otherwise engaged in the study and practice of composition as political work, this insight is essential; when engaging with *Triple Jeopardy* and other movement newspapers, we must understand political writing as intrinsically connected to organization-building.

The Alliance's orientation to movement writing as political work and organization-building resonated with the larger context of the Women in

Print Movement of the late 1960s and 1970s, which gave rise to a vibrant print culture via the production and distribution of newsletters, magazines, newspapers, political and literary journals, and books distributed in both local and national networks. These grassroots publishers and distributors connected via social gatherings like writing retreats and conferences (Pratt 1981, ii). The movement's focus on cultivating women producers of texts intentionally countered the "head/hand" dichotomy privileging intellectual and written labor over the physical production of newsletters. Travis writes that "women would never be truly free unless they first seized ownership of the means of cultural production and then restructured and de-hierarchalized that production, liberating the written word from the material regime that had grown up to enforce the oppressive epistemological and moral structures of capitalist patriarchy" (Travis 2008, 282). Part of organizing against the state from within it, then, required building autonomous women-run revolutionary spaces for knowledge production—from newspapers to political education spaces.

Because *Triple Jeopardy* was circulated to the other chapters of the Alliance, it also served as a method of internal education and coordination. Archives indicate that in addition to *Triple Jeopardy*, chapters also produced internal newsletters and bulletins to keep the group's membership updated on what the organization was doing, and to create a written record of the group's work. The West Coast chapter of the Alliance produced a newsletter, which in part functioned as an internal political education tool, and the Seattle chapter produced a newsletter titled *Seattle Third World News* that served a similar function. Within the organization, other publications were used for political education; these included *Pa'lante, Mohammed Speaks, Black Panther, Guardian*, and movement newspapers that reported on Vietnam (Romney 2021, 88).

It was in this larger context that *Triple Jeopardy* spread word of the Alliance's political education program. The "Tuesday Schedule," in particular, highlights the range of ways that the Alliance mobilized its base of self-identified Third World people living in the "belly of the monster" of U.S. empire, to quote the group's "Editorial: What Is the Third World?" The editorial linked the larger geographical concept of the Third World to a mass liberation struggle against oppression of man by man, nation by nation, and woman by man. To fight state power from within the "belly of the monster" required deep coalitional work among racialized women with different political and economic histories and lived experiences as they sought to synthesize these histories and experiences into a "U.S.-Third World" political consciousness. Political education played a central role in forging these coalitions, and the New York chapter of the Alliance's political education program, which engaged communities of color in "examin[ing] the intersections of racism, imperialism, and sexism through interactive theater and discussion groups," offered a key way to bring people into these spaces of organizing (Springer 2005, 102).

To more fully understand and contextualize the "Tuesday Schedule," it is important to note how central political education was to the Alliance's larger project of training lifelong organizers. Education created a social space where members "had the opportunity to learn from each other's histories and struggles and forge solidarity out of commonalities" (Lee 2007, 37). The West Coast branch of the Alliance, for example, would engage its members in collectively writing the histories of different women of color in the U.S., to build not only personal relationships but also a historical understanding of the interrelationship of women of color's migration histories, working conditions, and political struggles. The East Coast political education program did include traditional Marxist-Leninist and Maoist theoretical readings but also relied on embodied activities like theater.

In Patricia Romney's foundational book on the Alliance's history, *We Were There: The Third World Women's Alliance and the Second Wave,* she describes the power of the Alliance's guerrilla theater group, La Nueva Mujer. "Guerrilla theater" invokes the spirit of Che Guevara's writings on guerrilla tactics (which drew inspiration from Vietnamese anti-colonial writings); the word *guerrilla* is Spanish for "little warrior." When applied to theater, the word *guerrilla* suggests "unannounced, politically or socially motivated performances in public spaces for an unsuspecting audience"— in other words, performance that was not "officially" sanctioned ("History," n.d.). For one Alliance member, guerrilla theater served as a mode of personal expression and a way to push audiences to shift their thinking: "to act out my beliefs and do something about them, like maybe get people to agree with my ideas" (Romney 2021, 92). For another member, guerrilla theater built a culture of collaboration and interpersonal support, and offered a way to become critically conscious of everyday gender relations: "more than anything else, has given me a sense of true sisterhood, and working with the women in the group on the skits has really helped me a lot in recognizing the very subtle sexist attitudes that penetrate this society" (Romney 2021, 92). Rather than situating personal transformation as an end in itself, political education was understood as a necessary and ongoing corollary to collective action.

These tactics for political education mirror the articles in *Triple Jeopardy*, ranging from the intimate and embodied to the local to the global. The "Tuesday Schedule" and the Alliance's orientation to political education remind us that when we look at *Triple Jeopardy* and consider its long-term implications as a resource for scholars and students of the movement, we should also understand it as a tool for gathering people for transformative educational work. The multiple scales of struggle represented in *Triple Jeopardy* mirror the personal, relational, emotional, and analytic work that members of the organization undertook in their political education sessions and larger organizing work.

**Vani Kannan** is an assistant professor of English at Lehman College, CUNY, where she also serves on the steering committee for the Women's and Gender Studies program. Her research interests include social justice–oriented writing pedagogies, community literacies, social movements, and multimodal/multigenre writing. Her recent work has appeared in *constellations: a cultural rhetorics publishing space*, *Present Tense: A Journal of Rhetoric in Society*, and *Writers: Craft & Context*. She can be reached at arianevani.kannan@lehman.cuny.edu.

## Works Cited

Burnham, Linda. 2005. Interview by Loretta J. Ross. March 18, 2005. Voices of Feminism Oral History Project, Sophia Smith Collection, Smith College, Northampton, MA. https://www.smith.edu/libraries/libs/ssc/vof/transcripts/Burnham.pdf.

"Dear Cheryl." 1972. Third World Women's Alliance Papers, box 4, folder 2. Sophia Smith Collection, Smith College Libraries, Northampton, MA.

"Dear Friend." July 12, 1973. Third World Women's Alliance Papers, box 3, folder 4. Sophia Smith Collection, Smith College Libraries, Northampton, MA.

"Editorial: What Is the Third World?" n.d. *Triple Jeopardy: Racism Imperialism Sexism*. Women of Color Resource Center, Oakland, CA. https://www.flickr.com/photos/27628370@N08/2570007296/in/album-72157605547626040/.

"History." n.d. San Francisco Mime Troupe. Accessed June 26, 2017. https://www.sfmt.org/history.

Lee, Joon Pyo. 2007. "The Third World Women's Alliance, 1970–1980: Women of Color Organizing in a Revolutionary Era." MA thesis, Sarah Lawrence College.

Pratt, Minnie Bruce. 1981. *The Sound of One Fork*. Durham, NC: Night Heron Press.

Romney, Patricia. 2021. *We Were There: The Third World Women's Alliance and the Second Wave*. New York: Feminist Press.

Springer, Kimberly. 2005. *Living for the Revolution: Black Feminist Organizations, 1968–1980*. Durham, NC: Duke University Press.

Travis, Trysh. 2008. "The Women in Print Movement: History and Implications." *Book History*, no. 11: 275–300.

# How Do We Grow Grassroots Critiques of the State?
# A Close Reading of *Triple Jeopardy* from East Baltimore

Lenora R. Knowles

When I sit with the images, concepts, and community voices of the Third
World Women's Alliance (TWWA) in their *Triple Jeopardy* newspaper, I am
struck by how this movement publication served as a key mechanism for
the New York City chapter of the TWWA to grow leadership and critical
consciousness of the racial capitalist U.S. state among their base of Third
World women and Third World people more generally. In this first issue,
the TWWA elucidates how members were teaching and circulating Third
World political analysis and movement strategy, along with the meanings
and values of Third World movement leadership. As a revised organic intellectual, organizer, and *nepantlera*,[1] I find joy and possibility in the complex
process of growing grassroots movement leaders struggling for broadscale
social transformation. From its first issue through its last, *Triple Jeopardy*
offers important considerations for doing the relational and processual work
of political education and leadership development today. Below, I explore
how writers of *Triple Jeopardy* utilized the rhetorical device of the question
as a method for critical inquiry and political education. Moreover, I trace
how they mobilized radical critiques of the state at multiple scales, ranging from global regimes of violence to everyday trauma, in order to build
political unity. I suggest that these approaches provide invaluable tools for
the grassroots base-building and leadership development that I attempt to
practice while organizing in East Baltimore.

To better understand some of what this first issue teaches us about
leadership development, I provide a bit of context for the TWWA (see
Springer 2005; Farmer 2017), the stakes of their organizing and theorizing
within a Cold War context, and how they conceptualized the role of their

*WSQ: Women's Studies Quarterly* 51: 1 & 2 (Spring/Summer 2023)

grassroots publication. The TWWA was a radical women of color organizing collective that first took shape in New York through the leadership of Black women organizers Frances Beal and Gwendolyn Patton. The organizational life of the New York–based TWWA spanned roughly from 1969 to 1977; during this time, they created an organizing program and collectivist organizational structure that centered a Third World woman of color politics that was anti-racist, anti-imperialist, and anti-sexist. The collective's effort to develop a united front of Third World women necessitated multimodal work that was deeply personal, epistemic, collective, analytical, and embodied in nature. Their writings and organizing articulated a Third World women's consciousness among working-class women of color. They mobilized members around key local and international campaigns that promoted reproductive justice, opposed the Vietnam War, and resisted police and carceral violence. Their growing numbers demonstrated the resonance of the organization's intersectional analysis and its strategies for organizing among Third World women. In addition, their thriving base spoke to their increased organizational capacity. Thus, we might think about the TWWA's increased grassroots power in terms of its potential threat to the U.S. nation-state's stability and working-class women's allegiance to a U.S. status quo. By 1971 the organization expanded into the West Coast with the formation of the Bay Area and Seattle chapters. The national membership has been estimated to be somewhere around two hundred members.

While the NYC chapter mostly organized among Black diasporic and Puerto Rican women, the West Coast chapter expanded the membership of Chicana and Asian American and Pacific Islander women alongside African American women. The NYC chapter mobilized women for the annual International Women's Day and supported local workers' picket lines, as well as protests spearheaded by groups like the Black Panther Party, La Unión Latina, and the Campaign to Free Angela Davis. One of their first actions as a collective was participating in the 1970 New York women's strike, during which members publicly delivered a critique of the hegemonic white feminist organizations of the time (TWWA [1974?], 2). The organization challenged state and corporate violence domestically and abroad, most notably in their work to end the country's imperial intervention in Vietnam, state discipline of Black activists, and attacks on Third World Women's reproductive capacity.

The organization's revolutionary political ideologies were circulated most consistently via the publication of *Triple Jeopardy*. The newspaper, which had a national reach, functioned as a mechanism of both leadership development and political education on the failures of the U.S. state. In a 1974 meeting, the writers of *Triple Jeopardy* described their goal: to develop a publication that would be "working class oriented in choice of material, language, etc." (TWWA 1974). Throughout the life of the publication, writers covered a variety of subject matter, like the mass sterilization of women of color, the rise of white supremacy, revolutionary political uprisings unfolding across Latin America and Africa, the U.S.-based Black liberation struggle, and more. They employed a diversity of genres, including but not limited to interviews with women of color workers, poetry on state violence, journalistic accounts of U.S. imperialist foreign policy, letters from political detainees and prisoners like Kisha Shakur and Angela Davis, and book reviews on contemporary writings such as *Genocide against the Indians (Its Role in the Rise of U.S. Capitalism)* by George Novak. Issues also featured photography, especially portraits and protest scenes depicting Third World women, along with political cartoons critiquing Richard Nixon's presidency, visual tutorials for DIY projects, and the poster art of movement leaders like Johnnie Tillmon of the National Welfare Rights Organization. The criticisms they raised of the state and the coalitional nature of *Triple Jeopardy* did not go unnoticed by the state. According to redacted records, the FBI documented and annotated at least two years of content from *Triple Jeopardy* (FBI 1972, 1; FBI 1973b, 1), including articles (FBI 1973a, 2–3) and editorials (FBI 1973a, 6–8). From 1970 to 1974 the federal agency surveilled the organization (FBI 1970, 1; FBI 1974b, 1) including its anti-imperialist and socialist ideologies (FBI 1973a, 7), members' whereabouts (FBI 1973a, 16, 18), strategy (FBI 1973a, 7), meetings and events (FBI 1973a, 16), chapter developments (FBI 1973a, 6; FBI 1974a, 1), and their proximity to contemporary Black Power (FBI 1971, 2), New Left (FBI 1973a, 15–16), and anti-imperialist organizations (FBI 1973a, 16, 17).

This first issue of *Triple Jeopardy* offers a wellspring of material still salient today when it comes to developing frameworks for movement epistemology, pedagogy, and leadership development within the context of ongoing state-sanctioned violence. More specifically, this issue presents several fundamental practices to teach when attempting to spark critical consciousness about the state and to foster grassroots leadership among those most directly impacted by state violence: a practice of critical questioning, a profound appreciation of the nature of state power and the need to resist it on multiple registers, and a complex understanding of the interconnectivity of Third World peoples as a strategy and vision for social change.

The writers of *Triple Jeopardy* intended to create a movement text that was based on the quotidian experiences and material realities of poor and working-class women readers. This first issue included reporting, analysis, and images on the experiences of low-wage factory workers, the lack of affordable and safe childcare and public transit systems, the physiological makeup of the uterus and reproductive processes, surveillance of Black and Brown communities in urban contexts, and more. By engaging the everyday realities of poor and working-class communities of color, they created an opportunity for their readers to think critically about their quality of life and their relationship to state institutions and state power on a global scale.

Writers integrated thought-provoking questions that promoted a critical analysis among their readership of their personal experiences and relationships to the state. For instance, in the opening lines of the first article on the September 1971 Attica Prison Uprising the writers ask, "Where does justice lie in this country?" They expand: "Only those who live without it can say, for it is they—we, who can define it, who can implement it" (TWWA 1971, 2). Such provocations invite readers to engage the validity of the so-called criminal justice system, how they are implicated in it, and how communities might redefine it. In another piece, titled "anti-war demonstrations," the TWWA challenges readers to consider the deadly impact for the Vietnamese of the violent U.S. occupation of Vietnam, the inequitable toll of the war on poor and racialized communities living in the U.S., and the need for these communities to resist U.S. imperialism as a united front. They offer,

> Who is dying in Indochine? Chicano, Black, Puerto Rican, Asian and poor folks in general, are drafted into the army or forced to join due to the racist economic situation in the united states. This is money that we need for housing, education, health care and the establishment of day-care centers. How can a mass movement with the purpose of bringing soldiers home and stopping the bloodshed of our own people be classified a "white thing?" (TWWA 1971, 5)

These and other questions throughout this issue present a key lesson on how the ongoing practice of asking big and seemingly impossible questions based in everyday struggle can animate deeper thinking, loving, and resistance. Earlier in this same article, writers reflect, "We are taught not to ask questions, because supposedly the 'gentlemen in Washington' know what

is best for us. We are now asking how and why" (TWWA 1971, 5). The
TWWA teaches that the practice of critical inquiry in community—even
when it feels scary—can help us to name the contradictions of our shared
realities, call us into processes of accountability, discover new possibilities
for living outside of state-sanctioned violence and exploitation, and determine strategic openings for building community power.

I'm currently organizing alongside poor and working-class Black residents in East Baltimore to build community power, heal, and bring about
community control of land and housing. The writings of the TWWA offer
crucial insights on what it can look like to radicalize, support, and care for
our folks as leaders engaged in political struggle against uneven development on the east side. In the "Editorial" found on the final page of this first
issue, the TWWA positions the task of leadership development and training as one of its primary objectives as an organization. The writers explain,
"Women and our youth must become educated in revolutionary consciousness and practice. We believe that the political education, organization and
defense of our people are clearly positions that women can be responsible
for. Therefore, one function of the Third World Women's Alliance is to act as
a vehicle for developing and training women" (TWWA 1971, 16). For the
organization, leadership development was about creating space for Third
World women to participate in revolutionary practice and theory.

The task of how to nurture grassroots leadership has been fundamental
to my organizing for healing and community control of land and housing in
East Baltimore. Just the other day, I was in a base-building committee meeting. Those in attendance included a member who lives at a nearby public
housing development and has become increasingly involved in our collective. The purpose of this meeting was to orient and integrate this member
into the work of the committee. One of the qualities I admire most about
this emergent leader is how she regularly asks questions. During our regular
membership meetings, political education gatherings, and casual conversations, she asks clarifying questions about concepts, terms, and even the
questions facilitators pose during community strategy meetings.

Such questions facilitate a space for our collective discussion and
(un)-learning. This member-leader's questions have the power to move
our organization into more authentic accessibility and accountability to
each other and our broader community. In addition, I believe such critical questions have the power to expose the historic failures of the state in
regard to poor and working-class Black residents of Baltimore. Revisiting

this first issue reminded me of the power of critical inquiry in our movement spaces, so much so that I was moved to share my admiration of this
leadership characteristic found in this member-leader during this orientation meeting. Intentional and critical questioning is an essential practice
for any grassroots leader organizing against state violence.

The writings of the TWWA also illuminate the importance of having
grassroots leaders who have a working understanding of the multiple registers of state violence and surveillance domestically and globally, and how
Third World women and their larger communities can strategically challenge
such violence by forging political coalitions. One of the most prominent
themes in this issue includes the organization's foregrounding of the historic
failures of the capitalist and racist U.S. state. Writers make this critique
through their discussion of the state's refusal to provide public benefits like
childcare and education. In addition, they interrogate policing through an
exploration of the surveillance of Black and Brown communities in urban
centers, the dehumanization of incarcerated peoples, and the terrorizing of
political activists. We also might draw our attention to their examination
of a hegemonic capitalist culture that enables the lack of protections and
adequate wages for Third World women workers.

Writers also were keenly aware of, and explicitly discussed, the psychic
nature and reaches of state violence. They wrote, "We live with the constant
threat of drug addiction and the abuses that result from it. We endure miser-
able housing conditions and inflationary prices for the necessities of life.
These are all forms of violence. What other name can you give them, for
they have caused the physical death of some of our children, as well as the
mental and spiritual death of others" (TWWA 1971, 5). Their writings and
even their calendar of events speak to the multiple registers of state violence
and how we might contend with them. Thus, when considering the formation of grassroots leaders, we should teach how state power is experienced
by our communities through disinvestment, regulatory policies, and carceral
policing along with psychic, epistemic, and spiritual violence, and trauma.

Trauma, or the embodied and psychic impact of the historic state
violence committed against Black people living in East Baltimore and
across the city, is a defining characteristic of our organizing context. Our
community has often been pathologized and rendered deviant by mainstream media, scholars, government officials, and even middle-class Black
professionals because of a lack of critical analysis of the profound ramifica-
tions of state violence. Therefore, self- and collective healing is an important

frame for how we extend compassion to each other, build unity, and move toward generative states of being and relating. We strive to center holistic approaches and self-awareness in our day-to-day communications, internal power dynamics, meeting spaces, political education curriculum, strategic planning, organizational narrative, and broader work to reclaim and steward land for community benefit amid settler colonialism.

For example, we are organizing our member-neighbors to transform a vacant lot into a much-needed community-owned park for play, meditation, exercise, and gardening. The land sits within the shadow of two massive and contested redevelopment projects. Our efforts to reclaim this land from the city have been met with great opposition. We created our Saturday morning political education series to educate ourselves on the history of land and power, share stories about the human impact of uneven development enacted by state and private collaboration, and invite neighbors to empower the deepest parts of ourselves that are harmed through this systematic violence. Learning about the violence of inequitable development and displacement in the city weighs heavily on the mind and body. We take time in our sessions to practice intentional breathing, affirm our existence as Black people and our collective right to the city, and facilitate intermittent meditations on Black joy and our ancestral ties to the land on which we organize.

The TWWA was astutely aware of how experiences of state-sponsored physical, economic, and psychic violence were shared among racialized women living within the grasp of U.S. imperialism. In their centerpiece article, "Women in the Struggle," the TWWA present their history, foundational socialist ideologies, and their stance on the most pertinent social problems confronting racialized women at the time. The writers explain, "The development of an anti-imperialist ideology led us to recognize the need for Third World solidarity. Although, Asian, Black, Chicana, Native American and Puerto Rican sisters have certain differences, we began to see that we were all affected by the same general oppressions" (TWWA 1971, 8). Through their usage of the concept *Third World*, the collective engaged in a political identity, strategy, and philosophy of interdependence that continues to have the potential to rupture the strongholds of state power.

The TWWA taught a fundamental critique of state power, which they connected to a theory and practice of coalition and interdependence that is essential to the formation of any grassroots leader. Their solidarity continues to be an inspiration for why and how to build consciousness on the life-giving possibility of bridge-making. Their call for a Third World teaches us how to strategically harness shared experiences of not only oppression and trauma but more importantly our shared desires to have our communities flourish and get free.

**Lenora R. Knowles** is a Baltimore-based social movement practitioner. She is also a doctoral candidate in the Harriet Tubman Department of Women, Gender, and Sexuality Studies at the University of Maryland. Her dissertation explores the coalitional and anti-capitalist politics of the Welfare Rights and Third World organizers during the 1960s and 1970s. She can be reached at lknowles@umd.edu.

## Notes

1. The identities of organizer, revised organic intellectual, and nepantlera are distinct yet interconnected positionalities by which I attend to my work in community. I look to organizers and movement thinkers like the Third World Women's Alliance, Ella Baker, Alicia Escalante, Fannie Lou Hamer, Willie Baptist, Johnnie Tillmon, and others for inspiration. Italian philosopher and political activist Antonio Gramsci called for a new stratum of intellectuals to emerge from the ranks of the working class to create "an intellectual-moral bloc which can make politically possible the intellectual progress of the mass and not only of small intellectual groups" (2014, 333). I embrace the role of a movement intellectual who, while grounded in the quotidian lives and organizing of communities, facilitates knowledge creation for the success of movements and campaigns. However, I explicitly turn away from the exclusionary and elitist aspects of Gramsci's framing of the intellectual, which I do not have space to adequately discuss here. Thus, I use revised organic intellectual to articulate my critique of Gramsci's original concept. Chicana lesbian writer Gloria Anzaldúa theorized the Nahuatl concept "nepantla" as a transformative physical and conceptual in-between space and the *nepantlera* to be one who "facilitate(s) passages between worlds" (Anzaldúa and Keating 2009, 248). I am living on borders and in margins, including my lived experiences as a queer, working-class Black woman and Honduran American, grassroots organizer, scholar, and spiritual person. I harness these experiences and identities to bring about my personal, and our collective, transformation in Baltimore.

## Works Cited

Anzaldúa, Gloria, and AnaLouise Keating. 2009. *The Gloria Anzaldúa Reader.* Durham, NC: Duke University Press.

Farmer, Ashley. 2017. *Remaking Black Power: How Black Women Transformed an Era.* Chapel Hill: University of North Carolina Press.

Federal Bureau of Investigation (FBI). 1970. Third World Women's Alliance Racial Matters, December 11, 1970. Third World Women's Alliance Records, box 4, folders 11–12. Sophia Smith Collection, Smith College, Northampton, MA.

———. 1971. Third World Women's Alliance, March 16, 1971. Third World Women's Alliance Records, box 4, folders 11–12. Sophia Smith Collection, Smith College, Northampton, MA.

———. 1972. Third World Women's Alliance—Extremist Matters Memo, January 25, 1972. Third World Women's Alliance Records, box 4, folders 11–12. Sophia Smith Collection, Smith College, Northampton, MA.

———. 1973a. Third World Women's Alliance—EM Memo, April [5], 1973. Third World Women's Alliance Records, box 4, folders 11–12. Sophia Smith Collection, Smith College, Northampton, MA.

———. 1973b. Third World Women's Alliance—EM Memo, July 30, 1973. Third World Women's Alliance Records, box 4, folders 11–12. Sophia Smith Collection, Smith College, Northampton, MA.

———. 1974a. Third World Women's Alliance—EM Memo, March 7, 1974. Third World Women's Alliance Records, box 4, folders 11–12. Sophia Smith Collection, Smith College, Northampton, MA.

———. 1974b. Third World Women's Alliance—EM Memo, March 8, 1974. Third World Women's Alliance Records, box 4, folders 11–12. Sophia Smith Collection, Smith College, Northampton, MA.

Gramsci, Antonio. 2014. *Selections from the Prison Notebooks of Antonio Gramsci.* Edited by Quintin Hoare and Geoffrey Nowell-Smith. New York: International.

Springer, Kimberly. 2005. *Living for the Revolution: Black Feminist Organizations, 1968–1980.* Durham, NC: Duke University Press.

Third World Women's Alliance (TWWA). 1971. *Triple Jeopardy* 1, no. 1 (September–October).

———. 1974. "Meeting Minutes." September 27, 1974. Third World Women's Alliance Records, box 4, folders 2–3. Sophia Smith Collection, Smith College, Northampton, MA.

———. [1974?]. "Preparation for the Mobilizing Meeting on June 23, 1974—History of the Organization from It's Beginning in New York through December 1971 on the West Coast." Third World Women's Alliance Records, box 3, folder 9. Sophia Smith Collection, Smith College, Northampton, MA.

# The Making of *Triple Jeopardy*

Tiana U. Wilson

Over fifty years ago, Third World Women's Alliance (TWWA) members made their debut with the first women-of-color-focused newspaper of the New Left movement in the United States. The name of their newspaper, *Triple Jeopardy*, also reflected these activists' political standpoint and theorization of power—how it is constructed, maintained, and eradicated. In a telephone interview, cofounder and leading *Triple Jeopardy* editor Frances Beal reflected on the group's ideological contributions, explaining, "A lot of the academic people just talk about it in terms of identity, racism, sexism, and classism, and the intersection of those things. Well, we talked about it in terms of the struggles against racism, against sexism, and against imperialism, and the intersection of those struggles "(Frances Beal, pers. comm., October 3, 2022). The idea of triple jeopardy operated as a framework, a lens for understanding structural oppression on a national and international scale. Members also utilized it as a tool to connect Black, Latina, Asian, Middle Eastern, and Native American women's domestic issues to a larger movement against colonialism and global capitalism. Their newspaper thus served as a political education platform for members to map these intellectual and material linkages. As articulated from the very first *Triple Jeopardy* issue published in 1971, studying "revolutionary theory and tactics" was the primary avenue to changing women of color's socioeconomic conditions in the United States and abroad (TWWA 1971, 16).

More recently, scholars have begun to critically engage with the content of *Triple Jeopardy*, its internationalist, feminist, and revolutionary components. However, few explore the creation story of the newspaper and how members produced and disseminated copies. Examining the "behind the scenes" activities of the TWWA's newspaper launch contextualizes the

*WSQ: Women's Studies Quarterly* 51: 1 & 2 (Spring/Summer 2023)

group's pioneering efforts to envision a socialist society with women of color struggles at the forefront.

In my telephone interview with Fran Beal, she graciously shared her early memories of the newspaper and recalled names, events, locations, and dates of important and influential forces that shaped the TWWA's decision to develop *Triple Jeopardy*. Recovering the process of making the newspaper, especially its first issue, offers insight into the ways Black, Asian, and Latina women worked together under one collective to empower themselves and voice their concerns in national and international discourses of revolution and liberation.

Beal accredited two previous activist experiences with equipping her with the necessary skills to lead *Triple Jeopardy*'s editorial team. First, she learned the art of journalism from leftist French teachers while studying abroad in Paris between 1960 and 1966. Beal remembered, "I had a whole class on how to write an essay. I learned about the who, what, when, where, how, and why approach to journalism. [ . . .] And we recruited stories from some people. We didn't have that much luck with that. But we essentially taught ourselves to write stories" (pers. comm., 2022). When Beal arrived in Paris, she was planted in the strong African American expatriate community that had been well established since the interwar period, and she met Caribbean and African students from formerly French colonies. Beal advanced her journalism skills in an African diasporic environment, where students engaged in radical internationalist politics and debated strategies and tactics for the larger anti-colonial movement. Her time abroad sowed the seeds of her founding work with the TWWA's newspaper, which included a feminist and anti-imperialist analysis of international events relevant to Third World communities.

Organizing with the Student Nonviolent Coordinating Committee (SNCC) also prepared Beal to spearhead *Triple Jeopardy*. During her years abroad, Beal spent the summers in the United States, visiting family and working with SNCC. When she permanently relocated to New York in 1966 and took a research position with the National Council of Negro Women (NCNW), she also continued her activism with the local SNCC chapter. Beal joined the International Affairs Commission under the leadership of James Forman. By that time, SNCC's California branch was regularly publishing the organization's newspaper, *The Movement*, which covered domestic civil rights efforts and global liberation struggles. Beal drew inspiration from Forman, whom she recalled as the "one who said, we can print up pamphlets and articles ourselves and publicize them. A bestseller is ten thousand copies, we can do twenty-five or fifty thousand pamphlets." Beal continued, "He's the one, I think, that probably influenced me the most in terms of the importance of propaganda and the importance of information sharing and getting your side of the story out." On a practical side, Beal remembered learning two journalistic methods: "One was raising up and writing about issues that the mainstream media just didn't write about at all. And the second aspect was taking current events, particularly things that were in the mainstream media, and writing it and analyzing it from your perspective, and the impact it might have or might not have on women of color" (pers. comm., 2022). In the first *Triple Jeopardy* issue, readers can recognize how both methods are employed to discuss underexplored problems in mainstream news, like hypersurveillance in Black neighborhoods and misrepresented media coverage of political prisoners like Angela Davis and George Jackson (TWWA 1971, 3, 6, 15). SNCC offered Beal the blueprint that she then built upon to develop the TWWA's intellectual organ.

In making the physical newspaper, the TWWA relied on its members' volunteer labor to research, write, draw graphics, format, print, and distribute copies. They rented a commercial printer in New York's Chinatown that was popular among activists. Beal argued, "All of this was done in the sense of being self-sufficient, and we were training women to be able to do things. So people used what typing skills they had to become typesetters. We learned to lay out the paper [. . .] scratch in the headlines" (pers. comm., 2022). TWWA members, working in various organizations, reappropriated resources like pencils, pens, and Xerox machines when possible. Readers will notice that the first *Triple Jeopardy* issue does not include bylines or citations. This was done strategically and intentionally by members to evade being identified by the Federal Bureau of Investigation (FBI), which was surveilling the group's writings, activities, and political affiliations at the time, as evidenced by TWWA member Kisha Shakur's incarceration (TWWA 1971, 4).

Members collectively decided on the structure of the newspaper, which they agreed would serve an organizational component—bridging the different chapters—but also would go beyond this model. Voicing the group's original motives for creating a newspaper, Beal asserted, "We wanted to reach more women than we could in terms of just face-to-face." Beal explained, "We bonded our publication to be appropriated to talk about the issue that we were trying to raise [. . .] and we were concerned about the kind of language we would use, the class of people who we were trying to address" (pers. comm., 2022). They located and studied other radical newspapers at the time and discussed effective strategies for communicating with Third World communities. *Triple Jeopardy's* inaugural issue uplifted working-class women of color's struggles like affordable childcare services, medical racism, and economic exploitation: for example, TWWA members' published interview with Mrs. B, a Maryland factory worker who discussed the sexism and racism she experienced on the job. When asked if she worked because she was tired of staying at home, Mrs. B responded, "No, I worked there because I had to. The pay was lousy, the job was lousy, but me and my family had to eat!!!" (TWWA 1971, 14). Here, TWWA members pointed out the stark differences between mainstream white feminists—who wanted to enter the workforce en masse—and women of color's liberation goals, which went beyond participating in capitalism.

When designing *Triple Jeopardy*, the TWWA considered which activist circles to enter. Beal highlighted, "We ended up going through those who [were] radical, those who [were] progressives—talking about fundamental changes in terms of social change in America. So, in that sense, it's not like we were different from—we were in alignment with all the other left organizations that had an alternative press" (pers. comm., 2022). The Liberation News Service, a radical news agency founded in 1967, tied many underground and alternative presses together, providing inexpensive photographs, news articles, and opinion pieces on American politics, the Vietnam war, and other international struggles. Beal acknowledged how the TWWA used the Liberation News Service mainly for images, but sometimes on occasion for essays on Vietnam too. By the time the TWWA started imagining the material and structural components of *Triple Jeopardy*, members had a copious number of examples to draw inspiration from. In addition to SNCC, other radical and nationalist groups, including the Black Panther Party and the Young Lords, also had organizational newspapers. What distinguished *Triple Jeopardy* from any other alternative press at the time was the TWWA's focus on women of the Third World movement. When members entered the realm of underground print culture, they sought to disrupt hypermasculine framings of liberation and encourage women of color in the U.S. to take an active role in defining and articulating their freedom dreams and visions of societal changes.

In the inaugural issue of *Triple Jeopardy*, the TWWA announced the group's history, ideological platform, and political goals in the center spread of the newspaper, "Women in the Struggle." Members' decision to format their core beliefs at the center of *Triple Jeopardy* also played up the group's larger argument for Third World women to be situated at the heart of revolutionary struggles in the 1970s. The TWWA's "Women in the Struggle" essay outlined the group's ideological pillars under the subcategories of "Family," "Employment," "Sex Roles," "Education," "Services," "Women in Our Own Right," and "Self-Defense." Each description of these categories reframed women's role in the broader Third World community. At least three of these categories argued for women's bodily autonomy, challenging pronatalist advocates in communities of color. Under the "Family" category, TWWA activists boldly asserted their support for "communal households and the idea of the extended family" and called for a "socialization of housework and child care with the sharing of all work by men and women" (TWWA 1971, 9). These nontraditional household structures would shift the burden of care from mothers to other relatives. Members also argued against forced sterilization and mandatory birth control programs, naming these violent practices as "genocide" against poor Third World women. In the "Women in Our Own Right" section, the TWWA called out "so-called radical, militant, and/or so-called revolutionary groups" who failed to see women of color's humanity outside of their relationship with men (TWWA 1971, 9). Beal disclosed, "We had a lot of criticisms of the Panthers. [...] There was this contradiction between agreeing with their worldview, but disagreeing also with the militarization of their organization and their macho culture" (pers. comm., 2022). Differing from many male cultural nationalists, who also espoused an anti-sterilization position but supported pronatalist arguments, the TWWA advocated for women to have the right to choose whether they wanted children.

TWWA members also took up the controversial issue of heteropatriarchy in Third World liberation movements in the first *Triple Jeopardy*, further distancing their politics from other self-proclaimed revolutionary organizations in the United States. The discussion of "Sex Roles" challenged homophobia, contending that "the oppression and dehumanizing ostracism that homosexuals face must be rejected and their right to exist as dignified human beings must be defended" (TWWA 1971, 9). TWWA members identified the distinction between gender and sexuality while also linking them as inseparable from one another. Members debated the collective's stance on homophobia a year before announcing it publicly, when the group was still organizing as the Black Women's Alliance (BWA). For Beal, she saw it as politically "pragmatic" to organize against *all* forms of sexual oppression. A lesbian Black woman who went by the one-name Affrikka was a part of the BWA, and her Puerto Rican partner's interest in joining the group sparked a larger conversation that ultimately ended with a renaming of the collective to the TWWA. Remembering these early discussions, Beal justified her support of lesbians on the basis that the TWWA was already "being lesbian baited" for "having an independent women's organization and raising issues other than the racial aspect," which, she explained, back then was considered "divisive" to the broader movement. Unfortunately, the TWWA's sister chapter in the Bay Area would stray from the organization's anti-homophobic roots two years later when they voted against tackling issues related to homophobia in their community outreach and political education activism. The TWWA's founding chapter made an unconventional and controversial stance when they included a section on "Sex Roles" in their first *Triple Jeopardy* publication, a perspective critical to expanding feminist concerns in revolutionary rhetoric and practice in the United States.

After printing the inaugural *Triple Jeopardy* issue, these women then explored every avenue to share copies. This included hosting baked-good sales in Central Park and passing out their newspaper to anyone interested in talking politics. This could range from the movement to free political prisoners and national anti-war demonstrations to women's working conditions and bodily autonomy. Matching theory with practice, New York members also sent free copies to political prisoners and soon expanded the distribution to anyone incarcerated who requested an issue. The Bay Area sister chapter was in its early formation, so West Coast founder Cheryl Johnson also disseminated copies at local bookstores, cafes, and community centers.

An examination of the TWWA's process of developing *Triple Jeopardy* sheds light on the web of organizational and ideological networks that influenced members' decisions on what to write about, who to write to, and how to share these ideas. *Triple Jeopardy* was more than a news outlet. It was an intellectual space for TWWA members and newspaper contributors to forge international solidarities and theorize about the role of women in revolutionary struggles. Any Black, Latina, Asian, or Native American woman could pick up a copy of *Triple Jeopardy* and learn how their everyday experiences of patriarchy, poverty, and reproductive injustices were deeply interwoven in the fabrics of capitalism and imperialism that also impacted women in Third World countries. When reminiscing about the newspaper and people's reaction, Fran Beal revealed it was "very encouraging to us to know that we were speaking for women, on behalf of women, advocating for women, who were not yet prepared to speak for themselves" (pers. comm., 2022). Beal and other TWWA members knew the power of information-sharing, so joining the underground print culture was an opportunity to correct mainstream media's silencing and misrepresentation of working-class women of color's issues, nationally and internationally.

**Tiana U. Wilson** is a doctoral candidate in the Department of History with a portfolio in Women's and Gender Studies at the University of Texas at Austin. Her dissertation is an intellectual history of the Third World Women's Alliance. She can be reached at tianauwilson@gmail.com.

## Works Cited

Blackwell, Maylei. 2015. "Triple Jeopardy: The Third World Women's Alliance and the Transnational Roots of Women-of-Color Feminism." In *Provocations: A Transnational Reader in the History of Feminist Thought*, edited by Susan Bordo, M. Cristina Alcalde, and Ellen Rosenman, 280–89. Berkeley: University of California Press.

Farmer, Ashley. 2017. *Remaking Black Power: How Black Women Transformed an Era*. Chapel Hill: University of North Carolina Press.

Fernández, Johanna. 2020. *The Young Lords: A Radical History*. Chapel Hill: University of North Carolina Press.

Hong, Grace Kyungwon. 2018. "Intersectionality and Incommensurability: Third World Feminism and Asian Decolonization." In *Asian American Feminisms and Women of Color Politics*, edited by Lynn Fujiwara and Shireen Roshanravan, 27–42. Seattle: University of Washington Press.

Kannan, Vani. 2018. "The Third World Women's Alliance: History, Geopolitics, and Form." PhD diss., Syracuse University.

Romney, Patricia. 2021. *We Were There: The Third World Women's Alliance and the Second Wave*. New York: Feminist Press.

Springer, Kimberly. 2005. *Living for the Revolution: Black Feminist Organizations, 1968–1980*. Durham, NC: Duke University Press.

Third World Women's Alliance. 1971. "Women in the Struggle." *Triple Jeopardy* 1, no. 1 (September–October): 8–9.

Ward, Stephen. 2006. "The Third World Women's Alliance: Black Feminist Radicalism and Black Power Politics." In *The Black Power Movement: Rethinking the Black Power Civil Rights Era*, edited by Peniel E. Joseph, 119–44. New York: Routledge.

PART IV. **BOOK REVIEWS**

# The Anti-idealist Black Feminism of *The Other Side of Terror*

Roderick A. Ferguson

Erica R. Edwards's *The Other Side of Terror: Black Women and the Culture of U.S. Empire*, New York: NYU Press, 2021

Erica Edwards's *The Other Side of Terror: Black Women and the Culture of U.S. Empire* is a book that provides a necessary interpretation of African American women's literature within the context of twentieth-century U.S. imperial ventures. If it just did that, that would be enough. In providing this interpretation, it has helped us understand the impressions that war and conflict have had on African American cultural production and how some of its most celebrated producers—Black feminists—have responded powerfully to the imprint of state violence. As important as that intervention is, the book does even more. It uses the long war on terror to initiate a critique of the worrisome idealisms that currently constitute many of the conversations around Blackness, idealisms that conceal Blackness's relations with what Edwards calls "imperial grammars" and "the scenes of incorporation," relations that align Blackness with imperial violence and incorporate it into regimes of dominance.

Situating her investigation in the span of time between the rise of U.S. counterinsurgency in the 1960s and the years of the Obama presidency, Edwards defines the "imperial grammars of Blackness" as "the codes of cultural production and public discourse in linking the rationalization of US imperial violence abroad to the US public sphere's manipulation and incorporation of Blackness as the sign of multicultural beneficence" (21). As such, the book theorizes Blackness as existing in a dialectical relationship with U.S. empire in that it has been both the critic and the supplicant of U.S. imperial formations. In this, the book rejects Blackness as an idealism that is always the antithesis of dominant forms of power. Instead, the book favors a historically and politically grounded engagement with

**WSQ: Women's Studies Quarterly** 51: 1 & 2 (Spring/Summer 2023)

Blackness, determining its vulnerabilities to empire as well as its possibilities for anti-imperialist insurgency.

The imperial grammar of Blackness has direct bearing on the institutions that constellate the book—literature, the university, Black studies, and Black feminism. Those institutions set the stage for Blackness's incorporation into and rebellion against empire. About the scenes of incorporation, she writes the following:

> I wager, then, that the scenes of incorporation that tell the story of Black women's passing through the very fields through which I now pass— Black studies and literature in particular, universities and literary culture in general—might highlight a contradiction at the heart of contemporary Black (literary) studies, at the heart of English, at the heart of this book: that Blackness is as intimate with empire as the reader is with the book on-screen or on her lap, that the Black cultural text is, in other words, a transfer point, a too-short bridge, between the long war on terror's brutal practices of counterinsurgency and its smooth calls of advancement, inclusion, celebrity, and celebration. (188)

The contradiction that she wrestles with in the book is the one that designates Black people, Black literary studies, Black feminism as entities simultaneously minoritized by the U.S. nation-state and activated by U.S. empire. For her, Black womanhood is not free of these contradictions. As she argues, "That Black women were both the targets of state defense initiatives and authors of a national narrative of democratic righteousness meant that they were positioned along the fault lines of competing nationalist discourses" (58). As Black women were occupying these fault lines, Black feminism developed practices to assess and confront those contradictions.

This necessarily means that the book promotes and constructs a Black feminist archive that opposes the concealments of liberalism. Here, she points to the ways that liberal ideologies and apparatuses facilitate and obfuscate social violence by proclaiming the state's benevolence. As she says, "I will continue to call Black feminist literature—the work we might gather not as a collection of singular texts by great writers but rather under the banner of a collective project of marshaling the embodied practices of reading, writing, hearing and performing literature in the interest of abolitionist anticolonial social change—as a passing through that devastates the desires of the liberal literature teacher" (188). To the extent to which we cover up Blackness's relations to imperial projects is the extent to which we walk in step with the liberal literature teacher. We might, therefore, think of

*The Other Side of Terror* as the embodiment of a critical subject that strives to walk down other roads.

Lastly, the book is immediately impactful for the study of Black social formations. One way of thinking of Edwards's argument is to posit it as a thesis about how the long war on terror demonstrates the relational nature of Black social formations and discourses of Blackness. Contrary to much of the current conversation about Blackness, there is no isolationist or antirelational argument about Blackness in the book; instead, we see an engagement with Blackness and Black social formations through their geopolitical relations with empire. Indeed, the book forcefully implies that whether Blackness likes it or not, it is implicated in what happens in Latin America, Asia, and the Middle East. In this way, relationality is not a matter of volunteerism. It is a matter of how Blackness is constituted as a historical formation and how we Black people are constituted as social subjects. Black feminism, for Edwards, is the name of what can be done after we accept the fact that we are always and already implicated in the workings of empire.

For Black studies, this would mean a rigorously feminist return to the foundations of that critical practice. Recall that C. L. R. James insisted that Black studies could not be narrowed to the confines of identity—that it was about Black people as individuals removed from the larger historical struggles. He said instead that Black studies was the critique of Western civilization (James 1993). Edwards's book extends that definition to reveal that one of the most powerful articulations of Western civilization has been all the campaigns and social projects that make up the U.S. war on terror. Assessing them means reconstituting cultural archives that we presume we already know. The book enacts a profound service as it shows how Black feminism can be adapted to help us meet our most urgent geopolitical dilemmas.

**Roderick A. Ferguson** is the William Robertson Coe Professor of Women's, Gender, and Sexuality Studies and American Studies at Yale University and the author of *The Reorder of Things: The University and Its Pedagogies of Minority Difference*. He can be reached at roderick.ferguson@yale.edu.

## Works Cited

James, C. L. R. 1993. "Black Studies and the Contemporary Student." In *The C. L. R. James Reader*, edited by Anna Grimshaw, 390–404. Oxford: Blackwell.

# Recovering the Entangled History of Political and Sexual Radicalism

Zifeng Liu

Aaron S. Lecklider's *Love's Next Meeting: The Forgotten History of Homosexuality and the Left in American Culture*, Oakland: University of California Press, 2021

Many historical accounts of the U.S. gay and lesbian liberation struggle date the beginning of radical sexual politics to the late 1960s, when activist groups such as the Gay Liberation Front linked the attainment of sexual freedom to the eradication of racial capitalism, imperialism, and patriarchy. According to such studies, the possibility of an alliance between leftists and sexual dissidents before that decade of worldwide revolutionary fervor was precluded by the former's inability to incorporate sexuality into their analyses and visions of liberatory social transformation, if not their outright homophobia. While not downplaying the Old Left's contradictions and ambivalence in its attitude toward nonnormative sexualities, Aaron S. Lecklider's *Love's Next Meeting: The Forgotten History of Homosexuality and the Left in American Culture* recounts a pre-1960 history of queer advocacy that reveals the intimate imbrication of anti-capitalist politics and gay visibility, recognition, and liberation. These little-known queer-Left intersections helped shape the contours of later sexual activism. As with other scholars exploring political and sexual formations that fall out of the boundaries of the permissible, Lecklider mitigates the archival lack around the intimacy between leftist politics and queer life—due to long-standing anti-communism and sexual conservatism—through examining the representational, the aesthetic, and the pleasurable as sites where the engagement between political and sexual dissidents was most visible. He focuses particularly on leftist literary and cultural circles that offered space for radical, alternative representations and discussions of nonnormative sexualities. In tracing this underexamined relationship, Lecklider assembles an impressive multiracial cast of writers, artists, and thinkers, some better known than others, who intentionally

**WSQ: Women's Studies Quarterly** 51: 1 & 2 (Spring/Summer 2023)

and at times unknowingly drew gay men and women into the fold of radical politics and united the movement for sexual diversity with the struggle against the ravages of capitalism and white supremacy.

Lecklider convincingly explains the intertwining of political and sexual radicalism. Leftists and gay women and men were united by their shared geographical spaces, similar experiences of marginalization and exclusion from mainstream U.S. society, and comparable commitments to transgressing the confines of the acceptable and the normative. In particular, the entanglement of anti-Blackness, heterosexism, homophobia, xenophobia, and anti-radicalism and the resistance to it blurred the lines between political radicalism and sexual deviance. Organized both chronologically and topically, *Love's Next Meeting*'s exploration of the intersection between the Left and homosexuality unfolds in three sections.

The first part, consisting of the first three chapters, shows that political radicals, and in particular those who were sexually dissident, supported sexual liberation as an inseparable part of the fundamental political and economic transformation of the United States. They articulated that position in the pages of leftist literature and the leftist press. In agitating for radical social change, queer leftists in many instances were able to link their desire for same-sex intimacy to their commitment to anti-capitalist activism. These sexual radicals, at times, also struggled to balance the fulfillment of their affective and sexual needs with the waging of struggles against racial capitalism and imperialism. Within leftist networks, whose advocacy work around the issue of sexuality was often constrained by political and cultural rigidity as well as by heterosexism, gay women and men repurposed the language and conventions of leftist and anti-racist politics to explore sexual nonnormativities. For them, the repression of obscenity served the interests of the ruling class, and the embrace of sexual diversity was a hallmark of a classless society. Radical print culture thus abounded with discussions of nonnormative sexualities. Radicals also drew on narratives of Black solidarity with sexual dissidents against state repression, as well as leftist analyses of sexual deviants as members of the proletariat, in order to link the Left's anti-racist campaigns with the struggle for sexual freedom.

The second part argues that leftist theorizations of labor, "the woman question," and proletarian fiction laid the groundwork for a radical sexual politics that emphasized the mutual constitution of homophobia with capitalism, sexism, and racism. Effective radical labor organizing in industries that were presumed to be attractive to sexual dissidents enabled the mobilization of leftist institutions' resources, rhetorics, and representational strategies regarding the condition of the proletariat to connect queer intimacy and worker revolution. The incorporation of sexual diversity into radical worker movements led to the positioning of queer sex work as a labor issue and a survival strategy, which, while pathologizing sex workers, acknowledged their humanity. Similarly drawing on both the Left's feminism and its visual conventions, in particular the elevation of masculinity, queer women contested heteronormative expectations placed upon them and embraced nonnormative sexualities as holding revolutionary potential. In a similar vein, writers of color on the Left capitalized on the opportunities opened by proletarian literature's emphasis on representations of working-class lives to, with either naturalist or modernist techniques, articulate a radical sexual politics that exposed the moral and economic bankruptcy of racial capitalism and celebrated the radical possibilities of gender and sexual nonconformity in poor urban settings.

The third part, the final two chapters, shows that sexual dissidents were at the forefront of the struggle against fascism and the democratizing process in the United States during the Popular Front era. Queer radicals rode the surging waves of antifascist mobilization to link racism, capitalism, and heterosexism and step up their struggles for sexual freedom. The experience shared among gay volunteers of fighting in battles against fascism abroad connected internationalist militancy and sexual nonconformity. The Communist Party's new emphasis on forming a broad Left-liberal Popular Front in this political context of antifascism prompted queer radicals to forge solidarities across ideological borders, swell the ranks of anti-Nazi forces, and pursue sexual liberation through stretching the boundaries of full citizenship, though squarely within the framework of U.S. democracy and pluralism. This adoption of the rhetoric of 100 percent Americanism entailed compromises that blunted the radical edges of the movement for sexual diversity. This framing of the struggle against sexual oppression as an issue of minority rights and as resolvable through reform rather than a reordering of the United States along anti-capitalist lines, as well as the incorporation of sexual dissidents into the affirmation of the value of American democracy, was exemplified by the activism of the homophile movement during the early Cold War. However, the combination of the Red and Lavender Scares and the persistent conjoining of struggles against racial capitalism with visions of sexual liberation reinforced the linkage between sexual and political deviance.

In tracing the intertwined histories of struggles against capitalist exploitation and strivings for sexual justice, Lecklider presents biographies of a range of queer radicals who shared a commitment to the fusion of the pursuit of nonnormative sexualities and the construction of socialism but differed in, among other things, their particular understandings of the entanglement of class, sexuality, gender, and race; strategies to explore the relationship between transgressive sexuality and fundamental social change; and performances of gender and sexuality. Bursting from the pages of *Love's Next Meeting* are queer radicals filled with enthusiasm for life, love, pleasure, and revolution, and with agential power. Inside and outside the organized Left, sexual dissidents were not passive recipients of leftist organizations' resources, ideologies, and policies. Indeed, they attempted to navigate the twists and turns of the Communist Party's policies and the treacherous and shifting waters of domestic and international politics. They not only sought to push the Party to address gender and sexual oppression under capitalism but also deftly repurposed official conceptualizations, discourses, and artistic strategies to pursue sexual diversity.

In playing a crucial role in the Communist struggle against capitalism, queer leftists were also engaged in the Left's anti-racist work and drew on leftist analyses of how race and class interacted to produce and perpetuate Black unfreedom, linking their struggle to the long civil rights movement and advancing campaigns for sexual liberation. Lecklider is sensitive to how race, as a foremost organizing principle of economic, political, and social life in the United States, stratifies the lives of queer activists, as the book both offers portraits of Black queer radicals and points out the inadequacies of certain white sexual dissidents' views on Blackness. However, even as Lecklider recognizes the capaciousness of "queer," his exploration of sexual radicalism does not fully address how Black people experienced queerness differently. While Lecklider shows how certain queer radicals courageously pursued nonnormative expressions of desire, a consideration of how Black sexualities have been structurally positioned outside of heteronormativity, how nonnormative sexualities have been produced through anti-Black abjection, how queering can be a technology of racial exploitation and oppression, and how anti-Blackness and anti-radicalism are mutually constitutive might yield a richer analysis (Dillon 2018, 15; Haley 2013, 73; Burden-Stelly 2017, 344–46). These shortcomings, however, are outweighed by the book's contributions. In particular, *Love's Next Meeting* powerfully demonstrates the historical inextricability of the attainment of sexual and gender liberation, the eradication of white supremacy, and the fundamental transformation of society. It constructs a useful past to offer a reminder that a truly revolutionary queer politics must call for forging a broad coalition against racial capitalism, heteropatriarchy, imperialism, and colonialism. It is a book we sorely need in an era of attacks on women's bodily autonomy and setbacks in the pursuit of sexual freedom.

**Zifeng Liu** is a postdoctoral scholar in the Africana Research Center at Pennsylvania State University. His current research project explores Black leftist women's interactions with Chinese government officials and intellectuals during the Cold War. He can be reached at zql5527@psu.edu.

## Works Cited

Burden-Stelly, Charisse. 2017. "Constructing Deportable Subjectivity: Antiforeignness, Antiradicalism, and Antiblackness during the McCarthyist Structure of Feeling." *Souls* 19, no. 3: 342–58.

Dillon, Stephen. 2018. *Fugitive Life: The Queer Politics of the Prison State.* Durham, NC: Duke University Press.

Haley, Sarah. 2013. "'Like I Was a Man': Chain Gangs, Gender, and the Domestic Carceral Sphere in Jim Crow Georgia." *Signs* 39, no. 1 (Autumn): 53–77.

# Abolishing Settler Imperialism: Review of *Red Scare*

Juliana Hu Pegues

Joanne Barker's *Red Scare: The State's Indigenous Terrorist*, Oakland: University of California Press, 2021

Joanne Barker's *Red Scare: The State's Indigenous Terrorist* is a significant and necessary examination of state power's consolidation through the criminalization and surveillance of Indigenous peoples. Focusing on the historical and contemporary contexts in the United States and Canada, Barker argues that Indigenous peoples are both represented as terrorists and made representable as terrorists in order to establish, organize, and maintain state imperialism. Barker looks specifically to two figures, the Murderable Indian and the Kinless Indian, who act in tandem to fortify the authority of the state to regulate identity, punish opposition, and condition the possibilities for life itself. *Red Scare* offers an important analysis of state power through an intersectional Indigenous studies, which is in conversation with feminist studies, carceral studies, critical ethnic studies, and anti-imperialist scholarship.

Readers familiar with Lenape scholar Joanne Barker's work will recognize her incisive critique of colonialism and capitalism grounded in an Indigenous feminist framework. While her previous book *Native Acts* focused on Indigenous peoples' subjectivity within state formations of recognition and membership, in *Red Scare* she hones in specifically on how, and to what ends, state and corporate actors (often working together) deploy discourses of national security and public safety in order to enact materially and epistemically violent reprisals against Indigenous activists and Indigenous peoples' self-determination. Since the 1998 publication of Luana Ross's (Confederated Salish and Kootenai Tribes) foundational book, *Inventing the Savage: The Social Construction of Native American Criminality*, very few scholars have focused keen attention on the criminalization of Indigeneity and

*WSQ: Women's Studies Quarterly* 51: 1 & 2 (Spring/Summer 2023)

Indigenous peoples. Such analyses are critical, given disparities within the system of mass incarceration and the alarming yet underreported instances of police violence experienced by American Indian, Alaska Native, Hawaiian, First Nations, Métis, and Inuit persons and communities. Barker joins scholar-activists in Indigenous studies, such as Leanne Betasamosake Simpson (Alderville First Nation), Heidi Kiiwetinepinesiik Stark (Turtle Mountain Ojibwe), and Roxanne Dunbar-Ortiz, in centering the criminalization of Indigenous peoples as both sign and instantiation of colonialism's *longue durée* in the United States and Canada. *Red Scare*, moreover, locates the state's current strategies of counterterrorism, particularly in response to the pipeline opposition of Indigenous water protectors, as a continuation of ongoing imperial processes of anti-Indigenous invasion, occupation, extraction, and sexual violence.

Throughout the book, the concept of Red Scare functions as both an organizing analytic and a reading practice for studying state formation through this polysemantic phrase that invokes the fearmongering fueled by the discursive and affective imagery of, alternately, the red communist and the racialization of the Native Red Man/Woman. Though an inventive play on words, Barker moves past analogizing the multivalent meanings of the term to offer a historical reiteration of anti-Indigenous criminalization located in the shift from government scapegoating and the (extra)legal disciplining of communists, socialists, and anarchists during World Wars I and II, to a post–Cold War refashioning of subversive threat attached to a new cohort of racialized radicals, namely Indigenous, Black, Muslim, or queer. From the late 1960s forward, Indigenous activists in particular were considered communist sympathizers, or unknowing patsies for communist organizers, because of what was viewed as the inherently socialistic and anti-capitalist nature of Indigenous communities. In relation to state imperialist practices, Barker goes even further to explicate an additional Red Scare genealogy through the lens of extractive capitalism. In a section under the heading "Capital Oil," Barker brilliantly traces the development of oil economy and infrastructure alongside the ascendancy of American military hegemony, resulting in the equating of energy security with national security. Not only does this securitized economy depend disproportionately on energy and mineral extrication from Indigenous territories, but it underscores the reasons underlying the creation of the Indigenous terrorist, whose protection of the environment undermines national inviolability and public freedom. These are not incidental constructions. Barker excels in drawing these types of unexpected and nuanced linkages that, once understood, are the only way one can view them.

Joanne Barker most strongly makes her argument about the state's reliance on the Indigenous terrorist in her chapter on the figure of the Murderable Indian, starting with the stark fact that in every instance of anti-pipeline activism in the United States and Canada, state and corporate officials, alongside police and private security forces, have charged water and land protectors with terrorism. Within the Red Scare genealogy that Barker traces, she contends, the current state retaliation against Indigenous activists is notably different given new scales of global surveillance and carceral technologies. Barker focuses on two examples, the No Dakota Access Pipeline (NoDAPL) camps at the Standing Rock Sioux Reservation in North Dakota and the perhaps less well-known (at least to U.S. readers) Wet'suwet'en oil and gas pipeline protests in their territory in northwestern British Columbia. NoDAPL protestors were consistently labeled as terrorists by a conglomeration of state actors, oil company representatives, and mainstream media, to such an extent that even in the face of brute and severe violence including sicced dogs; detention without access to food, water, or bathrooms; mass arrests; and the use of water cannons in freezing weather, counterterrorism measures were deemed necessary and beneficial to the protection and rationalization of global economic interests. In the example of the camp established by the Unist'ot'en, a house group of the Wet'suwet'en, the Royal Canadian Mounted Police coordinated a raid with energy companies; notes gained from a strategy session detail that violence was encouraged, lethal force was condoned, and child apprehension by social services was considered. This last aspect, including the arrest of children and the elderly, underscores the need for Indigenous feminist critique such as Barker's to analyze the anti-relational, racist, and sexist intergenerational violence accorded to the expansive scope of the state's counterterrorism. Through the representational logics of the Indigenous terrorist, Barker compellingly demonstrates that it is not the figure of the dead Indian that animates state power but, instead, the Murderable Indian, who instills an affective terror and justifies the expansion of policing and punishment.

At first read, Barker's figure of the Kinless Indian appears to be less explicitly tied to the state's construction of the Indigenous terrorist, especially following the vicious material violence the state deploys against Indigenous protestors under the rationale of counterterrorism. As Barker proceeds through her examples of the Cherokee in the United States and the Métis in Canada, and the increased number of self-identified and unverifiable (kinless) claims to belonging to these two Indigenous nations, however, her larger argument about the imbrication of state power through control of Indigenous representation is made apparent. Fraudulent claims of Indigeneity are not simply absurd or insulting arguments for individual rights or spurious critiques of authenticity, but they ultimately authorize the state as adjudicator of who a (good) Indian is or can be, invalidating Indigenous sovereignty and self-determination in the process. Given current discussions in Indian Country and academia, Barker's trenchant analysis reminds us to not lose sight of power, particularly the state's investment in erasing Indigenous peoples from land and territory.

*Red Scare* is not only a study of how state power is operationalized through the organizing representation of Indigenous as terrorist: Barker also offers us the already present social alterity of land-based Indigenous relationality. As she affirms, "The future is not something we are waiting for, but rather is already embodied in our relationships with one another. These relationships anticipate the abolition of state imperialism and the real alternative of Indigenous governance" (25). Barker demonstrates why Indigenous sovereignty and self-determination, especially as conceptualized and enacted through Indigenous feminism, is central to abolition movements. As she contends, "Imperialism, colonialism, corporations, the military, security, and prisons are so fused to one another as to be impossible to distinguish. It will never be enough to reform or defund the police, the military, or security without also addressing corporate collusion. [...] Imperialism and colonialism must be undone, not as threads that pull at the others but as a woven amalgam of ideologies and institutions that must be obliterated" (115). Part of the University of California Press's series American Studies Now: Critical Histories of the Present, Barker's book is impressively accessible, even as it is paradigm-shifting. *Red Scare* is an immensely generative and teachable book, both within academia and beyond. Not only will this book be of great interest for students and scholars of Indigenous studies, feminist studies, carceral studies, imperialism, and the environment, but I expect *Red Scare* will have a lasting impact for Indigenous and community-based activists, and all those invested in a world beyond the state's imperial reach.

**Juliana Hu Pegues** is associate professor of literatures in English at Cornell University. She is also an affiliate faculty member in the American Indian and Indigenous Studies Program and the Asian American Studies Program. Her book *Space-Time Colonialism: Alaska's Indigenous and Asian Entanglements* won the 2022 Lora Romero First Book Prize from the American Studies Association and the 2022 Sally and Ken Owens Award for best book on the history of the Pacific West from the Western History Association. She can be reached at jhupegues@cornell.edu.

# Review of *Abolition. Feminism. Now.*

Barbara Ransby

Angela Y. Davis, Gina Dent, Erica R. Meiners, and Beth E. Richie's *Abolition. Feminism. Now.*, Chicago: Haymarket Books, 2022

Written by four of the sharpest and most respected scholar activists around, *Abolition. Feminism. Now.* gives us a powerful genealogy of the feminist roots of the twenty-first-century abolitionist movement and its urgent call to action. Angela Y. Davis, Gina Dent, Erica Meiners, and Beth E. Richie have the cumulative experience that covers a great swath of contemporary radical movements. The amalgam of that work, over many decades, deeply embedded in the work of many organizations, collectives, campaigns, and networks, has led all four coauthors to the place of "abolition feminism." In this book, they trace their collective journey and acknowledge all the "co-conspirators" they have embraced and worked with along the way. "Abolition feminism," the book reminds us, is both a "mode of analysis and a political practice." It insists that an end to state or interpersonal violence cannot occur without a larger feminist politics of justice, and conversely, feminists cannot rely upon oppressive carceral institutions to make women, LGBTQ, and especially trans folks, safe or free. The three major sections of the book address three questions implicit in its title: Why abolition? Why feminism? Why now? Abolition of prisons and the apparatuses of the prison industrial complex is what the new anti–state violence movement calls for.

Why abolition? This book insists that reforms alone cannot end the harm caused by policing and prisons. Making nicer, kinder prisons and nicer, kinder police just has not worked. Reform after reform has failed, and even the more robust reforms have been co-opted. The very logic and purpose of the "punishment industry," as Angela Davis calls it, is to harm, coerce, violate, and diminish those with whom it comes into contact. More-over, the system doesn't do much to heal or help the survivors and victims of harm either. The only real solution, *Abolition. Feminism. Now.* argues, is

**WSQ: Women's Studies Quarterly** 51: 1 & 2 (Spring/Summer 2023)

the dismantling of prisons and the building of alternative mechanisms to ensure safety and accountability.

The "building" aspect of abolition is underscored by the authors. They are not ignoring the importance of safety, but rather demanding that we think beyond guns and cages for ways to realize it. Holding up Black Youth Project 100's "Building Black Futures" campaign, and its corollary demand, "Invest/Divest," abolitionists have consistently foregrounded the need to allocate more resources for health care, affordable housing, quality public education, and jobs as critical ingredients for crime and violence prevention. They quote Ruth Wilson Gilmore, who insists abolition has never been only about "absence" but also about "presence" of critical resources and alternatives. Violence prevention is better than violent punishment, for everyone involved, and a plethora of restorative and transformative justice programs point to repair and healing as more ethical responses to "crime" than jails and prisons. In the case of poor and working-class women and femmes of color, often police intervention results in those women and femmes being further traumatized, jailed, or killed, even when they are the ones initially reaching out for help. The cases of Marissa Alexander, CeCe McDonald, Eisha Love, and Chicago's Bettie Jones are only a few examples.

Why feminism? The introduction traces the roots of abolitionist politics to a number of feminist thinkers and feminist-led organizations from Critical Resistance (CR) to INCITE: Women of Color Against Violence. CR was formed in California in the early 2000s in response to the growing and insatiable prison industry in the state and nation. A feminist politics was there from the beginning, insisting on a holistic approach: inclusion of incarcerated women and the families of incarcerated men and women, and a feminist analysis of violence as systemic and not simply an amalgam of individual cases. The Color of Violence conferences hosted by INCITE built upon this feminist praxis. They insisted that violence against women and femmes was not simply a domestic issue but had to be understood in the context of state violence, settler colonial violence, and violence caused by wars and occupations, as well as economic violence. Their perspective, as is that of Davis, Dent, Meiners, and Richie, is a global one.

As much as this book makes the case for abolition, it also fights for a robustly radical definition of feminism. The authors acknowledge the corrosive and dangerous effect of a kind of carceral feminism that needs to be opposed. Many who claim to be for gender justice, and the best interest of women and girls, accept and advance the notion that more cops and cages are needed to combat domestic abuse, rape, and other forms of sexual assault and misogynist, homophobic, and transphobic violence. The reality, we are reminded, is that police often perpetuate and aggravate dangerous situations rather than de-escalate and protect those *in* dangerous situations. This is especially true when those involved are people of color or live in low-income communities.

Why now? Citing both the numerous and widely publicized instances of police violence and the massive resistance that followed, the authors conclude that this is abolition's political moment. In other words, the gut-wrenching murders of Breonna Taylor, George Floyd, and others, coupled with the outpouring of protest, have created conditions for abolitionist solutions to finally be taken seriously by a wider audience. We live in urgent times, and we need to embrace radical solutions. But radical solutions are not isolated ones. The call for the abolition of police and prisons is, first of all, a process and not an event and, secondly, is part and parcel of a larger movement for far-reaching system change that dismantles not only police and prison but the entire system of racial capitalism. This message comes through loud and clear in each chapter of the book.

The collaborative approach taken to writing this book, as well as its humble acknowledgment of unanswered questions, reflects yet another set of feminist politics and sensibilities. The authors are conscientious about naming and honoring the work of dozens of individuals, organizations, and campaigns that are part of the larger abolitionist feminist ecosystem. Groups like Love and Protect, Dignity and Power, Black Mamas Bailout, Survived and Punished, No New Jails NYC, Project Nia, and the list goes on.

Abolitionist organizers are engaged in hard and tedious work. Joy and optimism have to be at the center for this kind of work to survive and persevere. Adorned with moving abolitionist graphics that chronicle local and national campaigns, *Abolition. Feminism. Now.* has both intellectual heft and historical resonance, and it does not fail to celebrate the radical imaginary. One poster beautifully illustrates the relationship between prisons and immigration detention, demanding that elected officials "Dismantle Prisons (and) Abolish ICE [Immigration and Customs Enforcement]," with images of butterflies that migrate across borders and dandelions that grow freely. "The Networkers" poster by Molly Costello is a design that celebrates not only what negative things need to go but what positive efforts can be, and are being, created. With a free-floating organic background, Costello shows adults caring for children, one person coming to the aid of another, and yet a third person working away, presumably problem-solving, on her laptop computer. The inclusion of these illustrations reminds us of the importance of art in making change and imagining the future. Gina Dent and Rachel Nelson's *Visualizing Abolition* multimedia project at University of California, Santa Cruz, is one of many examples.

Finally, for those who might say "abolition" is a lofty ideal but there is nothing concrete to do to advance it, the authors have a concrete response. The appendix of the book highlights a poster, titled "Reformist Reforms vs. Abolitionist Steps to End Imprisonment," that provides a kind of blueprint for abolitionist practice while drawing detailed distinctions between "reforms that create or expand cages" and efforts that move toward decarceration. The introduction to the appendix poster concludes with the following: "In all decarceration strategies, we must utilize tactics that will improve life for those most affected and make space to build the worlds we need." This is also the overall message of this powerful and hopeful text.

**Barbara Ransby** is an author, activist, and historian and Distinguished Professor and John D. MacArthur Chair in the Departments of Black Studies, Gender and Women's Studies, and History at the University of Illinois at Chicago, where she directs the Social Justice Initiative. She is a founding member of Scholars for Social Justice and a Marguerite Casey Foundation Freedom Scholar. She can be reached at bransby@uic.edu.

PART V. **POETRY**

# trans*imagination

Alan Pelaez Lopez

\* \* \*

The asterisk is a portal and a pause.

The asterisk is not a signifier of a destination.

A destination, here, is a form of violence.

The asterisk is an invitation to meditate on a material condition with legal, social, and cultural consequences in the hopes that one can depart from that reality.

The asterisk is not a star; it is not a burning rock, but some might argue that it is a rock that burns.

The asterisk feels. It is a feeling of stillness and prolonged puncture.

The asterisk is alive, but one cannot insist life onto it.

The asterisk is not a person or an identity.

The asterisk has been attended to and perhaps, it does not want to exist anymore. This is why the asterisk is a portal and a pause.[1]

The asterisk is not an arrest, it is a pause.

*WSQ: Women's Studies Quarterly* 51: 1 & 2 (Spring/Summer 2023)

The asterisk is not a hold, it is a portal, but the asterisk [temporarily] embraces the hold [of the ship :: belly :: sigh :: breath].

The asterisk is not a signifier of gender or race or nation-states; all those kill, kill, kill.

The asterisk is a portal and a pause.

*  *  *

On Zoom, Omi Salas-SantaCruz shares that one of the problems is that people always want to start with "the human" when extending care to the trans* experience. And that's the problem. The cis think they're extending care. But each attempt at care ends up in a desire for intelligibility. And what if the radical potential of trans* liberation is not legibility and uniformity but the endless possibilities within the simultaneity of experimentation, abstraction, opacity, and reworlding?

A trans* future necessitates the undoing of mastery. If the trans* subject must first be human, then doesn't that limit all other trans* possibilities? Lock all understandings of trans* to a medicalized (or at least, psychoanalyzed) Western understanding?

The cis spin planets to understand *trans*interiority*. And the tea is that there is no need for understanding. trans* is. That's it. trans* is trans*temporal, trans*hemispheric, trans*gressive, trans*imaginative, in trans*it, in trans*it always. There need be no more language.

*  *  *

On university campuses, there are classes on capital *t*, Trans Studies. Sometimes, Indigenous understandings of spirit, kinship, and land are subjugated to "transgender." And that's the limit of study. In the West, study does not always mean abolitionist planning or a rethinking of epistemologies and epistemes. In the West, to study is to lay out genealogies deemed legible to those who have been appointed the power to story :: those who have been gifted with the weapon of authorship. In the Global South, Indigenous, gender-expansive, and agender peoples self-author:fashion:make every single day. And that's interesting to the West. Some of us in the Global South call it existing, or being, or the everyday, or the latest formation of the self. And the Global North sees it, marks it, and authors it as a Trans performance, Trans subjectivity, Trans articulation, Trans gesture, and it goes on and on and on.

Sometimes, not everything is Trans. Sometimes, everything is trans*. Sometimes, things just are what they are when they are still.

* * *

I'm only trans* when gender(ing) is projected onto me.
        (Maybe that's a lie but right now, it feels true)

When I am lying in bed and the room is spinning and my inhaler + nausea dissolvable pills + vertigo meds are too far away from my nightstand and I reach out to grab something and everything falls to the ground and I open my eyes and there is more spinning and suddenly everything is white, I am not Trans in that moment. I'm just a person trying to understand my body and my needs. But wait, "I'm just a person trying to understand my body and my needs" will be ejected, coded, and theorized as Trans by a lot of [      ].

Sometimes, I forget that I am a gendered person. I do not forget that I have a body though. The body is often in too much chronic pain to think of gender when it is solely thinking of staying alive.

When I have not left my apartment in days, I tend to forget that I "live" in a gender. My favorite thing about my bathroom is that there is no air vent. When I shower, the mirror gets foggy. I step out and there is no gender in the mirror. There are specks of flesh. In the absence of an air vent, there is me and there is flesh, and then there is me and flesh together.

* * *

I was born in "México." Like my Afrodescendant ancestors, I was forced to migrate to another country. Saidiya Hartman names a reality such as this "the afterlife of slavery."[2] Sometimes, both my country of birth and the country I was forced to migrate to feel like different continents though they're only separated by one border. That's the frightening power of settler-conquistador violence: lands that should be familiar to the Indigenous Black subject feel foreign.

I think that when Indigenous peoples are removed from land, our bodies become the closest claim we have to land :: memory :: origin :: kin.

To be Indigenous in this moment then, is to have an intimate and ongoing relationship to trans*itioning.

There is no way to trans*ition into or out of settler colonialism. The structure must be abolished.

\*\*\*

In *Solastalgia*, Demian DinéYazhi' writes, "I want to go back / 500 years but that / means you would / not be here."[3] When I first read the poem, I couldn't move. I thought about *it* for days. The desire to go back and change anything would change *us* :: fragment who we are now :: perhaps disembody us :: maybe disappear us? So many ugly things have happened in the *before* to arrive at the *now*. We are always arriving and trans*itioning.

To live *here*, we must surrender to the trans*ition.

\*\*\*

Erendira and Luis ask me to develop a workshop for mostly single moms. They think sharing my experience with gender might help. I take out Expo markers, find an empty space in their tiny office, and get to work. A few days later, I get in the back of Luis's pickup truck, and we drive for an hour. Minutes after leaving León, Nicaragua, I can tell that there's something *wrong* about what I'm about to do. So, I take out a notebook and add "DE LAS POSIBILIDADES" instead of leaving it just as "EJEMPLOS." Invoking words like NO BINARIA, TRANS, TRAVESTI, TRANSEXUAL, ANDRÓGINA, MUJER, HOMBRE, INTERSEXUAL, feels too binary, or should I say, too West. After all, everyone knows I'm from México and not from Nica. I'm literally the oppressor here :: the "activist" from one of Latin America's empires. So, I lean on DE LAS POSIBILIDADES to gesture toward something other than the West, other than México, other than the North, other than gender. Perhaps this possibility is spirit, or the land, or time . . .

[In México, everyone *knows* the gays have rights, in the same way that everyone *knows* that in México, the gays can be murdered and/or disappeared in public at any moment.]

More than halfway through the workshop, I can't explain NO BINARIA. Me, the nonbinary facilitator, can't explain NO BINARIA. I guess no one had ever asked me to lay out all my business. So, I tell them: Ser una persona que no tiene necesidad, deseo o interés de insistir en un género. Cuando eres tú mismo/a y la expresión de género no es necesariamente algo que te atraiga a imitar, vigilar o dar a los demás. I feel like I'm wrong. But can language capture the essence of rejecting a settler gender (and at times, a settler sexuality) and in that same rejection not only unsettle the world but unsettle oneself in the knowledge that one knows oneself, but one doesn't know if one is safe in the world one claims to know?

"Entonces yo creo que soy no binaria," a mother utters just loud enough for me to hear. The other mothers turn their heads to meet the eyes of the speaker. I kill the mosquito on my arm and successfully kill another on my neck. I cannot remember how I reply to the comment, but I know I acknowledge it. The comment stays with me. Still does. Perhaps, everyone who was sitting outside in that burning sun still thinks about the comment. The articulation :: statement :: testimony :: declaration :: assertion.

Erendira, Luis, and I reflect on our drive back. The three of us are unsure if the mother meant it, but we believe; we must.

\* \* \*

Less than a year before I was born, Marsha P. Johnson's body was found in the Hudson River. There is no photo, video, or audio that can attest to what happened at the Hudson :: the piers.

If the Hudson could speak, what would the Hudson say? How many names would it utter before it spoke of anything else? Are there enough years in someone's lifetime to bear witness to all the names the Hudson would honor?

How long can a memory live in water? How long can a vision of a world that has not come live in water?

This poem is not an attempt at asking, *what happened* in the days leading up to *the event*?

In many ways, the *what* is answered every day. The *happening* is unbearable.

\*\*\*

"If you're Trans, why do you dress manly?"

\*\*\*

On my penultimate day in Mexico City before I must pack too many suit-cases and return to the U.S. so as not to have U.S. immigration consider my time in México, my country of birth, an "abandonment" of U.S. residency, I walk by Plaza de la República, and from afar, I can spot graffiti on the metal bars shielding the Monumento a la Revolución.

"NO TRANS"

The message is clear. A feminist future *here* means a future without trans* people.

When I was younger, I used to say that México taught me how to be a femi-nist. I was wrong. A nation-state can never teach such a thing. What I meant back then was that Black and Indigenous rural women in México taught me all I know about feminism.

I take a photo of the words. I'm not sure why I want to memorialize this event that is actually a non-event because for something to be an event it must have a start and endpoint. I do not know if this has either of those two requirements, and thus, a non-event. This is longer than an event is.

A trans* future in México is a future where trans*-exclusionary feminism ends.

Over a Google Meet call, Diego tells me that TERFism is getting worse and worse in the country.

A few weeks prior to bearing witness to "NO TRANS," I am on hour eleven of a bus ride to Pinotepa Nacional. I fear arriving at the terminal at 5am and someone seeing me in my (very bad) masculinity and seeing my faggotry :: my trans*-ness. Then I remember that faggotry and trans*-ness doesn't operate in Oaxaca as it does in the West, and I breathe with ease.

A trans* future in México is a future where Indigenous languages are rehabilitated by their communities; a future where we no longer label things as Trans just because the West tells us to. A trans* future in México is bound to a Black Indigenous future that reorients our understanding(s) of gender(s), sexuality, sex acts, kinship, and more.

The present-future of "NO TRANS" is in direct opposition to a Black Indigenous future.

Settler feminisms must be abolished.

**Alan Pelaez Lopez** is the author of *Intergalactic Travels: poems from a fugitive alien*, a finalist for the International Latino Book Award, and *to love and mourn in the age of displacement*. They are an assistant professor of race and resistance studies at San Francisco State University. They can be reached at alanpl@sfsu.edu.

## Notes

1. Christina Sharpe, *In the Wake: On Blackness and Being* (Durham, NC: Duke University Press, 2016). Christina Sharpe utilizes the term "Trans*Atlantic," defining the asterisk as a symbol that "speaks to a range of configurations of Black being that take the form of translation, transatlantic, transgression, transgender, transformation, transmogrification, transcontinental, trans-fixed, trans-Mediterranean, transubstantiation, transmigration, and more" (2016, 30). My theorizations of the asterisk in *trans*\* account for Sharpe's conceptual framework, which is why the poem names that the asterisk has already been attended to.

2. Saidiya Hartman, *Lose Your Mother: A Journey along the Atlantic Slave Route* (New York: Farrar, Straus and Giroux, 2007).

3. Demian DinéYazhi' and Jess X. Snow, *Solastalgia: A Queer Eco-Feminist Poetry Tour* (self-pub., 2016).

PART VI. **ALERTS AND PROVOCATIONS**

# Reimagining the State

Lisa Duggan

What is the state? How do we grasp it, engage it, transform it? These are the broad questions to which this issue of *WSQ* is addressed. The articles and reviews here take concrete historical approaches to the dilemmas that social movements face in relation to state formations, as they are intertwined with racial capitalism and with shifting arrangements of intimacy and care. Right now, it can seem that the primary options are (1) grassroots organizing against the punitive, coercive, violent carceral and surveillance state, as in prison abolition and campaigns to defund the police; (2) social democratic reforms to claim state resources, as in the fight for universal accessible health- and childcare; or (3) organizing to protest the exploitation and violence at the nexus of corporate and state profit machines, as in protests of oil pipelines and environmental degradation. As this issue shows, the landscape of possibility is more complicated—these options overlap and are always shifting. And the deep intersections of formations of class, race, Indigeneity, gender, sexuality, religion, and ability defy any easy division between class and so-called identity politics. The materiality of everyday life draws us into the ways class is lived as race, gender is deployed by religion, and Indigenous history upends common assumptions about states and sovereignty.

In this essay, I want to provide two examples of political dilemmas and interventions that illuminate some dead ends and some new thinking about social movements and the state. The first is from Latin America and the second from Palestine.

*WSQ: Women's Studies Quarterly* 51: 1 & 2 (Spring/Summer 2023)

## Latin America

During spring 2021, I signed an open letter addressed to the editors of the socialist journals *Monthly Review* and *Jacobin* complaining about their coverage of the 2021 election in Ecuador. The two hundred signers of the letter are all aligned with left projects and formations. Our complaint was focused on the journals' representation of the candidate of some Ecuadoran Indigenous social movements, Yaku Pérez, and his political party, Pachakutik. They portrayed him as a Trojan horse for the left's most bitter neoliberal enemies (Signatories 2021).

The election came on the heels of the unpopular government of Lenín Moreno, the successor to the decade-long dominance of Rafael Correa of the Alianza País. Moreno had moved substantially to the right of Correa's left-wing socialist, anti-imperialist, anti-neoliberal government. The election of Correa had been an achievement of the "pink tide" in Latin America, but over time that government's reliance on extractivist practices for income generation, and their severe crackdown on dissenting social protest movements, generated opposition among anti-extractivist Indigenous groups. The Indigenous movement and its political party, while far from politically or ideologically monolithic, generated alternative visions for left governing, including feminist and queer components and offering an eco-socialist conception of land and resource use along with visions of radically inclusive democracy. The first round of elections in February 2021 at first looked like it would result in a runoff between Correa's candidate, Andrés Arauz, and the Pachakutik candidate, Yaku Pérez. But the surprising result was a runoff between Arauz and the neoliberal banker Guillermo Lasso.

The conflict surrounding the runoff on the left was fierce (Peralta 2021). Pérez charged electoral fraud, and Pachakutik advised their supporters to spoil their ballots rather than vote for either of the two remaining candidates. Pérez had himself been assaulted, arrested, and imprisoned for protest activity. The general criminalization of protest and the extension of extractivist policies by Correaists meant that an Arauz victory loomed as an existential threat to the existence of the Indigenous movement. There could be no support for a neoliberal Lasso government either. This was a strategic gambit, not an ideological choice. But understandably the Arauz forces considered this position a profound betrayal of the overall left project. Not only Correa supporters specifically, but sections of the international left saw the failure of Pérez and his allies to support Arauz against a neoliberal banker as evidence of hidden neoliberal sympathies. Thus the Trojan horse charge.

The point of the open letter was to push back against that charge of betrayal of the left, to situate Pachakutik and Pérez in the contested space between two intolerable alternatives: neoliberal rule and the dominance of a form of left statism that deploys police-state tactics to suppress left opposition, in part in order to continue planet-destroying extractivist practices. That space of opposition to both sides of the political polarity can feel strategically untenable, especially when the reaction of the repressive left is to view all opposition as neoliberal sabotage.

The dilemma of Ecuador's election was reflective of our impasses on the global left. There is a history of left governments that turn to patriarchal repressive policing to maintain power, and to destructive environmental practices to generate income, often in the face of lethal global capitalist opposition. The left's need to centralize power and deploy military tactics develops in a context of genuine existential threat. From the Bolsheviks to Cuba, or Venezuela and Ecuador, the sense of threat and the need for a powerful defense of the socialist project is real. Alongside these formations, various left social movements work to build alternative models of power that are cooperative, inclusive, democratic, and anti-patriarchal as well as anti-capitalist and anti-imperialist. These formations can be disorganized, incoherent, and transient. Often, they are easily crushed by police power (e.g., the Paris Commune, Occupy). In the face of existential threat, they can seem like a distraction from the overwhelming task at hand—winning collective power against the forces of global capital.

But we cannot remain trapped in a humanly intolerable binary of Correa vs. Lasso ad infinitum. The only way to develop alternatives is to develop alternatives. When the left itself dismisses or even violently crushes those alternatives, we are left to face a future of repressive policing and/or human extinction on a dying planet. We can criticize Pérez and Pachakutik, and indeed many open letter signers disagree with many positions and decisions the movement and its leader made! But if left governments like Correa's work to crush rather than engage and incorporate the creative forces of left social movements, if Pérez and company are left to face assault, jail, or exile for their political thinking and organizing, what do we expect them/ us to do? Like initially pro-Bolshevik Emma Goldman in the wake of the victory of the Russian revolution (which she celebrated), facing its subsequent evolution toward Stalinism, we are left in utter despair (Goldman 1923). You don't have to be an anarchist to feel it.

One of the key features of the Marxist left attacks on Pérez et al. is its patriarchal Eurocentrism. Indigenous thinking does not proceed from the dilemmas of Euro-America in 1968, or indeed from the Paris Commune through the Bolshevik revolution to the pink tide. The Eurocentrism of left binary thinking is strangling the political imagination of the left in the Global North. A deep engagement with the history of racial colonialism, with decolonial theory and practice, and with Indigenous ways of thinking and living, accompanied by eco-socialist, feminist, and queer strains within and alongside them, can help lead us out of the impasses of the entrenched binaries, the unwavering attachment to individual European male thinkers, the enmeshment in European histories, the dependence on extractivist economies.

In the Latin American context, Verónica Gago's *Feminist International: How to Change Everything* offers a brilliant reimagining of the politics of the state. Drawing on the women's strikes in Argentina and around the world, she shows us how concrete organizing around everyday life and labor can produce both massive and effective mobilizations and connect apparently disparate zones of life under conditions of precarity in new ways. This is a *transversal* left feminist politics that fully incorporates demands for reproductive justice and sexual and gender freedom within critiques of neoliberalism and neo-extractivism. For this new feminist-led politics, we do not need to choose class or identity, opposition or engagement, mass organizing or intimate consciousness-raising. These shift and combine in community assemblies and on the streets. Of course this is not the utopian solution to the dead ends and conflicts we face, but a process for working through that allows for ongoing conflict and change (Gago 2020).

### Palestine
The forces arrayed against Palestinian liberation are overwhelming, violent, and intransigent. Up against the appalling alternatives of an increasingly out-of-reach "two state solution" that offers only a shrunken and dependent form of limited sovereignty, and a "one state solution" of second-class citizenship in apartheid Israel, some Palestinians are searching for a "no state solution"—a way out of the impasses of the violent present. Scholar Rana Barakat and others have called for Palestinians to look to the decolonial practice of Indigenous resurgence, alongside the critique of Israeli settler colonialism, for practices and methods of liberation in the here and now as

well as the future (Barakat 2017). In "Designing the Future in Palestine," a dazzling article in *Boston Review*, human rights lawyer Noura Erakat outlines the approaches being introduced by the Palestinian Feminist Collective (PFC) and a collection of Palestinian architects and urban planners. Indigenous resurgence reframes decolonization, turning away from the state to focus on Indigenous nationhood and relations with the land and communities. The PFC is embedding gender liberation within a national liberation framework while the architects redesign demolished villages suitable for the diaspora upon return. As Erakat explains, "Statist approaches concentrate power among a political and economic elite, disempowering a popular base—historically Palestinians' greatest asset" (2022).

Erakat is also careful to point out that this shift does not reject state-centric efforts or abandon the fight against settler colonialism and apartheid. Rather, Indigenous resurgence in this context works alongside other approaches. This shift is not an abandonment of anti-imperial uprising but a way to make hopeful things happen in grim and dire circumstances. Putting care for people and land into the center of political focus transforms the horizon of immediate possibility, supporting life against death-dealing violence through everyday practices like seed harvesting and village building.

What the work of Verónica Gago and Noura Erakat offer us is not simply prefigurative politics, as opposed to the fights to oppose and transform the state. These thinkers, both deeply embedded in activist projects, offer us instead a way to get from here to there in company with diverse others, a way to connect and create new socialities, new institutions, and new conceptions of power on our way to reimagining the state.

**Lisa Duggan** is a queer feminist and leftist journalist, activist, and professor of Social and Cultural Analysis at New York University. She is the author of *Mean Girl: Ayn Rand and the Culture of Greed*, *Sapphic Slashers: Sex, Violence, and American Modernity*, *Twilight of Equality? Neoliberalism, Cultural Politics and the Attack on Democracy*, and other books. Duggan was president of the American Studies Association from 2014 to 2015. She can be reached at lisa.duggan@nyu.edu.

**Works Cited**

Barakat, Rana. 2017. "Writing/Righting Palestine Studies: Settler Colonialism, Indigenous Sovereignty and Resisting the Ghost(s) of History." *Settler Colonial Studies* 8, no. 3 (March): 349–63.

Erakat, Noura. 2022. "Designing the Future in Palestine." *Boston Review*.
    December 19, 2022. https://www.bostonreview.net/articles/
    designing-the-future-in-palestine/.

Gago, Verónica. 2020. *Feminist International: How to Change Everything*.
    Translated by Liz Mason-Deese. London: Verso.

Goldman, Emma. 1923. *My Disillusionment in Russia*. New York: Doubleday,
    Page & Company.

Peralta, Pablo Ospina. 2021. "The Divided Left in Ecuador." *Dissent*.
    April 9, 2021. https://www.dissentmagazine.org/online_articles/
    the-divided-left-in-ecuador.

Signatories. 2021. "Open Letter to Editors of *Jacobin* and *Monthly
    Review*." *New Politics*. March 2, 2021. https://newpol.org/
    open-letter-to-editors-of-jacobin-and-monthly-review/.

# Tulsa Studies in Women's Literature

Spring 2023, Vol. 42, No. 1

Featuring articles on:

Mary Wortley Montagu • Maria Edgeworth • Almira Hart Lincoln Phelps • Martha Gellhorn • Toni Morrison • Toni Cade Bambara • Alice Walker

@TSWLJournal
utulsa.edu/TSWL
Like us on Facebook